W9-BCZ-954

THE CASE FOR BUREAUCRACY

CHATHAM HOUSE SERIES ON CHANGE IN AMERICAN POLITICS

edited by Aaron Wildavsky
University of California, Berkeley

THE CASE
FOR
BUREAUCRACY
A Public Administration Polemic

CHARLES T. GOODSELL
Virginia Polytechnic Institute and State University

CHATHAM HOUSE PUBLISHERS, INC.
Chatham, New Jersey

Wingate College Library

094174

THE CASE FOR BUREAUCRACY
A Public Administration Polemic

CHATHAM HOUSE PUBLISHERS, INC.
Post Office Box One
Chatham, New Jersey 07928

Copyright © 1983 by Chatham House Publishers, Inc.

All rights reserved. No part of this publication may be reproduced, stored in a retrieval system, or transmitted in any form or by any means, electronic, mechanical, photocopying, recording, or otherwise, without the prior permission of the publisher.

PUBLISHER: Edward Artinian
COVER DESIGN: Lawrence Ratzkin
COMPOSITION: Chatham Composer
PRINTING AND BINDING: Hamilton Printing Company

LIBRARY OF CONGRESS CATALOGING IN PUBLICATION DATA

Goodsell, Charles T.
  The case for bureaucracy

(Chatham House series on change in American politics)
  Bibliography: p.
Includes index.
  1. Bureaucracy--United States. I. Title. II. Series.
JK421.G64 1983 353'.01 82-14795
ISBN 0-934540-17-9

Manufactured in the United States of America
10 9 8 7 6 5 4 3 2

For Amanda

Contents

PREFACE

This book is a polemic. I consider it a gentle polemic in that I avoid ad hominem attacks and take the trouble to back my position with evidence. But it is a polemic nonetheless.

I have been moved to write a polemic out of growing irritation with a view that has long been dominant in popular culture and the social sciences, namely, that governmental bureaucracy in the United States is a generalized failure and threat. This viewpoint comes to us from all directions. Political conservatives insist that bureaucracy blunders constantly and threatens the superior instruments of private enterprise and market organization. Political liberals reject bureaucracy as a tool of the elitist establishment and as an oppressor of the hapless individual. The press finds bureaucracy to be a splendid source of interest-arousing horror stories. Academics within several disciplines — who, above all, should know better — make extravagant, outraged claims as to bureaucracy's overall breakdown and oppressive nature.

I am not claiming that bureaucracy is perfect or anywhere near that wondrous state. Any large administrative apparatus, including that found in the United States, is riddled with individual instances of inefficiency, maladministration, arrogant behavior, repressive management, and abused power. My point is simply that in America, at least, these deficiencies are particularized rather than generalized and that they occur within tolerable ranges of proportionate incidence. They do not constitute a comprehensive inadequacy or overarching threat within the society or political system. Bureaucracy is, instead, a multitudinous, diverse reality in which is found a vast mix of performance and quality. Within this mix, acceptable and responsible conduct is far more common than unacceptable or irresponsible behavior. The drumbeat of antibureaucratic criticism, emanating as it does from multiple sources within the society, supports a powerful myth that wildly exaggerates shortcomings in government's performance and invariably underestimates government's achievements. A main objective of the book is to expose that myth, although I have no expectation of destroying it.

To many, the word "bureaucracy" in itself means bad public administration. To defend something that is admittedly "bad" would be difficult, to say the least. Although I find myself in a polemical mood, I am not prepared to try the impossible and make a case for evil. I wish only to make a case for something that most Americans mistakenly consider evil.

In the pages that follow the term bureaucracy refers collectively to governmental administrative agencies found in the United States; that is, American public administration. My defense of bureaucracy is not necessarily limited to its U.S. manifestation, although for reasons of strategy and inadequate information I choose to make a case for American public administration alone at this time. Surely, however, some of my observations apply to some other countries, and perhaps students of the subject in those countries will be moved to reconsider the total performance record of their executive institutions.

I should like to emphasize that the book is not a defense of the status quo or a restatement of theoretical orthodoxy. I do not make a case for bureaucracy out of loyalty to current regimes or a commitment to existing managements of organizations. The position I take is, in fact, radical to the study of public administration, as anomalous as that may seem to the outsider. The field tends, amazingly enough, to condemn categorically rather than approach sympathetically or at least with an open mind the institutions it purports to staff and advise. While other writers within public administration have in the past stated views parallel to my own, the active case for bureaucracy has been presented in limited scope and in a fragmented manner. Meanwhile, articulate bombast from bureaucracy's critics has dominated the scene. One of my aims is to help correct this imbalance.

The book is addressed, therefore, in part to my fellow students and teachers in the field. Additionally, I hope to find a substantial audience among lay citizens. My reasoning is that citizens have a right to grant legitimacy to their public institutions to the extent that these institutions earn it through performance. This is true with legislatures, courts, political parties, presidencies, and governorships, as well as with bureaucracies. But the near-monopoly of a one-sided view of public administration within the output of the mass media and the utterances of politicians and professors does not permit a fair judgment of it. Unjustified delegitimization of publicly owned institutions is, in a way, robbing the people of what is due them.

Several persons helped make this book better than it would have been. The initial idea for the volume was discussed more than five years ago with a former colleague, John L. Foster, and on reviewing the final product he suggested a number of concrete improvements. A current colleague, John A. Rohr, spent many tedious hours with the draft, uncovered hundreds of major and minor flaws, and accompanied all of them with constructive suggestions. Two individuals who are not "colleagues" organizationally but are intellectual co-workers with all scholars of public administration because of their prominence in the field, Dwight Waldo and Aaron Wildavsky, made useful comments at one stage or another of the project. My favorite high school science teacher, citizen participant in local and state government, candidate for public office, and personal critic of bureaucracy—Barbara G. Clark—identified in the manuscript many examples of stuffiness and needed clarification. My publisher, Edward Artinian, demonstrated infectious enthusiasm for the undertaking throughout, and my typist, Beth Burch, exhibited uncommon technical skill and personal good will. A sincere "thank you" to all these individuals.

CHAPTER 1

BUREAUCRACY
DESPISED AND DISPARAGED

To make the case for bureaucracy: What a ridiculous idea! The author must be an earthbound Screwtape or plain mad. Only a diabolic polemicist would present a brief for evil. Only an insane mind would come to the defense of the indefensible.

I hope that the reader, as he or she turns these pages, quickly revises this initial impression. The first point to make is that the discussion is not bound by the pejorative definition of "bureaucracy." That usage in itself refers to incompetent, indifferent, bloated, and malevolent administrative departments of government. The need to escape this definition points to a fundamental error commonly made in interpreting American government: the tendency to downgrade and malign U.S. public administrative institutions regardless of their tasks, limits, and record. Contrary to first impressions, this book neither defends evil nor exhibits insanity but argues that such a tendency is both unjustified and productive of inaccurate understanding. Stating the book's thesis in a positive way, the case is made that American administrative agencies of government function surprisingly well. In other words, bureaucracy in the United States is not nearly as "bureaucratic," in the pejorative sense, as commonly thought.

To clarify my definition of bureaucracy right away, in this book "bureaucracy" refers simply to American public administration. The reference is a collective one and includes all administrative agencies at all levels of American government, not just those in Washington, D.C. Individual "bureaucracies" are single examples of those agencies.

This descriptive category is, then, vast. Also, it embraces a hodgepodge of institutions. Yet the variety of public bureaucracies in a country like the United States is itself a basic truism that we must incorporate in our understanding of American public administration. This hodgepodge nature itself argues against quick and simple generalizations about bureaucracy, whether cynical or not.

Academic writers on bureaucracy often use the term in a quite different way. To them "bureaucracy" often refers to a type of organization. Originally conceptualized by the German sociologist Max Weber, the bureaucratic model of organization possesses these characteristics: large size; a graded hierarchy, formal rules, and written files; and employment of salaried, full-time staff hired for long periods to perform stated duties using technical knowledge.[1]

This kind of organization is usually, and rightly, thought of as dominating government within most societies. In fact, Weberian organization is often associated with governmental administration. The bureaucratic form, nevertheless, has great importance beyond the public sector—for example, within the corporate world of American society. In any event, for the most part, American public administration is highly "bureaucratic" in the Weberian sense (the main exception being that governmental organizations are often much smaller than expected). Hence, making our case for bureaucracy inescapably involves defending the use of Weber's model. Students of the subject will immediately recognize that such a step flies in the face of much well-known and long-worshiped academic theory. Weberian organization is attacked in most emphatic terms as unworkable and even immoral in not just one but several disciplines. Thus, the reader should be forewarned that by making the case for bureaucracy, this book not only rejects much popular wisdom but steps on a number of intellectual toes.

DEPICTIONS IN POPULAR CULTURE

Let us begin by elaborating common depictions of public bureaucracy so that we can appreciate what making the case for it confronts. As for portrayals in mass media, we encounter a relatively simple picture, confidently expressed. The employee of bureaucracy, that "lowly bureaucrat," is seen as lazy or snarling, or both. The office occupied by this pariah is viewed as bungling or inhumane, or both. The overall edifice of bureaucracy is pictured as overstaffed, inflexible, unresponsive, and power-hungry, all at once. These images are agreed upon by writers and groups of every shade of opinion. One is hard pressed to think of a concept more deeply ingrained and widely expressed in American cultural life.

To exemplify popular culture's image of bureaucracy, a newspaper feature on the subject describes it as "a brontosaurus of unimaginable size, appetite, ubiquity and complexity." At the federal level alone, the feature notes, this dinosaur owns 413,000 buildings, leases 228 million square feet of space, operates 450,000 automobiles, and owes a trillion dollars in debt.[2] In another illustration, a columnist likens American bureaucracy to "several hundred lidless baskets of snakes placed in a single room," with confusion rampant within and between baskets.[3] A Sunday supplement article solemnly proclaims that despite the tradition of individualism in America, bureaucracy is reducing us to "a nation of paper-shuffling petitioners, forever waiting for permission from some government office for our next step, continually putting aside the work of the world in order to fill out forms."[4] An article in a monthly magazine declares that "the performance of the bureaucracy constitutes the biggest crisis facing our country today," comparable to Watergate or Vietnam.[5] In short, the phenomenon of bureaucracy is seen as so terrible that metaphors of snakes and Jurassic monsters are needed to describe it, and disasters like military defeat and presidential perfidy are required as standards of comparison to indicate the magnitude of crisis involved.

What evidence do the popular writers have for their attacks on bureaucracy? If we asked them, they would rephrase the question by wondering where evidence to the contrary could be found. One source the popular critics always draw upon is that item found in almost every edition of every daily newspaper, the bureaucratic horror story. This is the graphic and sympathetic account of how some poor citizen has been mistreated by incompetent bureaucrats or how in some other way a great bureaucratic error has been committed. Here are summaries of a few such stories:

- A Chicago woman undergoing chemotherapy for cancer of the breast applied for Medicare. She received a computer-produced letter indicating she was ineligible since she had died the previous April.
- A chronic alcoholic was arrested and mistaken for another man. When he protested, his claims of misidentification were diagnosed as paranoia and schizophrenia, and he was committed to a mental hospital.
- The Department of Energy set out to declassify millions of documents inherited from the Atomic Energy Commission. Eight of the released documents contained the basic design principles for the hydrogen bomb.
- A woman on welfare ran up astronomical medical bills because of terminal illness. She was denied Medicaid on grounds that her welfare payments created a personal monthly income $10.80 above the eligibility maximum.
- A unit of what is now the Department of Health and Human Services sent fifteen chimpanzees to a Texas laboratory for the purpose of launching a chimp-breeding program. All were males.

All right, you will say, these stories were newsworthy precisely *because* such horrible and ridiculous things happened. And "bureaucracy" let them happen! Is this not *proof* that bureaucrats are heartless, asinine, and plain stupid?

Notice, however, that the bureaucratic horror story is usually short. Often not many details of the case are included, and those that are given stress the citizen's anguish or the incident's adverse effects. Certainly any extenuating circumstances or the government's side of the story are not covered. Journalists are perfectly aware that what arouses reader interest is the maligned citizen and the horrific outcome, not restrictions faced by bureaucrats in terms of rules with which they must live and workloads with which they must cope. With respect to the Chicago breast cancer case, for example, who would care that a new computer-based information system was at the time being installed and many bugs had yet to be worked out? As for the misidentified alcoholic, how many readers are interested in the fact that another man with the same name, similar physique, and almost identical birth date was entered on police records? On the Medicaid case, how newsworthy is the fact that personal income maximums are not set by local welfare departments and, if exceeded by them in any amount, result in an adverse state audit and charge-back?

Another point on bureaucratic horror stories has to do with what social scientists would call a sampling problem. The cases appearing in print are selected for attention and not because they are representative. This is so despite the implication often given that repeated occurrence is precisely why these stories are published so often. (One story begins, "Brace yourself. It's more bureaucratic madness."[6]) Actually, a random selection of cases would yield routine and thereby uninteresting subject matter; nothing could be less newsworthy than the smoothly processed eligibility claim or by-the-book police arrest. Moreover, a selection of instances of unusual government efficiency would violate the media's desire to appear independent by being skeptical.

What *is* of interest, to journalists and readers alike, is the bizarre case. In a country as large as the United States, and in a society as efficient in transmitting news as the American, plenty of bizarre cases can be singled out each day. But by definition they are atypical. Especially of interest is the atypical case that reinforces stereotypes of bureaucracy and thereby strikes a responsive chord. All citizens old enough to have conscious memory have experienced incidents from time to time in which officials have acted toward them in baffling and frustrating ways. Hence, everyone can relate personally to the bureaucratic horror story. That is why it is printed. Nevertheless, such stories are not a good research source for finding out how bureaucracy actually operates.

Another kind of evidence frequently cited by popular critics is poll results that reflect the negative overall image of bureaucracy propagated in the media and ingrained in our culture. This is a highly abstract, depersonalized image that I later analyze as central to a grand bureaucratic myth. The polls quoted by critics tap this abstract level almost exclusively, which merely reinforces the conventional wisdom. Gallup, for instance, asked a national sample whether federal employees "work harder or not so hard as they would in nongovernmental jobs." He also questioned whether the federal government "employs too many or too few people to do the work that must be done."[7] In both instances he was surveying abstract images of the federal government and not personal, concerete experience with its agencies or personnel. We are not surprised that about two-thirds of the sample said bureaucrats work "not so hard," and a similar proportion replied that government "employs too many." The conclusion then drawn is that Americans are alienated over poor government services. Yet the questions asked are nicely set up with dichotomous phrasing, and there is little doubt as to the "right" answer in terms of accepted norms. Also, the questions reflect national frustrations that go beyond bureaucratic performance; pollsters have found an erosion of confidence in almost all national institutions in recent years. When we move, in the next chapter, to survey questions where citizens are asked specifically about past personal experiences with government agencies, a radically different picture emerges. This more meaningful set of survey results is ignored by the high priests of popular culture—it is too damaging to their preconceptions and intentions.

To frame this discussion in terms of "evidence" actually elevates popular discussion of bureaucracy above its usual level. Most of the antibureaucratic commentary assumes everyone hates bureaucracy and does not bother substantiating its negative attributes. The impression is given that consensus is so complete on this issue that the time and trouble needed for verification are unnecessary. Bureaucracy is portrayed as so wicked that its sins could hardly be subject to exaggeration.

It is easy, then, for individuals and enterprises to exploit this fixation against public bureaucracy without fear of being called to account. Their interest is not in describing American government but in using antibureaucratic sentiment to their own ends. Countless politicians run for office (including the highest posts in the land) on platforms that blame society's problems on "the bureaucrats" and their burdensome rules, wasteful extravagance, social experimentation, and whatever else nettles. Candidates promise that when they are elected, they will deal fiercely and conclusively with these enemies; when, after the election, neither the bureaucrats nor the perceived problems disappear, voters conclude that the survival of the former has caused the perpetuation of the latter.

The exploitation of antibureaucracy sentiment is not restricted to politics. Comfortable livings are made from the phenomenon. Numerous amusing books are written that ridicule government servants and agencies, and they sell well. Public lectures are given on the subject at substantial fees. Parlor games on evil bureaucracy are manufactured and marketed. Literary reputations are made by fictional depictions of bureaucracy that use the imagination of the novelist to satisfy the keenest cravings for cynicism and despair. Futurists make best-seller lists by contending that the rejection and replacement of bureaucracy is the inevitable wave of the future—and indeed is already upon us.

It could all be considered harmless. After all, politicking by scapegoat and buck-chasing by entrepreneurship are the American way. Yet, as a result we are treated to the spectacle of the opinion molders of a national culture bent on reinforcing dismal perceptions of a government that is unusual by world standards. It is a government subject to periodic review in relatively honest elections. It is a government massively constrained by law and constitution. It is a government widely admired by foreigners for organizational innovation and technological prowess. Is American bureaucracy really that bad?

DEPICTIONS IN ACADEMIC WRITING

Meanwhile, academic writers on bureaucracy address the subject not only from the standpoint of breakdown of a particular set of institutions but also from the perspective of inherent problems of the bureaucratic (Weberian) form of organization. Yet, since American public administration is largely in accord with that form, the two orientations end up addressing essentially the same topic.

With few exceptions, academic analyses of bureaucracy are pessimistic and condemnatory. Using different vocabularies and contrasting conceptual models to be sure, professors from disparate disciplines conclude overwhelmingly that bureaucracy in the United States and elsewhere has served mankind disadvantageously, to put it mildly. One might organize their criticisms in various ways, but at least three evils are perceived as paramount: unacceptably poor performance, dangerous manipulation of political power, and intolerable oppression of the individual.

As for bad performance, the notion that bureaucracy fails to work properly is arrived at through various chains of deductive reasoning. We might first mention the market-oriented economists. They are hostile to government bureaucracy on the grounds that competitive markets and profit-based incentive systems are the only feasible means to attain economic efficiency, which is their distinctive definition of the public good. The basic problem perceived is that bureaucracy does not respond to a market of multiple consumers, but rather to a single "buyer" in the form of an appropriations committee or budget bureau. Also, bureaucracy does not face competition with other producers but enjoys a legal monopoly in its mandated field of operation. As a result, output does not conform to true demand, and incentives for efficient operation are absent. The consequence is unlimited budgetary expansion in the absence of need and an economically inefficient allocation of resources to and within the public sector. Meanwhile, governmental activity is said to add nothing to the economy's productivity, while the taxes needed to finance it dampen private investment and fuel inflation.[8]

Next come the functional sociologists. They believe that bureaucracies are destined to work against themselves, that is, be "dysfunctional." Because of their structural characteristics, it is said, these organizations will inevitably take on countereffective, "pathological" behavioral patterns. One of the most important of these patterns is an obsessive conformity to rules. We are told this creates a phenomenon known as "goal displacement," or placing the means of bureaucratic action ahead of its ends. Another diagnosed pathology is a deep-seated and persistent conflict between superiors and subordinates, which results in petty game-playing and eventually organizational breakdown. Still another perceived dysfunctionality is that the hierarchical chain of command automatically generates vertical communication blocks and distortions that destroy any chance for informed decisions and leadership. Also, bureaucracy is perceived as inherently rigid, incapable of innovation, and riddled with fighting cliques and scheming careerists.[9]

A third academic setting from which comes despair about bureaucratic performance is the policy analysis community. This relatively new field does not seem to detest bureaucracy so much as have little or no faith in it. Although national or state legislatures pass laws and appropriate money to solve social problems, it is duly noted the problems somehow persist. The difficulty is often diagnosed as a failure by bureaucracy to do its part of the job, that is, carry out the policy and deliver the services. Bureaucrats, used to and committed to old policies, are characterized as not liking change and hence resisting it or delaying action. Also, they are said to fail to define objectives, establish performance standards, gather sufficient information, predict program effects, and avoid political interference. Bureaucracies, while not pernicious perhaps, are at least highly irrational.[10]

Another whole range of academic castigations of bureaucracy is concerned with political power rather than instrumental achievement. Public bureaucracy is perceived as not just bungling but outright dangerous. One wonders how bureaucracy could be both inept and menacing at the same time, but that seeming contradiction has not dampened accusations on either score.

Again, different themes appear. One of the earliest attacks on bureaucracy from the standpoint of ominous political power was made by Max Weber.

Although there is a common tendency to portray Weber as a friend and propo-
nent of bureaucracy, he also represented it as a threat to parliamentary democracy. Once bureaucracy is established, Weber said, it becomes almost impossible to destroy. Moreover, it serves as "a power instrument of the first order—
for the one who controls the bureaucratic apparatus." Weber also seems to
doubt that even "the one who controls" can truly do so, for bureaucracy is
both indispensable to society and highly technical and secretive in nature. The
elected politician, supposedly bureaucracy's master, becomes to Weber an im-
potent dilettante.[11]

Contemporary students of Weber and later German or Austrian scholars
carried the political danger argument substantially further. They identified it
with authoritarian and totalitarian government. One writer considered bureaucracy a form of "oriental despotism" created by the technical imperatives
of public works projects associated with the use of water. Others analyzed it in
terms of having reached its fullest and therefore potential expression in Nazi
Germany and Stalinist Russia. A more recent commentary in this teutonic tradition of analysis argues that bureaucracy has become "the basic problem of
our times" by crushing the individualism released by the disappearance of feu-
dalism and rise of liberalism.[12]

A third theme in the political analysis of bureaucracy is that, even if not
necessarily totalitarian, bureaucracy possesses an elitist bias and is capable of
distorting the political process in proestablishment ways. Bureaucracies are
portrayed as inevitably oligarchic and conservative organizations. Bureaucrats are described as unrepresentative of the masses, automatically favorable
to the regime, and invariably allied with powerful interests in the society. As a
consequence they are said to be opposed to meaningful change, bent on maintaining stability and order, and determined to keep all real power in traditional hands. Furthermore, bureaucrats engage covertly in the formation and manipulation of policy, despite an official ideology that separates politics from
administration. They are seen as taking bold initiatives, abusing discretion,
forming alliances, and coopting other centers of power in order to steer the
ship of state in the desired conservative directions. In short, representative
government is sabotaged, and democracy becomes overwhelmed by bureaucracy.[13]

Even Marxists—who are not always committed to democracy—express
various acute anxieties about the political power of bureaucracy. Marx himself, who perceived the principal enemy as the capitalists rather than the bureaucrats, nevertheless worried at various times in his life about "parasitic
officialdom" and the possibility that the bureaucracy could become an autonomous political force. This was so despite his view that the state is mere super-

structure and a pawn of underlying class struggle. For his part, Lenin despised the Tsarist bureaucracy but, after initial attempts at dismantling it, went on nonetheless to perpetuate and elaborate it. Many neo-Marxists have similarly denounced large bureaucracies as oppressive, viewing them as hateful abstractions comparable in stature to the business corporation, industrial technology, and the bourgeoisie. Yet while many Marxian critics steadfastly decry state bureaucracy in the Soviet Union, they are far more tolerant of the same phenomenon in China and Cuba.[14]

A final political theme to be mentioned has to do with bureaucracy's growth. Bureaucratic expansion is said to be perpetuated by various forces related to career advancement and organizational aggrandizement within the organization. In addition, external factors are identified as having a growth-perpetuating effect out of a need for the capitalist, elected, and welfare state to continue to ameliorate economic crises, buy support, and pacify angry masses. The picture one gets of bureaucracy is that of an imperialist superpower totally out of control.[15]

Interestingly enough, other scholarly voices simultaneously preach the opposite doctrine. According to one point of view, the need for small, flexible, and egalitarian work groups means we are now "beyond bureaucracy" and rapidly departing from its constraints. Another theory being advanced is that bureaucracy as a "sociobiological form" is becoming extinct in the evolutionary process and hence will eventually disappear. To those terrified by uncontrollable bureaucratic imperialism, the prospect of its early demise must be reassuring.[16]

The final broad category of academic condemnation of bureaucracy deals not with performance failures or power problems but with organizational oppression in various forms. Bureaucracy is said to treat human beings callously at the minimum and crushingly in all likelihood.

One major category of victims is employees of bureaucracy. The principle of hierarchy is seen as instituting an intolerable pattern of inequality. Authoritative direction and rule making are viewed as insults to individual freedom. Specialized work creates narrow, humdrum routines that are impossible to bear day after day. Security and economic needs are served at the expense of attaining "self-actualization." Employees are kept psychologically subordinate, required to behave in immature ways, and called upon to abandon spontaneity and genuineness. In addition, they are forced to make decisions in a fear-ridden atmosphere where failure to achieve planned outcomes results in ruined careers and broken personalities. The bureaucrat's psychological health and personal identity are—in the more extreme statements of this position—destroyed.[17]

A second general grouping of victims of bureaucracy is its clients. Toward these human beings bureaucracy allegedly commits several crimes, a leading one being the treatment of the person as a mere "case." The organization supposedly forgets that the welfare applicant or citizen in some other supplicant capacity has rights and emotions. The bureaucrat treats the citizen as an impersonal object within the context of rules defining eligibility or forbidden behavior. The official does not consider the "whole person" but limits attention to that narrow and abstract slice of the client which is of programmatic relevance. As a consequence, bureaucratic behavior toward clients is characterized by remoteness, manipulation, and an absence of authenticity. The client, outraged by the fact that he or she is not dealt with as a unique and total person, then becomes deeply alienated to "the system" writ large.[18]

Other forms of client mistreatment supposedly stem from internal needs and drives of the "bureaucratic personality" or "bureaucratic mentality." The bureaucrat is perceived as a low-level subordinate whose own position within the hierarchy is that of repressed victim. To compensate for this dire circumstance the bureaucrat then lashes out officiously at the hapless citizen. Rules are interpreted without regard for genuine human needs, and the client is addressed in authoritarian and incomprehensible language. To avoid responsibility for handling borderline cases or unusual circumstances, the bureaucrat bucks all such matters to superiors or another office. Procrastination, put-offs, and put-downs result. Red tape, arrogance, and evasiveness abound.[19]

Another syndrome of client abuse blamed on bureaucracy is repression of the disadvantaged. This includes the poor, racial minorities, and "difficult" cases. Bureaucracies are viewed as essentially middle-class institutions that are incapable of serving the "underclass" on its own terms. Poor, urban blacks do not understand the culture or language of bureaucracy and hence a "war of cultures" is waged across reception counters and in agency waiting rooms. Clients who operate outside bureaucracy's norms are said to be ignored because they are messy to deal with, sometimes dangerous, and contribute little to success rates. Bureaucrats working with wide discretion at the "street level" have ample opportunity to exercise racial and class prejudices. Spheres of working autonomy are constructed in which the bureaucrat manipulates information and selectively enforces rules in order to cope with overwork and uncertainty. The costs of being a client are deliberately increased by staged "degradation rituals" that force many citizens to withdraw or not request help in the first place. As a result, government services, in inner cities in particular, are supposedly characterized by low participation rates, poor delivery quality, and high levels of client alienation.[20]

Beyond all these rather concrete ways in which bureaucracy supposedly oppresses is its involvement in a general hoodwinking of society, which we are told occurs. The accusation is made by "critical theory" advocates in public administration and organization theory, whose currently fashionable intellectual orientation is based on the Frankfurt School of social philosophy. The central notion of this point of view is that human beings are deeply alienated from an imposed order of rational authority, positivist science, exploitive capitalism, and dominating bureaucracy. Despite this alienation, however, the victims do not realize their fate; they suffer a "pathology of consciousness" or live in a "psychic prison," depending on which metaphor you pick. Because of their unknowingly dominated condition, men and women cannot realize their potential, are unable to communicate competently, are distracted from self-reflection, and are manipulated by powerful interests for selfish purposes. As for public bureaucracy, its role in this unrecognized suppression is to control the definition of problems; focus attention on narrow questions of technique; and perpetuate values of discipline, obedience, and regulation.[21]

RECONSIDERING A HATE OBJECT

Bureaucracy, then, is despised and disparaged. It is attacked in the press, popular magazines, and best sellers. It is denounced by the political right and left. It is assaulted by molders of culture and professors of academia. It is castigated by economists, sociologists, policy analysts, political scientists, organization theorists, and social psychologists. It is charged with a wide array of crimes, which we have grouped under failure to perform; abuse of political power; and repression of employees, clients, and people in general. In short, bureaucracy stands as a splendid hate object.

Beginning with the next chapter we shall, despite all this, have the temerity to make a positive case for bureaucracy. But before doing so we would be well served to examine these attacks on their own terms. Denunciations of this common hate object are fashionable, appealing, and make us feel good. They invite no retaliation or disagreement since almost everybody agrees bureaucracy is bad. Government agencies do not, moreover, sue for libel. But fashionable contentions are not necessarily solid ones. Are the allegations against bureaucracy inherently believable? Have contrary views been expressed that are also persuasive?

Let us begin with the observation that the attacks are almost always made in a tone of unremitting dogmatism. They are usually unqualified in portraying wicked behavior and inadequate outcomes. The pessimistic picture presented seems unbroken. This absolutism itself, it would seem, cannot help but strain our credulity. How can we believe that *all* public bureaucracies, *all* of the time, are inefficient, dysfunctional, rigid, obstructionist, secretive, oligarchic, conservative, undemocratic, imperialist, oppressive, alienating, and discriminatory? How could any single human creation be so universally terrible in so many ways?

Second, it should be pointed out that bureaucracy cannot be everything the critics are in effect demanding it to be. If we insist that bureaucracies become efficient, they will have to treat clients as mere "cases." If we demand they be externally controllable, internal rules and hierarchical authority will be necessary. If we want them to stop protecting the status quo and reconstruct society, we will have to give them plenty of political clout. Bureaucracy cannot be everything to everybody. "There are inherent limits to what can be accomplished by large hierarchical organizations," James Q. Wilson reminds us.[22] Christopher Hood equates "anti-bureaucracy utopianism" with impatience with any kind of administration,[23] which may be the real reason for applying impossible standards. Perhaps even the societal bête noire deserves a fighting chance.

It should be further noted that condemnations of bureaucracy are often, in the felicitous language of Alvin Gouldner, "a theoretical tapestry devoid of even the plainest empirical trimmings."[24] Purely deductive models abound. They are bandied about more often than they are empirically tested. Commentators prefer to exploit the negative symbolic power of bureaucracy or engage in the championing of subjectivist epistemologies rather than take a balanced or detached view. When empirical study is undertaken, single cases illustrating the desired conclusions are selected. Nicos Mouzelis charitably comments, "The writers, usually sociologists, in undertaking such investigations, have in their minds certain hypotheses, certain theoretical problems which influence the method of observation and the kind of data which are collected."[25]

As we have seen, these hypotheses and problems are multiple. Unified only by abhorrence of the hate object, they enunciate a wide range of discrete bureaucratic noxiants. Bureaucrats are portrayed as fear-ridden yet arrogant, incompetent yet ominous, Milquetoasts yet Machiavellians. Bureaucracy is rigid and at the same time expansionist. It poses a grave danger to the Republic but is inevitably disappearing. While amusingly comical in its blundering, bureaucracy also represents the terrors of the police state. One begins to react to this mixed barrage of allegations like the juror who hears the country lawyer summarize the 101 good and bad arguments supporting his case, hoping that at least one will take. "Many writers, it seems, have abandoned their minds to denunciations of bureaucracy," observes Stephen Miller. "During the past twenty years bureaucracy has come to stand for all that is wrong with the modern world."[26]

No doubt these multiple and often contradictory attacks stem from the fact that different people see the modern world as wrong in different ways. Bureaucracy is a visible and appealing scapegoat for numerous discomforts. For political conservatives it symbolizes expensive government requiring heavy taxation and the unpleasantness of outsiders interfering in the management of one's firm. For political liberals, bureaucracy represents the failure of government social programs to achieve miraculous results in helping the disadvantaged. Leftists find attacking bureaucracy emotionally satisfying because its supposedly insidious repression helps explain why the American masses have not revolted. Rightists lose few opportunities to flail at bureaucracy as they conjure up the imminent arrival of communist totalitarianism.

Various influential occupational groups also find bureaucracy a convenient target of loathing. Commenting on how many contemporary novelists "have spoken of bureaucratization as the disease that pervades all advanced industrial societies," Miller speculates that bureaucracy serves nicely as a vehicle for attacks on banality, confusion, and meaninglessness. In the play of creative artistry all bureaucracies, whether big or small, awesome or mundane, ruthless or law-bound, are lumped together. "The notion that modern societies are, for the most part, madhouses where confusion and oppression reign is a lazy man's wisdom," writes Miller, "that enables writers to avoid the hard task of making distinctions not only about different societies but about different persons as well."[27]

Social scientists as a group also find attacks on bureaucracy both useful and satisfying. In the first place, by concentrating on the problems, disorders, and dysfunctions of bureaucracy rather than on what is working rather well, academics confirm their own diagnoses of breakdown and demonstrate the need for their own solutions. Furthermore, such emphasis reveals levels of skepticism and cynicism considered appropriate to the normative orientation of the intellectual calling. A "metaphysical pathos" described by Gouldner as underlying theories of bureaucracy stresses dark constraints, oligarchic tendencies, and threats to democracy, never liberating features or democratic commitments. One gets the impression, Gouldner says, that "some social scientists appear to be bent on resurrecting a dismal science." This gloomy outlook, while fashionable in academia, helps to form myths that affect the whole society. "Woven to a great extent out of theoretical whole cloth, much of the discussion of bureaucracy and of organizational needs seems to have provided a screen onto which some intellectuals have projected their own despair and pessimism, reinforcing the despair of others."[28]

Furthermore, according to Victor Thompson, sociologists studying bureaucracy have traditionally tended to view the organization as only a natural system, not an instrumental tool as well. Bureaucracy is depicted as an entity that survives, grows, and takes on an independent life, rather than—in addition—a deliberately created implement of the polity. This frame of reference

Wingate College Library

directs attention to informal and irrational aspects without admitting the possibility of external control. Thompson also believes that many antibureaucratic writers in effect call for a denial of external control by legitimate state authority, on the grounds that disadvantaged constituencies should be directing
their own programs. This Thompson sees as a form of theft.[29]

Finally, Charles Perrow contributes the interesting argument that social
scientists castigate bureaucracy because they themselves dislike organizational
constraints. "For many social scientists, rules are a nuisance; the emphasis
upon rules in organizations is bad enough, but the existence of a hierarchical
ordering of offices and authority is a barely tolerable evil." Although the university setting is of course not without hierarchy, the simplistic concept has
taken root among academics that professionals cannot perform well when employed in a bureaucratic context. The result, Perrow says, is an entire line of
literature that mistakenly argues the incompatibility of professionalism and
bureaucracy.[30]

THE CASE FOR BUREAUCRACY PREVIEWED

Permit me now to state briefly what is undertaken in each of the remaining
chapters of this book, thereby previewing my case for public bureaucracy in
the United States.

In chapter 2, "The Water Glass Viewed Differently," data are presented
that form the opening wedge in behalf of our case. It is discovered that, contrary to popular abstractions and academic deductions, the performance of
bureaucracy is acceptable or satisfactory in the preponderant majority of actual encounters with citizens. The data are taken from a variety of surveys of citizen experience with bureaucracy plus some direct performance measures. A
point of considerable interest in this material, in addition to the highly favorable light it casts on bureaucracy, is the extent to which ordinary citizens perceive bureaucracy differently from most professional students of the subject.
The John Does and Mary Smiths of this land seem to know something about
bureaucracy the experts do not.

In chapter 3, "Some Suspicions, Some Surprises," bureaucracy is studied
comparatively in various ways. The great heterogeneity of administrative institutions is underscored when formally identical agencies and normally stereotyped behaviors are discovered to exhibit drastic differences. Empirical
data on treatment of minorities and the poor, on the one hand, and governmental performance in comparison to private business, on the other, force us
to reconsider images of a repressive and inefficient public bureaucracy. Also,
comparisons are drawn between American public administration and bureau-

cracy in other countries, and once more the hate object looks much less ominous on closer scrutiny.

"Great (But Impossible) Expectations," chapter 4, pursues the question of demanding unrealistic achievements from bureaucracy. We create no-win situations for agencies by asking them to meet inconsistent and contradictory goals. We have in effect hobbled American administration in achieving even reasonable goals by too often using indirect methods of administration through intergovernmental grants, contracts with the private sector, and government credit. We expect bureaucracies not merely to expend maximum possible effort in solving societal problems but to dispose of them entirely, whether solvable or not. Finally, we fail to appreciate bureaucracy's role in social change by misunderstanding the function of administration and misconceptualizing the nature of change.

In chapter 5, "Bureaucrats as Ordinary People," various stereotypes concerning the employees of bureaucracy are explored. Public bureaucrats are found to mirror the demographic makeup and attitudes of the general population quite faithfully. The concept of a distinctive "bureaucratic mentality" evaporates into nothingness when subject to empirical examination. Survey studies of bureaucrats disclose that they do not feel nearly as put-upon or oppressed as the critical literature alleges. It is discovered that low-prestige images of the bureaucrat are more prominent among upper-class Americans than lower, suggesting something of an elitist bias in antibureaucracy sentiment.

In chapter 6, "Bigness and Badness Reconsidered," we discover that far from constituting a generally huge-scale phenomenon, bureaucracies in the United States tend to be of moderate size. In fact, most are extremely small, incredible as that may seem. Other surprises are that bureaucracies do not invariably grow bigger; bigger bureaucracies do not necessarily perform less well than smaller; and older bureaucracies are not necessarily more ossified than younger. Also, although bureaucracies possess and represent highly significant political power, this power is not unchecked. Contentions that bureaucracy perpetuates socioeconomic inequities and contributes to policy drift are, moreover, not nearly as damning as they sound.

The book then concludes with a brief of the case for bureaucracy. An explanation for what is exploded by this case, the grand bureaucratic myth, is offered. Compelling reasons must exist, it is speculated, for why something that works reasonably well and is so close to our daily lives becomes grossly underestimated and wildly ridiculed. The book concludes with some advice to colleagues in the field of public administration, which they will not—I expect—unanimously and immediately follow.

CHAPTER 2

THE WATER GLASS
VIEWED DIFFERENTLY

Imagining bureaucracy as a partially full glass of water with the empty portion representing bureaucracy's failings and the contents its achievements, it is possible to fasten attention on either the partial emptiness or the partial fullness of the vessel. To some extent, I suppose, choices of this kind depend on one's personal view of the world. Yet in the instance of this particular water glass, the choice is essentially imposed on us. The accepted cultural and academic view of bureaucracy as incompetent and malicious forces attention upon the emptiness and not the fullness. In fact we expect the water level to be very low indeed—the glass of bureaucracy is assumed to be nearly empty.

In the present chapter we test the water level of bureaucratic performance and consider whether the glass should be viewed differently. We conduct this test at a point that is critical, at least within my scale of values. This is the point of service delivery to individual citizens. In a democratic polity that proclaims public responsiveness as a major goal and respect for the individual a central tenet, the immediate encounter between bureaucracy and citizen would appear to be the crucial testing ground for public administration. At this final end-point in the chain of collective action, bureaucracy's moment of truth arrives, so to speak.

The prevailing view is that bureaucratic service to clients is terrible. Such a judgment is typically developed from purely deductive reasoning, if any attempt to support it is made at all. Illustrative is the argument of one scholar that "organizational behavior leading to client dissatisfaction is inherent in the very structure of government itself." The author then predicts structure-induced dissatisfactions in the form of insensitivity to individual clients' problems; extreme pigeonholing of responsibility; and inflexible, hostile, and self-interested behavior by officials. Whether even the writer is convinced of this reasoning is questionable, however, inasmuch as it is admitted that "in most cases, the client or public receives the services requested or entitled to. Similarly in most cases treatment is fair, courteous and quick."[1]

Doubts about "ritualized degradation" of bureaucratic clients have arisen elsewhere from time to time. This is even true in the public welfare field, which, in addition to law enforcement, has probably the worst reputation with respect to citizen treatment. Speaking of the current welfare system and alternative proposals for "service integration," Morris and Lescohier ask:

> Is the present complex system really all that unsatisfactory to most of the users? Critics too often assume that dissatisfactions voiced by some reveal widespread dissatisfactions with existing arrangements. But is this necessarily true? Good data are lacking, and the lack of overwhelming evidence to the contrary leads some critics to argue that consumers do not press for significant changes because they do not know what better arrangements might be developed. A contrary interpretation is just as reasonable — that most consumers are fairly well satisfied with the present system and are reluctant to force a major change which may, at best, benefit a relative few — and that that benefit is not certain.[2]

This chapter provides some "good data." They will consist of reports directly from clients with supplemental performance information from agency records. This evidence is not, by the way, without its faults in terms of proven validity and representative completeness. But it is vastly superior along these lines compared to the largely nonempirical deduction so commonly used in assessing client service. Moreover, the evidence to be presented permits us to assess *proportionate* levels of satisfaction-dissatisfaction or success-failure, and not be reduced to forming an unbalanced impression from bureaucratic horror stories or the political statements of assorted axe grinders.

SURVEYING THE SURVEYS

Survey research is, of course, not without inherent problems of validity and bias. The Gallup polls mentioned in the previous chapter illustrate how the wording of questions can affect outcomes, for example. We should not, however, permit the current disenchantment (which I personally share) with surveys in social science to obscure their advantages. These advantages include flexibility in collection of new data (we need not depend on existing information), relatively inexpensive and thus high-count observation, and opportunities for the systematic sampling of large populations. Nor should we allow current interest in interpretive orientations to social research — which deny the existence of an objective reality in the first place — to persuade us that surveys are meaningless. Even if surveys reflect only the "constructed" realities of those surveyed, such constructions form the basis for evaluation of daily experience by the populations studied. Moreover, it can be argued, subjective realities of bureaucratic experience on the part of numerous citizens far outweigh in importance those of some antibureaucratic interpretivist professors.

Numerous surveys have been conducted that bear on citizen opinion regarding bureaucratic service or treatment. These vary considerably in quality and original purpose. In describing these many studies, we begin with relatively fragmentary and localized surveys and then move on to more definitive and nationwide investigations.

Probably the earliest citizen survey on perceived bureaucratic performance was conducted by Leonard D. White, a principal founder of the field of public administration. In 1929 White published the results of a survey he conducted in Chicago of 4,000 residents of that city. One question asked was: *"Do people generally think more highly of employment in the city hall than of employment with private corporations?"* Fifty-eight percent replied in favor of the private corporations. Another of White's queries was: *"Have your own dealings with public employees and officials been satisfactory?"* The outcome was 69 percent "yes" or equivalent. White was struck by the difference between these two responses. He speculated that the bad image of machine politics in Chicago accounted for the low reputation of city hall employment, while, and in spite of this, the machine's bureaucrats delivered services more than adequately. Stating a conclusion that should not have been forgotten this past half century, White suggested that "the great bulk of city officials and employees are more sinned against than sinning."[3]

Today, many students of government are, in effect, following White's lead by asking residents of communities their opinion of municipal services. In fact, citizen surveys of urban services have become something of a fad among city governments that view themselves as progressive and concerned with program evaluation. Officials of Normal, Illinois, asked citizens, *"Have you ever been treated discourteously by a town employee?"* Eleven percent answered yes, 85 percent said no, and 4 percent gave no response.[4] Dallas, Texas, which has been something of a leader in this area, annually asks a sample of its citizens to evaluate the response by city hall to telephone calls making complaints or requesting services. The 1978 results regarding quality of response to complaints and emergency calls and speed of response to emergency calls are given in table 2.1 We note that 58 to 80 percent of those sampled declared the city's performance to be either excellent or good.[5]

As mentioned, welfare and law enforcement are probably the areas of service delivery with the worst reputations. Nonetheless, the Dallas survey cited found that 79 percent of citizens sampled perceived the police as "generally fair" with only 8 percent viewing them as "generally unfair." As for welfare,

TABLE 2.1. EVALUATION OF CITY RESPONSIVENESS, DALLAS

	Excellent	Good	Only Fair	Poor
Response to complaints	26%	32%	20%	22%
Response to calls	47	33	14	7
Speed of response	53	27	10	10

the Milwaukee County Department of Social Services is required by local ordinance to submit an evaluative questionnaire to each consumer of county-purchased services. Tabulations for 1977 showed that 70 percent of recipients of unwed-parent services felt "their social worker treats them with respect." Ninety percent of those benefiting from group foster care said they have been "treated with respect and understanding."[6] Another analysis, conducted of its own operations by the Maine Bureau of Social Welfare in 1972, involved structured interviews at the homes of more than 1,700 clients of social services. Ninety to 95 percent placed their social workers in these categories: "Are friendly towards you," "Treat you with respect," "Really listen to what you have to say," and "Explain things so that you can understand." Also, 57 percent stated they had either completely or mostly reached the goal they and the social worker had agreed upon.[7]

As for evaluations of welfare service delivery at the federal level, in 1974 Social Security Administration staff interviewed a sample of more than 1,200 recipients of Supplemental Security Income (SSI). When asked, *"Have you been treated with courtesy and respect?,"* 79 percent said "Always." The question *"Have you gotten your checks on time?"* resulted in an "always" response from 83 percent, while 82 percent answered similarly to *"Does the SSI check include the full amount to which you are entitled?"*[8] In another Social Security study, conducted in 1975, contracted interviewers surveyed a small sample of that agency's clients on the premises of four district offices around the country. Prior to intake, 67 incoming clients were asked *"How satisfied were you with the outcome of your last visit to Social Security?"* The responses were:

Very satisfied	22%
Satisfied	50
Dissatisfied	19
Very dissatisfied	7

When in the same study 105 clients were interviewed after a Social Security transaction and were asked, *"How did your interview turn out?"* 71 percent said, "fine, okay"; 11 percent, "got what was expected"; and 8 percent, "poorly." Asked to evaluate the Social Security representative dealt with on an over-all basis, 64 percent said "excellent," 32 percent "satisfactory," and only 3 percent "unsatisfactory."[9]

In short, even police and welfare bureaucrats receive good to excellent marks when graded by most citizens. But the surveys mentioned to this point, with the exception of White's, were all conducted by bureaucracies themselves. Naturally, self-interest would dictate designing and executing the studies so as to reflect as favorably as possible on operations. Thus we need to examine evaluations carried out by other parties as well.

A study of Wisconsin state administrative operations was conducted by the University of Wisconsin Extension organization. More than 6,000 residents throughout the state were questioned. The responses in table 2.2 were from citizens of the state who had had telephonic or personal contacts within the past year with state employees involved with transportation (i.e., highway patrolmen and driver's license examiners).[10]

TABLE 2.2. EVALUATION OF CONTACTS WITH
STATE TRANSPORTATION PERSONNEL, WISCONSIN

	Excellent	Good	Fair	Poor	Depends
Courtesy of treatment	49%	36%	12%	3%	1%
Helpfulness of employees	46	37	11	4	1

Also, researchers from the University of Dayton surveyed 972 residents of that city on the quality of municipal services. One question asked about expectations of service in this manner: *"If you were to call a city official about a complaint or service request, how likely is it that the official would do something about it?"* A helping response was anticipated as "very likely" by 24 percent, "somewhat likely" by 43 percent, "not very likely" by 20 percent, and "not at all likely" by 13 percent.[11]

Another examination of citizen evaluation of urban services was conducted by the Bureau of Public Administration of the University of Tennessee. Within a sample of 438 surveyed individuals, 70 percent were satisfied with police services, 57 percent with education, 78 percent with sanitation, 87 percent with fire protection, and 47 percent with street services. Aggregatively, three-quarters were satisfied with at least three of the five services, and almost half were satisfied with at least four of them.[12]

As for independent research on citizen assessments of police work alone, researchers at Indiana University asked residents of three Indianapolis neighborhoods and three suburban communities what kind of job they thought the

TABLE 2.3. EVALUATION OF POLICE PERFORMANCE,
INDIANAPOLIS AND SUBURBS

	Indianapolis	Suburban
Outstanding	12%	31%
Good	42	44
Adequate	37	23
Inadequate	9	2

police were doing (table 2.3). Most of the citizens questioned did not feel the police accepted bribes, and the vast majority believed police response time was very rapid or quick enough (84 percent in Indianapolis, 97 percent in other communities).[13]

Independent studies by academicians of client perceptions of welfare case-workers are also suggestive. In six counties of Wisconsin it was shown that 77 percent of 558 clients were not bothered "at all" in discussing their personal budget with a caseworker. In reply to being asked whether this discussion is helpful, 24 percent said "very," 18 percent said "usually," 32 percent said "some," while 26 percent said "not at all."[14] Interviews of clients waiting in line in a Louisiana employment office showed that while most of them did not perceive a particularly "caring" attitude among the officials there, two-thirds saw the office as fair and impartial, and 84 percent believed the interviewers took enough time "to consider all the facts" and did not "hurry through" and fail to consider the client as an individual.[15]

MORE DEFINITIVE SURVEYS

The survey results described in the preceding section show favorable response rates on questions concerning bureaucratic performance that are almost never below 50 percent, usually above 70 percent, and not infrequently in the 80 and 90 percent ranges. In light of attacks on bureaucracy's treatment of clients, the consistency with which citizens evaluate their personal experiences with public agencies in a positive light is remarkable. We find high levels of approval of bureaucratic services rendered at the town, city, county, state, and federal levels. Responses are proportionately favorable with respect to complaint handling, quality of service, speed of service, absence of corruption, and degree of courtesy and respect shown. Satisfaction is expressed with services in areas of social welfare, law enforcement, transportation, sanitation, and fire protection.

Let us now compare these findings from several rather small-scale studies to the outcome of several bigger and more ambitious surveys. We examine, first, three public opinion surveys conducted with nationwide samples in the early 1970s.

In 1973, the Harris polling organization undertook an extensive study of public attitudes toward government in behalf of the Senate Subcommittee on Intergovernmental Relations. A random sample of 1,596 respondents was selected in 200 locations throughout the country, with interviews conducted in the respondents' homes in the usual pollster manner.

In one sequence of questions put by the Harris interviewers, respondents were asked if they had ever gone to the federal, state, or local government "to get them to do something" not related to routine matters such as paying taxes or applying for licenses or Social Security. Those indicating they had sought an important personal objective in the halls of bureaucracy were then asked two questions, with responses recorded for each level of government. The queries and corresponding results are shown in table 2.4.[16]

TABLE 2.4. HARRIS POLL OF PUBLIC ATTITUDES TOWARD GOVERNMENT

Did you find the people you went to at (the federal/your state/your local) government helpful or not helpful?

	Federal	State	Local
Helpful	73%	66%	64%
Not helpful	24	29	34
Not sure	3	5	2

Did you come away from that experience with (the federal/state/local) government highly satisfied, only somewhat satisfied, or not satisfied at all?

	Federal	State	Local
Highly satisfied	46%	39%	39%
Only somewhat satisfied	29	26	26
Not satisfied at all	24	34	35
Not sure	1	1	0

Points of interest in these data include the finding that two-thirds or more found bureaucracy helpful, a level generally consistent with the surveys discussed earlier. This is particularly important since a nonroutine matter was involved. As for satisfaction levels, respondents who regarded themselves as highly satisfied seem relatively few in comparison to the earlier survey evidence until we note how the question's options are stated; the only intermediate option between "highly satisfied" and "not satisfied at all" is the coolly phrased choice "only somewhat satisfied." Those less than completely satisfied but still favorably disposed had no choice other than the second answer. If we sum the response rates in the first two option categories, the 65 to 75 percent range of approval found earlier is repeated. In any case, those perceiving bureaucracy as definitely not helpful or satisfying were in the minority, at levels of 24 to 35 percent. We note finally that experience with federal bureaucracy was more favorably perceived than with state or local government. This differential should confound those who insist that the federal government is more "remote" from the citizenry and thus must render poorer service.

Another pertinent national poll was conducted about the same time by researchers at the University of Michigan's Survey Research Center. Once again a sample of about 1,500 was used, with home interviewing according to a structured schedule. Although carried out as part of the SRC's annual omnibus survey, the study was designed and its results were interpreted as an integrated investigation specifically focused on citizen encounters with bureaucracy.

In one set of questions respondents were asked if they had ever gone to a government agency for help in a number of indicated areas, from finding a job to securing public assistance or obtaining retirement benefits. Those with such experiences were then asked a number of specific questions regarding their perceptions of the offices and individuals encountered. Aggregate results from four of these questions are shown in table 2.5 on page 24.[17]

On the first question, 69 percent expressed themselves as very or fairly well satisfied with the way the bureaucratic office handled their problem. This figure is within the 65 to 75 percent range found in the Harris query on satisfaction. As for the somewhat more specific questions on effort, efficiency, and fairness, positive replies were given in the 73 to 76 percent range.

Two other kinds of questions asked by the Michigan researchers are of particular interest. In one, interviewers sought to discover whether the problems the clients had brought to the offices had in fact been solved. The overall percentage of responses coded as favorable in this regard was 59. Also, the Michigan project attempted to investigate the respondents' abstract images of bureaucracy, as against their concrete experiences with it. To a certain extent these images seemed less favorable to bureaucracy than reports on experiences. This led analysts to conclude that generalized attitudes toward bureaucracy are based not so much on concrete experiences as "the cumulative impact of the mass media and the accepted beliefs in the culture." While unpleasant encounters lower general evaluation of government, they suggest, successful and acceptable ones do not raise it.[18]

TABLE 2.5. UNIVERSITY OF MICHIGAN SURVEY OF
SATISFACTION WITH BUREAUCRACY

*How satisfied were you with the way the office handled your problem?
Would you say you were very satisfied, fairly well satisfied, somewhat dissatisfied, or very dissatisfied?*

Very satisfied	43%
Fairly well satisfied	26
Somewhat dissatisfied	12
Very dissatisfied	14
Don't know, no answer	5

*How much effort did the people at the office make to help you? Would
you say it was more than they had to, about right, less than they should have,
or no effort at all?*

More than they had to	16%
About right	57
Less than should have	12
No effort	9
Don't know, no answer	6

*How efficient did you think the office was in handling your problem? Was
it very efficient, fairly efficient, rather inefficient, or very inefficient?*

Very efficient	43%
Fairly efficient	31
Rather inefficient	9
Very inefficient	11
Don't know, no answer	6

Do you feel you were treated fairly, or unfairly, by the office?

Fairly	76%
Unfairly	12
Mixed	5
Don't know, no answer	7

A third important national survey conducted in the early 1970s was done by researchers at Ohio State University's Mershon Center. Interested particularly in the client application process, the survey team asked about 6,500 respondents to evaluate agency behavior upon applying, within the past year, to any of some 16 service programs. Inasmuch as some respondents had applied to more than one program, data were collected on the basis of applications, not respondents. Three of the principal questions asked with resultant aggregated answers are given in table 2.6.[19]

TABLE 2.6. OHIO STATE SURVEY OF APPLICANTS FOR GOVERNMENT SERVICES

In your opinion, how helpful (is/was) this agency to you? Would you say that it (is/was) very helpful, somewhat helpful, or not at all helpful?

Very helpful	57%
Somewhat helpful	22
Not at all helpful	17
Don't know, no response	5

In your opinion, how fair (is/was) the agency in its dealings with you? Would you say that it (is/was) very fair, somewhat fair, or not at all fair?

Very fair	60%
Somewhat fair	23
Not at all fair	10
Don't know, no response	7

In your opinion, how considerate (are/were) the people at this agency toward you as a person? Would you say that they (are/were) very considerate, somewhat considerate, or not at all considerate?

Very considerate	60%
Somewhat considerate	24
Not at all considerate	9
Don't know, no response	7

We note that in these application events the bureaucratic agency was recalled as very or somewhat helpful 79 percent of the time, a figure even higher than the Harris results on helpfulness. Similarly, the 83 percent of cases where the agency was evaluated as very or somewhat fair is substantially above the outcome on the Michigan fairness question. On considerateness, an even higher favorable total is found in 84 percent. Proportions of negative responses were correspondingly lower than those found in the other two polls, in a mere 9 to 17 percent range.

Like the Michigan study, the Ohio State project also examined the outcomes of bureaucratic encounters. It was determined that 82 percent of the applications had been accepted, with benefits being received in 74 percent of the cases at the time of the survey. Only 11 percent of the applications had been rejected, while 7 percent were pending.[20]

We turn now to two other surveys of bureaucratic clients, both carried out in the late 1970s. These did not utilize complete national samples or involve thousands of respondents, but each adds an important dimension to our understanding of client evaluation by employing a distinctive survey method.

Stuart Schmidt contacted current or past clients of the Wisconsin State Employment Service and asked them to fill out a mail-back questionnaire on their views of the service rendered. This agency works with two clienteles, job seekers and employers. Schmidt obtained completed questionnaires from 300 job applicants and 183 businessmen who had dealt with three district offices of the organization. Four of the questions asked are given in table 2.7 (queries to applicants are literally quoted, while employer questions were parallel in phrasing but not identical).[21]

Job applicants checked the top two favorable options on the questionnaires only 49 percent of the time for quality of service but from 61 to 67 per-

TABLE 2.7. RESPONSES TO QUESTIONNAIRE,
WISCONSIN STATE EMPLOYMENT SERVICE

From your experience, how would you rate the quality of the services that you received from the State Employment Service office?

	Applicants	Employers
Excellent	15%	7%
Good	34	45
Fair	30	21
Poor	20	17
Not ascertained	—	11

Do you feel that the people in the State Employment Service office look out for your interests in their dealings with you?

TABLE 2.7 *(Continued)*

	Applicants	Employers
Very much	25%	11%
Fairly much	42	49
Not so much	23	23
Not at all	11	4
Not ascertained	—	14

Do you feel that the people in the State Employment Service office tried to adapt their rules and methods to meet your needs?

	Applicants	Employers
Very much	16%	11%
Fairly much	47	54
Not so much	18	23
Not at all	18	8
Not ascertained	—	5

How satisfied are you with the services provided by the State Employment Service?

	Applicants	Employers
Very much	26%	13%
Fairly much	35	39
Not so much	19	21
Not at all	20	14
Not ascertained	—	14

cent on the other three criteria. These proportions do not seem inordinately low in view of the fact that probably only a minority of the applicants had found a job through the Employment Service. Even though the questionnaires were handled anonymously and the applicants had no fear of retribution, expressed levels of outright dissatisfaction were only in the 20 to 39 percent range. Most interesting is the fact that the employers, who as businessmen might have ideological reasons to be hostile to bureaucracy, indicated similar levels of approval. They did not mark the most favorable response option as often as the applicants did, but neither did they select the least favorable as frequently.

The other distinctive survey of the late 1970s to be mentioned is an "exit poll" conducted by this author outside welfare offices in four U.S. cities. The first twenty clients to emerge from the office during the middle of a business day were approached on the sidewalk or in the parking lot in front of the agency's building. Perhaps surprisingly, approximately 90 percent readily agreed to be interviewed. Structured questions were asked of 240 clients of public welfare, unemployment compensation, and Social Security offices in San Francisco, St. Louis, Duluth, Minnesota, and Evansville, Indiana. Prior to commencing each interview I identified myself as a teacher doing research and not connected in any way with the office inside. (This was true, although prior permission had been obtained from officials to conduct the interviews.)

Once again, reports on bureaucracy were favorable, at least in contrast to popular stereotypes. In response to the question *"Did you get done what you came for?"* 75 percent said they did. When asked how long they had had to wait prior to conducting their business with a worker, 29 percent indicated that they were taken care of right away and 15 percent more said they waited less than ten minutes. Only one-fourth had to wait a half hour or more. Sixty-eight percent of the interviewees stated the person assigned to them "really listened" to what they said, and 67 percent felt the worker "really tried" to get them their benefits. Generally, the personnel encountered in the office were regarded as very courteous by 66 percent, very efficient by 52 percent, and very sympathetic by 37 percent. If one adds to these figures the "somewhat" responses, they come to 90, 91, and 66 percent, respectively. Only 7 percent stated they had argued with personnel in the office. When asked, *"Overall, how satisfied were you with the way the office handled your problem?"* the responses were:[22]

Very satisfied	50%
Fairly satisfied	23
Somewhat dissatisfied	10
Very dissatisfied	17

A final survey to be reported concerns what might be regarded as the foremost bureaucratic hate object in the nation, the U.S. Postal Service. Every citizen heaps scorn on this organization when mail is delayed, and attacks on the post office are one of the most popular themes in press criticism of bureaucracy. Yet, how do citizens evaluate postal performance in light of their overall experience with it?

The Postal Service, understandably self-conscious of its image, regularly contracts with a private polling firm to collect data on attitudes of its "household customers," namely private citizens who have used the mails within the past thirty days. Surveys are conducted two times a year by structured interviews in a random national sample of approximately 1,000 homes. Three of the generalized questions asked in each survey are shown in table 2.8 on page 30, with the results recorded each April given.[23]

Incredibly, even the universally castigated Postal Service receives largely favorable ratings when overall evaluations, rather than momentary ire over a late letter, are considered. Over the past nine years 79 to 85 percent of respondents have rated their experience as recipients of mail "good" or better, with 75 to 83 percent saying the same as senders. Moreover, "excellent" ratings almost always surpass "fair" or "poor" ones, and often even the sum of the two. As for the total impression question, it yields a 74 to 80 percent summarized favorable rating and an 11 to 20 percent unfavorable. Moreover, these patterns are quite consistent down through the years, suggesting a basic core of citizen approval whose presence is verified by repeated surveys.

REFLECTIONS ON THE SURVEYS

These national opinion surveys and additional studies substantiate the conclusions of surveys discussed earlier. Citizens perceive their concrete experiences with bureaucracy in a generally favorable light. Usually the preponderant majority of persons asked describes their recollections or immediate experiences in highly approving terms. Most positive evaluation response rates are at least at the two-thirds level, and many reach beyond 75 percent. Disapproval levels are almost always in the distinct minority, and most fall well below one-third. The vast majority of clients of bureaucracy reports itself as satisfied with the encounter and transaction therein. In most instances bureaucratic personnel are described as helpful, efficient, fair, considerate, and courteous. They are, furthermore, usually perceived as trying to assist, ready to listen, and even willing to adapt the rules and look out for client interests. Also, the actual performance output of bureaucracy is usually praised. The picture presented by citizens in their assessments of bureaucracy appears, in sum, as an almost complete contradiction of the hate image depicted in popular media and academic writing.

One response to this contradiction has been most interesting. It has been an attempt to discredit citizen evaluation of bureaucracy. Incapable of accepting the idea that, despite bureaucracy's reputation, citizens usually have good experiences with it, some academic authorities have attempted to blunt the impact of the surveys by raising methodological doubts about them. In short, rather than use the surprisingly favorable findings as a reason to rethink fun-

TABLE 2.8. CUSTOMER SURVEYS, U.S. POSTAL SERVICE

Overall, how would you rate the service the Postal Service provides to you as a receiver *of mail?*

	1973	1974	1975	1976	1977	1978	1979	1980	1981
Excellent	23%	25%	25%	22%	23%	19%	24%	19%	20%
Very good	27	28	28	26	25	27	29	29	26
Good	29	31	31	32	35	35	32	35	37
Fair	15	13	13	16	13	14	11	13	13
Poor	6	3	3	4	4	5	4	4	4

Overall, how would you rate the service the Postal Service provides to you as a sender *of mail?*

	1973	1974	1975	1976	1977	1978	1979	1980	1981
Excellent	21%	24%	23%	19%	17%	17%	18%	16%	16%
Very good	24	24	24	23	25	26	28	28	27
Good	34	35	34	33	38	37	37	38	38
Fair	14	13	14	19	15	16	14	14	15
Poor	7	4	5	6	5	4	3	4	4

Which of these phrases best describes your impression of the U.S. Postal Service?

	1973	1974	1975	1976	1977	1978	1979	1980	1981
Very favorable	37%	42%	41%	33%	35%	36%	38%	38%	35%
Somewhat favorable	37	38	38	37	41	41	41	40	40
(Sum favorable)	(74)	(80)	(79)	(70)	(76)	(77)	(79)	(78)	(75)
Neither favorable nor unfavorable	10	8	9	10	10	10	9	11	12
Somewhat unfavorable	12	10	9	15	11	9	10	9	10
Very unfavorable	4	2	3	5	3	4	2	2	4
(Sum unfavorable)	(16)	(12)	(12)	(20)	(14)	(13)	(12)	(11)	(14)

damentally the prevalent intellectual models of bureaucracy, these critics argue that simple citizens cannot be giving us "correct" information.[24]

Five principal objections are raised to citizen surveys:

1. Citizens are said to expect so little from bureaucracy initially that they are pleasantly surprised when it performs at all.
2. The questions asked are said to be too abstract and global to be meaningful.
3. Respondents are claimed to answer with approving statements because of social pressures of the interview situation.
4. The questions posed in the surveys are regarded as phrased in such a way as to induce positive answers.
5. Regardless of their quality, survey results are considered as inferior to objective program statistics, which, it is said, often disagree with them.

Let us consider each of these objections.

As for the argument that citizens are so pessimistic that even mediocre performance seems good, let us for a moment recall the question asked by the Dayton researchers on expectations. Respondents were invited to state the probabilities that the city would do something about a complaint or request for service. Such a response was declared "very likely" by 24 percent and "somewhat likely" by 43 percent. Thus, positive expectations were entertained by a combined total of two-thirds of the sample—somewhat more optimism than the critics would lead us to believe.

Moreover, bureaucratic interactions that are *ongoing* in nature could hardly build unrealistic expectations. Clients would learn to know all along what to anticipate. We found evaluations by welfare clients of their caseworkers—whom they see periodically and often very frequently—as highly favorable. The Milwaukee study showed 70 and 90 percent agreement with statements concerning caseworker respect, and the Maine survey yielded a parallel finding in the 90 percent range. In the Wisconsin county study, we found that 74 percent of welfare clients believed personal budget talks were helpful to some extent. In my own exit interviewing, 67 percent of visitors to public welfare offices said their caseworker really tried to help them, with 66 percent declaring him or her very courteous. The Postal Service is clearly another recurring encounter with bureaucracy, and we have seen that rated favorably over the years at about the 75 percent level.

With respect to the abstract and global nature of the questions, it is true that many ask vaguely about "helpfulness," "fairness," "satisfaction," and the like. But such terms do tap general impressions of bureaucratic experiences.

Moreover, a number of other queries are exceedingly specific. Favorable responses were received in questions about response to complaints, the speed of emergency services, the corruption of police, and the courtesy of officials. Other questions concerned such concrete matters as the promptness and correctness of checks, the duration of office waits and whether an argument with officials was initiated. These highly specific questions yielded no less positive results.

An assumption behind the objection concerning vagueness is that in responding to general questions citizens simply acquiesce to the social situation of the interview or to their unconscious socialization to legitimated authority and reply in an automatically favorable way. Such "positive bias" is more the product of methodological speculation than empirical demonstration, however. One can just as persuasively argue that citizens, accustomed to the daily diatribes of bureaucracy they encounter in the culture at large, will automatically give negative answers in order to appear sophisticated and in touch with the "real" world of knowledgeable insiders.

Regardless of which line of speculation is more valid, we found that two of the cited surveys did not involve a social situation in which positive-bias dynamics could occur. Surveys involving the Milwaukee Department of Social Services and Wisconsin State Employment Service both used anonymous, mailed questionnaires. Furthermore, my own sidewalk and parking lot interviews convinced me that no degree of social pressure or system socialization would keep genuinely upset clients, who had walked out the door of bureaucratic offices a moment earlier, from expressing these feelings. Those few who were mad were plainly mad, and they told me so.

The fourth objection has to do with the positive phrasing of questions. It is very true that some questions induce a favorable answer, such as White's *"Have your own dealings with public employees and officials been satisfactory?"* and the Social Security Administration's *"Have you been treated with courtesy and respect?"* Yet many other questions used were neutral in wording, such as the contracted Social Security study's *"How did your interview turn out?"* and the questions asked in the national polls where the range of response options was included in the query itself. At least one question in the surveys cited was intentionally negative in phrasing, namely, the Normal, Illinois, question *"Have you ever been treated discourteously by a town employee?"* Furthermore, in a study not mentioned above, an evaluation for the Maine Bureau of Social Welfare on contracted social services, extremely negative questions were posed. For example, clients were asked the extent to which they agreed with the statement *"I don't feel that this service is really helping me."* Only 10 percent agreed; 84 percent disagreed. Another question was

"Could you use more help than you're getting now, not just from the agency but from anywhere?" Only 37 percent answered yes, with 56 percent responding no.[25]

A last objection to client surveys is that they yield subjective evaluative data that are inferior to objective, "harder," program statistics. Certainly citizen impressions are subjective, whether from the standpoint of the positivists' "perceptual sleeve" or the interpretivists' "constructed reality." But, as we shall see in a moment, nonsurvey performance data can also be very favorable in the picture they paint of bureaucracy. Moreover, the case is sometimes made by writers on program evaluation that in terms of sheer measuring value, it is difficult to find anything superior to citizen satisfaction. Blanche Blank and her co-authors state that "satisfaction is a particularly relevant output for American public bureaucracies because it is possibly the only manageable calculus in a democracy. It offers a method of measuring specific goal attainment in a highly complex system of undifferentiated public goals."[26] Taking another tack, Margo Koss and her associates comment in reference to the welfare field:

> Overall, it seems that clients themselves are the most practical source of reasonably reliable data on client outcomes. Clients are in a sense the "experts" on their own feelings and problems, and they have more up-to-date information than records or caseworkers have. Even though their judgment about their problems might at times be questionable, and their reports might not always be accurate, complete, or fully frank, they still seem to be the best source of data.[27]

I would prefer, however, to make the case for paying close heed to client satisfaction in normative rather than practical terms. In a society and polity where approval by the citizenry of government is valued in its own right, citizen perceptions should count as *innately* important. It would seem undemocratic to contend otherwise. Of course lay citizens are not well informed on program eligibility requirements, bureaucratic rules and procedures, budget-necessitated priorities, and other "objective" realities. They are not experts, and thus will not evaluate bureaucracy as experts. Nevertheless, they are the ultimate judges of whether government works and is thus acceptable. Moreover, for them the system's success is not merely a matter of intellectual debate but high-stake issues such as whether one waits two hours in an office to see the right person, whether one is treated by the people there as a human being, and whether one's government check actually arrives and on time. How better to evaluate bureaucracy?

DIRECT PERFORMANCE MEASURES

We now supplement this citizen survey data with other information capable of shedding light on the proportionate performance of bureaucracy. Government agencies develop directly statistics and records of many kinds that are useful for indicating, in a systematic way, relative levels of achievement or failure. I include this kind of evidence in our reexamination of the water glass of bureaucracy to satisfy those who insist that it is only such "factual" information that tells the true story.

In selecting recorded statistics I deliberately chose from policy areas where bureaucracy's performance is especially suspect as inhumane or inefficient. If this beast of society is so ugly, let us find out right away by looking at some of its least attractive parts.

As we know, that part of bureaucracy handling welfare is often thought of as its most pernicious. Program statistics available for welfare that measure proportionate levels of success concern application acceptance rates, agency error rates, and the speed of eligibility decisions.

With respect to the first, 66 percent of applications for Aid to Families with Dependent Children (AFDC) were approved on a state-average basis in 1974-76. In the first half of 1976 the mean state turndown rate on grounds of noncompliance with procedures was 5 percent. Discontinuance of existing AFDC eligibility for procedural irregularities was at a rate of less than 2 percent. Proclient actions with regard to cases are not necessarily "right" technically, of course, but the higher their rates, the less valid is an image of an anti-client, obstructive bureaucracy.[28]

As for error rates, incorrect AFDC eligibility decisions were made by agencies in 5 percent of cases audited in the first half of 1976 (state average). These involved 4 percent of the payments made. Wrong payment-level decisions were made in an additional 18 percent of the cases. Six percent of audited food stamp rejection or termination actions were found to be invalid. In these comparatively few errors, the incidence of giving clients more than the rules call for far exceeded granting insufficient assistance or withholding it.[29]

On the speed of bureaucratic action in welfare, in 1976 the average time needed for determination of AFDC eligibility was 23 days (mean of 25 states for which data were available). With respect to unemployment compensation, 83 percent of successful state unemployment insurance claims were paid within two weeks in 1979. Within three weeks, 91 percent of successful claimants were receiving checks.[30]

Program statistics are also available for the frequently castigated Postal Service. As with public opinion of mail service, the Postal Service monitors mail delivery times by means of a nationwide, periodic sampling system. Ac-

cording to its statistics for 1980, 95 percent of all first class mail correctly addressed to a local destination and deposited before 5 P.M. was delivered the
next day. Eighty-six percent of such mail going to locations generally within a
600-mile radius arrived in two days, and 87 percent of that moving farther was
delivered in three days.[31] In the first quarter of 1981, the average first-class
mailing arrived in 1.73 days with 5.07 days needed for parcel post and 5.58 days
for other fourth class.[32]

Also, the post office makes studies of the behavior of postal window
clerks. These are done by sending confederate "customers"—hired by a contractor—into representative post offices around the country and having them
engage in predesigned transactions. The confederates then leave the post office
and fill out a reporting form, without local postal officials knowing they have
been observed.

One thing such investigation shows is that the vast majority of postal
transactions is handled with considerable dispatch. One study found customer
waiting times five minutes or less in 92 percent of the test cases and transaction
times five minutes or less in 83 percent ($N = 1,440$). Another conclusion is that
clerks usually, but not always, handle transactions with technical correctness.
For example, in one study the correct charge was levied 75 percent of the time
for several transactions, each of which was especially designed as out of the
ordinary and demanding a thorough knowledge of the rules. Interestingly
enough, errors were particularly frequent when clerks were presented with the
dilemma of enforcing the rules or inconveniencing customers. A COD pack-
age was accepted for delivery to an APO (military) address 61 percent of the
time, for example, even though this should not be done. An undersized letter
was similarly accepted 78 percent of the time; and a parcel wrapped in flimsy
paper, sealed with masking tape, and marked "fragile" was accepted 75 percent of the time.[33]

An area of deep suspicion regarding performance in perhaps all bureaucracies is response to complaints. We have already seen that citizens are not
necessarily pessimistic about the outcome of complaints. But for those of us
who may remain skeptical, a large-scale study of what agencies actually did in
response to citizen complaints was conducted under the Technical Assistance
Research Program of the Office of Consumer Affairs of the former Department of Health, Education, and Welfare. In a rather unusual methodology,
the evaluators (employed by an outside contractor) directly examined the
complaint files of twelve federal agencies. By so doing they assessed the agencies' responses to approximately 250 citizen complaints. Agency action was
largely evaluated according to two criteria: appropriateness, or whether the
agency adequately tailored its response to the specific nature of the citizen's

problem; and clarity, meaning whether the response was written at a level of readability commensurate with the citizen's probable educational level. The percentage of files examined where an affirmative finding was made for these criteria is shown in table 2.9, for the agencies named.[34]

TABLE 2.9. QUALITY OF AGENCY RESPONSE TO CITIZEN COMPLAINTS

	Appropriateness	Clarity
Civil Aeronautics Board	97%	99%
Consumer Product Safety Commission	93	98
Federal Communications Commission	43	46
Federal Energy Administration	56	90
Federal Trade Commission	72	93
Food and Drug Administration	100	97
Housing and Urban Development	60	87
Interstate Commerce Commission	93	100
National Highway Traffic Safety		
Administration	95	97
Office of Consumer Affairs, HEW	78	93
U.S. Department of Agriculture	78	93
U.S. Postal Service	91	98
MEAN PERCENT	80	91

We note that for half the agencies, an appropriate response had been made in more than 90 percent of the cases and a clear response at that level in ten out of twelve agencies. Mean percentages for the twelve were 80 for appropriateness and 91 for clarity. Only one organization of those studied, the FCC, fell below 50 percent levels. The researchers also noted that average response times varied from 9 to 45 days, with the overall being 19 days. Apparently even the supposedly impersonal, unfeeling, unresponsive "ten-ton marshmallow" of the federal bureaucracy is capable of being successfully prodded by John Q. Citizen.

In welfare actions, postal service, and citizen complaints, then, proportionate statistics are available that portray bureaucracy as not perfect but working fairly well most of the time. Two-thirds of AFDC applications are accepted, procedural rejections of applications are rare, errors are committed in a definite minority of AFDC and food stamp cases and then usually in favor of the client, eligibility decisions are usually fairly prompt, the vast majority of mail arrives on time, most postal transactions are quick and accurate, and most federal agencies adequately respond to complaints and do so reasonably fast. Perhaps bureaucracy should be thought of as not so much a terrible beast as a fairly good used car, quite old but well maintained and functioning not all but most of the time. It is those mornings when the car does not start—perhaps once or twice every winter?—that we recognize the machine's fallibility and then malign it furiously. For a fundamental feature of bureaucracy is that it continually performs millions of tiny acts of individual service, such as approving applications, delivering the mail, and answering complaints. Because this ongoing mass of routine achievement is not in itself noteworthy or even capable of intellectual grasp, it operates silently, almost out of sight. The occasional breakdowns, the unusual scandals, the individual instances where a true injustice is done, are what come to our attention and color our overall judgment. The water glass of bureaucracy is quite full, and we have difficulty realizing it.

CHAPTER 3

SOME SUSPICIONS, SOME SURPRISES

Having begun our case for bureaucracy by looking at its proportionate levels of achievement, let us continue to build the case by examining patterns of variation and contrast. These patterns will be found to be contrary to what many lay observers, as well as professional students, suspect to be the case with respect to American public bureaucracy. In some instances, suspicions held against governmental administration are allayed; in others, unexpected patterns are uncovered.

The chapter debunks false notions and highlights overlooked features on four fronts. First, the implicit assumption in much bureaucratic analysis of homogeneity among public agencies is put to rest, using some rather unusual evidence. Second, the belief that governmental organizations systematically discriminate against underprivileged subgroups of the population is reexamined. Third, the expectation that public bureaucracies, in comparison to private businesses, are inefficient, inflexible, and noninnovative, is subject also to reconsideration. Finally, the seldom acknowledged but plain fact that American bureaucracy outperforms, overall, most other national bureaucracies of the world is brought forward for us to ponder.

BUREAUCRACY AS STEREOTYPE

In legitimating a cause it is convenient to have enemies, and to lump one's enemies together into a single, essentially homogeneous category. This places them all on an equally evil and ominous plane and dramatizes the "we versus they" dichotomy of good guys against bad guys. What emerges from this gross oversimplification is the appropriately pejorative stereotype, a simplistic and therefore distorted model of reality that can be easily conceptualized, absorbed into popular culture, and perpetuated over time. The image of "Bureaucracy" as a single, unified, and capitalized enemy is found everywhere, from the editorial writer's blast at "the runaway Bureaucracy" to the scholar's unqualified pronouncement that "Bureaucracy does not work well."[1]

This kind of reductionist thinking is silly. Whereas the verbal category "bureaucracy" embraces phenomena with sufficiently similar characteristics to fall into a single descriptive classification such as the Weberian model, the range of differences among bureaucracies is obviously enormous. The point is self-evident. Yet it must be underscored, inasmuch as acceptance of the unitary, negative stereotype of bureaucracy runs so deep and wide in our thinking. It has become not merely a standard piece of our mental baggage for public administration but a central image we utilize in visualizing government generally.

Let us point up the differentiation within bureaucracy by describing two kinds of empirical study. The first is a series of two-case, "twin" research projects in which bureaucracies formally identical or similar are compared on actual behavior. If the bureaucratic stereotype had any predictive power at all, the two would be the same informally as well as formally. But are they?

James Thompson compared two Air Force wings. Both units operated under the same regulations, directives, and tables of organization. Both reported to the same headquarters and were comparable in equipment, personnel, age, and mission. Yet Thompson found them to be extremely different in frequency of internal communication, the arrangement of true power hierarchies, and even whether command-staff or functional control channels were favored. Thompson concluded: "Despite its many characteristics of 'bureaucracy,' in the technical sense of that term, the roles in an Air Force wing are not completely standardized."[2]

Another study, this one by James Price, examined ways in which new scientific knowledge was absorbed by two wildlife management agencies of the same state, Oregon. The Fish Commission and Game Commission of that state were agencies of similar size, related jurisdiction, and comparable organization. Both even had a specific program in common, fish propagation. But in utilizing newly discovered knowledge about natural spawning methods, hatchery workers in the Fish Commission resisted change out of antipathy toward the biologists in the organization. The agency was typically "bureaucratic" in the pejorative sense of structured resistance to innovation. In the Game Commission, however, a close bond existed between hatcherymen and biologists, and the new knowledge was quickly absorbed—the organization was not "bureaucratic" in this sense.[3]

Still another comparative study was conducted by William Turcotte of two state liquor agencies. Both organizations ran statewide wholesale and retail operations and hence possessed an identical mission. Yet whereas one was politicized, loosely run, and characterized by store autonomy, the other employed the latest managerial techniques of integrated control, planning, and accounting. The latter bureaucracy's operating expenses as a percentage of sales were a fraction of the former's, and its profits per employee were almost double. In short, one was more "businesslike" than the other.[4]

A final example to be given of this kind of twin organizational study is Tana Pesso's examination of two intake units of the Massachusetts Department of Public Welfare. She observed them directly for two months. The units were comparable in size and structure. But in one office the intake clerks dealt with applicants in an abrupt, impersonal manner, while in the other clients were handled in a helpful and sympathetic way. Whereas in the first office workers called clients from the waiting room with a shout, in the second they were summoned quietly and politely. Interviews were conducted impersonally and without privacy in the former unit and informally, with the door closed, in the latter. Also, workers explained applicant sign-off statements more fully in the second office and made themselves more easily accessible to telephone calls and subsequent visits from clients.[5]

We turn now to a second kind of differentiating empirical study. We examine not all contrasts between two organizations but selected differences among many. The areas selected for analysis are typically perceived as especially marked by consistent uniformity. In these areas—two in number—the uniformity is believed totally bad. Both topics concern that bureaucratic bugaboo, public welfare.

With almost complete unanimity, theorists of bureaucracy and urban service delivery depict the welfare waiting room as a dreary spot at best and scene of systematic degradation and mortification of the poor at worst. These expectations derive not so much from actual visiting of welfare waiting rooms, but from deductive reasoning. The welfare client is seen as a powerless and pathetic individual with zero prestige. Hence, why should welfare departments give them cheerful places to wait prior to seeking their dole? Some writers on social services also theorize that welfare officials like to use every opportunity possible to demonstrate their superior power and status. Also, the officials are supposed to want to drive applicants out of their offices so as to reduce workload and expenditures.[6]

In studying the subject firsthand with few prior expectations, I personally visited 28 welfare waiting rooms in 14 cities and towns across the United States. These were located from coast to coast and in both frostbelt and sunbelt. They included Social Security, AFDC-food stamp, and unemployment compensation offices, about equally divided (part, but not all, of these visits were in conjunction with the exit polling described earlier).

I entered each waiting room as if I were a first-time client and waited in line or sat in reception chairs. I then absorbed the scene open-endedly for several minutes and took notes. What struck me as the project unfolded was the extreme differences among rooms. Instead of being consistently dreary, degrading, or Kafkaesque, the chambers were highly differentiated. This was so along several dimensions.

Upon reflection, the 28 sites seemed categorizable into five fairly distinct types. To express freely the essence of each I labeled it with a spatial metaphor. "Dog Kennel" rooms were characterized by a labyrinthine layout of rooms and hallways. They imparted a sense of crowdedness and projected a coercive and suppressive atmosphere by means of armed guards and threatening signs. A second type, "Pool Hall," was distinguished by large, open space, empty drabness, and a disinterested rather than coercive atmosphere. Clients were ignored more than threatened. "Business Office," a third group, displayed blandness of decor and an air of efficiency, much like a commercial establishment. Still another type, "Bank Lobby," was impressive—even sumptuous— in both exterior facade and interior appointments and displayed mood cues stressing physical security. A final category, "Circus Tent," was full of color, commotion, and animated conversation. Even some degree of institutional "heart" was portrayed in this last category, such as posters urging interpersonal courtesy and offers of help for a number of personal problems. In short, not only were the five categories of anterooms greatly different from one another, the last three of the five are not anticipated by any of the literature condemnatory of bureaucracy in general and welfare bureaucracy in particular.[7]

A second aspect of welfare bureaucracy that is often thought of as uniformly bad is the application given out to clients. Government forms, in general, are believed to be characterized by gobbledygook, officialese, excessive verbiage, and authoritarian language. Welfare forms, in particular, have been attacked as requiring far more education to read than most welfare clients possess.[8]

Three colleagues and I examined on a systematic basis the communication effectiveness and "tone of voice" of a sample of 157 wildlife, park, income tax, and welfare documents, all issued by state governments. In the welfare area we studied AFDC application forms and instructions. While overall the AFDC materials were evaluated as less readable and more negative in tone than documents in the other three categories, the welfare forms surpassed the others in terms of topographical space delimiters, useful placement of instructions, and inclusion of statements on personal rights and appeal procedures.[9]

The point of importance here is that the various AFDC forms differed among one another very substantially. Those used by Massachusetts and the District of Columbia were excellent communicators compared to those distributed in Alabama and Connecticut. The New York documents were very positive in the way they addressed and, by implication, regarded clients compared to those issued in Oregon.

To give a concrete idea of the contrasts encountered with respect to tone, note the differences among the following initial sentences in instructions accompanying AFDC application forms:

Notice: The law provides for a fine of up to $500 or imprisonment up to 6 months for anyone who obtains or attempts to obtain public assistance by deliberately withholding information or giving false information. (Delaware)

You must fill out this form so that we can determine if you are eligible for assistance or not. (Michigan)

The following is a statement of facts about your situation. Please read each question carefully and answer each one. (Washington)

You may have a friend, relative, minister, employer, agency worker, or anyone of your choice help you complete this form. (Kansas)

If you and the people who live with you have little or no income right now, you may be eligible to receive food stamps within a few days. (New Mexico)

Under Minnesota's Data Privacy Act, you have the right to know why the information we request is needed and how it will be used. (Minnesota)

I am in need of money for _____ (number) adults and _____ (number) children. (Maryland)

Which opening sentences do you find "best"? No doubt some disagreement would occur among readers on this question, since more than one value should probably be stressed in a document of this kind. One point is certain, however: The welfare bureaucracies of these seven states have made sharply different decisions on the mix of values they wish to "present" to welfare applicants, as well as to those who review the forms for one reason or another.

BUREAUCRACY AS DISCRIMINATOR

We now move to a second common suspicion about bureaucracy. This is the allegation that public administrative agencies systematically discriminate against certain underprivileged subgroups of the population. These subgroups are usually defined as the poor and nonwhites. With respect to the latter, the charge of "institutional racism" is sometimes made by liberals and critics of the American urban scene. Following the turbulent 1960s, students of urban sociology and politics were attracted to the notion that the riots and protests of that era were in part justified by failures of municipal bureaucracies.

Theoretical argument supporting discriminatory bureaucracy can be divided into two bodies of contention, although they are interrelated. One is that public bureaucracy in urban areas encourages the creation of and perpetuates an "underclass." This consists of blacks, other racial minorities, and residents of low-income neighborhoods. Black citizens are assumed to be subject to racial prejudice on the part of white bureaucrats, but this is only the starting point of the underclass thesis. In a kind of two-culture argument, bureaucracy is seen as organized according to white, middle-class norms while members of the underclass operate outside these norms. Thus the poor are less competent and knowledgeable, by definition, when playing the bureaucratic "game." Further, middle-class bureaucrats approach their downtrodden clientele with an air of superiority and implicitly condemn them in terms of moral worth. The barriers that result from this situation are exacerbated by the fact that problems brought to the bureaucracy by the underclass are especially difficult to interpret and difficult to solve. This leads bureaucrats, who want impressive records of success, to push aside hard cases while taking on more doable ones.[10]

Meanwhile, at a geographic level of argument, as conditions in poor districts of the city deteriorate, officials are seen as ignoring these areas as less worthy of attention while concentrating resources on better neighborhoods. Conditions in inner-city ghettos are made worse by estrangement from white-dominated police and fire departments, whose personnel move to the suburbs. These difficulties are further compounded by the inability of the administrative departments to induce the most competent staff to work in the deprived areas.[11]

Complementing the underclass thesis in many ways is the model of the "street-level bureaucrat." This theoretical construct, developed by Michael Lipsky and subsequently accepted by many others, portrays the urban, front-line provider of service to nonvoluntary clients as facing a set of dilemmas. Public school teachers, policemen, welfare workers, building inspectors, and the like encounter particular stresses in the poorer parts of the city. These include physical fear, a variety of psychological pressures, a shortage of resources, and contradictory expectations on the part of others as to how they should behave. As a result, the bureaucrat responds by creating client stereotypes based on racial and class biases in order to simplify decisions. The official adopts defense mechanisms such as treating citizens differentially in accord with racial and class stereotypes. As a result, self-fulfilling prophecies are set in motion that reinforce racism and class prejudice; to illustrate, the police watch adolescent blacks especially closely, find more occasion to arrest them, and hence perceive them as having greater criminal tendencies than adolescent whites.[12]

These theories are plausible. Also, they are highly appealing to those troubled with the inequities of capitalism or the injustices of historical racial discrimination in this country. Like most Americans, I am deeply disturbed about such inequities and injustices and the deplorable economic and social conditions found in urban ghettos. But the question remains: Do urban bureaucrats and bureaucracies systematically discriminate?

One kind of evidence that convinces many that they do is the opinions of minority citizens. When questioned about their attitude toward urban services, blacks and other minorities usually indicate lower levels of satisfaction than whites. In the Dallas and Dayton surveys described in the previous chapter, as well as the three national opinion polls, nonwhites have a less favorable view of the service experienced by a margin of approximately 10 to 20 percentage points. Other citizen surveys in Milwaukee, Denver, and four Illinois cities indicate a distinctly less approving attitude toward urban services on the part of residents of poor neighborhoods.[13]

This differential is inherently troubling from the standpoint of the perceived legitimacy of the American political system. Yet when reflecting on it in terms of our subject, several points should be borne in mind. First, the lower levels of satisfaction are not in themselves complaints against bureaucratic discrimination. Few of the surveys ask respondents if they feel they have been treated equitably or inequitably. When such inquiry is made, in fact, minorities do not see themselves as persecuted by government bureaucrats. When blacks were asked by the University of Michigan researchers, *"Do you feel you were treated fairly or unfairly by the office,"* 68 percent answered "fairly," 18 percent said "unfairly," and 4 provided a mixed interpretation.[14] In a survey of fifteen American cities, Schuman and Gruenberg asked the question, *"Thinking about city services like schools, parks, and garbage collection, do you think your neighborhood gets better, about the same, or worse service than most other parts of the city?"* Only 24 percent of the black respondents said worse, while 65 percent said the same, and 11 percent answered better.[15]

Second, many of the surveys show, despite the differentials, percentages of satisfaction among racial minorities that are still quite high, with most such citizens not dissatisfied. Some 58 percent of sampled blacks in Dallas, for example, said the police there are generally fair. According to the Harris survey, 83 percent of blacks found local government offices helpful when visited, and 88 percent said this for federal offices. In a separate study of Mexican Americans in Omaha, a sample of this ethnic group expressed satisfaction with various government services at levels ranging from 68 to 94 percent, with the police rated at 82 percent.[16]

A third observation is that studies attempting to interrelate variables of race, perceptions of service, and other factors usually find that lower levels of dissatisfaction are linked more to neighborhood of residence than race or income class. This was found to be the case by Schuman and Gruenberg in their fifteen-city study and by Aberbach and Walker in a research project on Detroit. Whites living in poor neighborhoods have less favorable views than suburban whites, and blacks residing in middle-class areas have more favorable ones than their ghetto counterparts.[17]

Nonetheless, even if the survey-opinion differential does not involve perceptions of discrimination, dissatisfied majorities, or racial causation, the widespread acceptance of underclass and street-level theories alone compels us to investigate whether evidence related to actual performance substantiates the notion of discriminatory bureaucracy. In a famous legal case involving Shaw, Mississippi (population 2,500), federal courts found this to be the case. That part of the town in which whites lived was provided with paved streets, sanitary sewers, five-inch water mains, mercury vapor street lamps, and plenty of fire hydrants. By contrast, black neighborhoods of Shaw had almost no paving and sewers, three-inch mains, incandescent lighting, and few hydrants.[18] How typical is this unfortunate pattern of performance for American urban bureaucracy?

With respect to street conditions, empirical equality-of-service studies have been conducted in Oakland, California, Chicago, and Tuscaloosa, Alabama. In Oakland, Levy, Meltsner, and Wildavsky found that street improvements are not allocated in accord with whether neighborhoods are rich or poor or even in response to a pork-barrel process. Instead, decisions are made by engineers in accord with professional standards intended to meet the specific objectives of improved traffic circulation and increased motorist safety.[19] Similarly, Kenneth Mladenka found in Chicago that citizen requests for new traffic signals or stop signs are handled not by the criterion of whether the wards concerned are black or white, but according to professional decision rules concerning accident rate, traffic volume, and the location of elementary schools. Mladenka found a similar situation with respect to street improvement in Chicago.[20]

In a study of Tuscaloosa that employed ingenious statistical methods, Philip Coulter calculated varying standards of equity for services and then analyzed departures from those standards. With respect to numbers of miles of unpaved and repaved streets, he found severe inequity within the city, but this did not correlate with predominantly black census tracts. Physical measurements of the roughness of streets (using a Mays Ride Meter) also were not correlated. Random counts of street lights did show significant correlations by black tracts, but they were inconsistent: Blacks had fewer lights per mile of street but more lights per capita.[21]

Robert Lineberry studied the extent of equality in numerous public services in San Antonio, Texas. He found several instances of inequality, but many actually favored minority and low-income neighborhoods because of such "ecological" factors as the age and density of these neighborhoods. This was true with respect to distances from fire stations, public libraries, and city parks, for example. Many of these facilities were built prior to suburban expansion and hence were closer to more central areas where the poor live. Also, Lineberry discovered that property tax assessments as a proportion of housing value were actually higher in higher-class neighborhoods, perhaps because assessments there had been more recently calculated. Water mains were discovered to be of smaller diameter in poor sections of the city, but they had been laid in an earlier era when engineering standards differed.[22]

Public facilities such as fire stations, city parks, and public libraries were also found to be frequently closer to black and poor residents in Chicago, Houston, and Tuscaloosa. But what about the *quality* of service rendered by such institutions?

Coulter's study found that fire response time in Tuscaloosa was not significantly slower for black census tracts. Such areas actually had more fire hydrants per square mile than white areas, and inequities with respect to actual fire incidence were minor.[23] As for parks, Lineberry's analysis of San Antonio's system revealed no systematic discrimination with respect to park acreage or the quality of sports fields, playgrounds, or swimming pools.[24] Mladenka found the same thing in Houston. In Chicago, Mladenka discovered equality in park acreage but inequality in park facilities, with black wards receiving fewer. This inequity lessened between 1967 and 1977, however.[25]

With respect to libraries, Lineberry reports that the quality of service in San Antonio's branch libraries is uneven but only weakly related to attributes of neighborhoods. Houston's branch libraries, according to Mladenka, have comparable equipment and conditions, but higher-income neighborhoods possess branches with more books and librarians, larger budgets, and more qualified personnel. This appears to be related to the fact that circulation in those libraries is greater. A similar situation was encountered in Oakland.

In the area of refuse collection, Coulter found that more litter remained uncollected in black compared to white census tracts of Tuscaloosa (studied by photographs) but that inequities in response to complaints about garbage pickup actually favored black neighborhoods. Mladenka noted that whereas black wards of Chicago had fewer refuse trucks assigned to them, the difference disappears when level of home ownership is held constant; a city ordinance there prohibits public garbage collection from large apartment dwellings. In a study of service delivery in Detroit, Bryan Jones also found more trash trucks operating in better neighborhoods, but this was because those areas generated more trash. Jones noted too that environmental enforcement (e.g., cutting weeds in vacant lots and towing away abandoned cars) took place disproportionately in high-income areas of Detroit—yet more complaints came from there.[26]

As for public schools, Mladenka discovered that predominantly white schools in Chicago had the most experienced and best educated teachers. Still, minority schools ranked first on teacher-pupil ratios because of special education programs. Levy and associates found an almost identical situation in Oakland, with the result that the distribution of educational dollars to income and racial groups formed a U shape, with the richest and poorest areas benefiting over those in between.[27]

Police behavior, perhaps, is the target of greatest suspicion regarding discriminatory treatment on the urban scene. As for distribution of police resources, Lineberry discovered disproportionate allocations of San Antonio's police manpower to predominantly white and predominantly minority districts, again the U-shaped pattern. John Weicher, an economist, analyzed police patrol expenditures in Chicago and concluded that their income redistribution effects benefit the poor at the expense of middle-income citizens.[28] On speed of response to calls for help, Mladenka and Hill found no evidence of slower response to black and low-income neighborhoods of Houston. In fact the police arrived slightly sooner there.[29] In Tuscaloosa, Coulter noted a significant *positive* correlation between proportion of black population and quickness of police response. Approximate equality on this matter was found by Robert Worden in St. Louis, Rochester, New York, and Tampa and St. Petersburg, Florida.[30] In other aspects of police behavior, Michael Maxfield discovered no greater incidence of nonrecording of emergency calls ("load shedding") for poor and black areas of Chicago than for middle-class precincts of the city.[31] In an observational study of police deference to citizens, Sykes and Clark noted officer disrespect to be relatively uncommon; when it occurred, it was slightly more frequent toward whites than blacks.[32]

With respect to other selected public services, Naomi Kroeger examined awards of supplementary grants to welfare clients in a large metropolitan public assistance agency. She found no significant differences in the rate of approval or size of these benefits by the ethnicity, age, or education of welfare clients. In fact, blacks and Hispanics received slightly higher grants than whites.[33]

In a study of wait times in the emergency departments of public hospitals in Cook County, Illinois, Barry Schwartz discovered that the black patients were required to wait more than twice as long as the white patients when their cases were nonurgent and the department was very busy. But for true emergencies and under lower-volume conditions, race made no significant difference.[34]

In sum, despite obviously inequitable conditions within American society, and despite the deductive persuasiveness of the underclass thesis and street-level model, significant levels of antiminority, antipoor discrimination in urban service delivery are not substantiated by the available empirical evidence. Despite lower levels of satisfaction toward services on the part of underprivileged citizens, minority and low-income groups are often shown to receive treatment not significantly distinguishable from that afforded others. We found this to be so in fire, parks, and welfare services, for example. Unequal services do appear in other areas but often have nonracist explanations. Street improvements are determined by traffic, safety, and budget considerations, not the race or income of residents. Smaller water mains are found in older neighborhoods only because of prevailing engineering standards. Differences in demand levels also affect distribution: Libraries with more patrons get more books, areas generating more refuse are visited by more refuse trucks, people making more complaints about weeds get more weeds cut. In some cases inequities actually favor the disadvantaged, as in the concentration of government buildings and primary parks in the center of cities; again, this results from historical migration patterns and not discriminatory policy. Then, too, some inequities are U-shaped, as seen in education and some law enforcement. Still others are inconsistent or relatively inconsequential, as in street lighting, police deference, and emergency medical care. A deliberate, regular, repeated pattern of serious racial or economic discrimination by urban bureaucracy is simply not verified by considerable study of the subject. Discrimination has been and is practiced in America, to be sure — but the bureaucrats cannot be blamed for the sins of a total society and the legacy of its history.

Bureaucracy as Bungler

If the facts disappoint political liberals committed to a concept of a bureaucracy that oppresses the poor, will the data be similarly uncooperative for political conservatives who insist that government cannot do the job as well as private business?

The critique of bureaucracy from the political right includes, but is not limited to, allegations of its relative incompetence, inefficiency, unresponsiveness, and inflexibility. Belief in these supposed shortcomings may spring simply from ideological dislike of big government, taxation, and regulatory inhibitions on business. This normative orientation is also well anchored in the prevailing values of an essentially capitalist society. Moreover, as we saw in chapter 1, conservative theorists produce well-developed arguments for why bureaucracy cannot perform well. These center on its lack of "market exposure"—few if any incentives are said to exist to reduce costs, increase productivity, and produce a product or service that people actually want. As a consequence, bureaucracy is said to be wasteful, unresponsive, not attuned to innovation, and inimical to an efficient allocation of society's resources. Since bureaucracy's leadership need not beat out competitors and satisfy investors by showing a good profit, according to this line of contention, it need only survive, promote expansion for its own sake, and appease political constituencies.[35]

The "business is superior" school of thought supplements these economic arguments with others related to control and authority relations. Government imposes more legal restrictions and accountability channels on public operations than private enterprise, it is said. As a result, public managers possess less autonomy and flexibility than entrepreneurs. The lack of clear, consistent, and quantifiable goals means public managers have less motivation or opportunity to assure high levels of performance within the organization. The merit system presumably constitutes a specific obstacle to performance by blocking discretion in hiring, firing, and promoting. This undercuts both executive control and subordinate motivation. Further, the rigidity of bureaucratic rules and the political safety found in "not rocking the boat" supposedly make bureaucracy uncreative, rigid, and nondynamic in comparison with private enterprise.[36]

Let us respond to this point of view by making some observations that are relatively axiomatic yet are necessary to avoid launching our discussion of the viewpoint on the basis of false premises. First, distinctions between government and business are not always that clear. The dichotomy of private versus public enterprise is vivid enough in classroom debates over capitalism versus socialism. But in the modern industrial world the interaction between sectors is so complex and pervasive that borderlines become fuzzy and the notion of a dichotomy itself approaches irrelevancy. Thus the issue of private versus public performance is not always relevant.

Second, business corporations are themselves organized bureaucratically. Hence comparative statistics are not between bureaucracy and nonbureaucracy but between kinds of bureaucracy. Corporate critics like Mark Green allege that the supposed diseases of government bureaucracy, such as wastefulness, lack of true innovation, and a preoccupation with conservative strategies, are currently infecting large corporations.[37] Rather than accept this speculation at face value, let us counterspeculate that large corporations operate better than small, family-held businesses by being less encumbered by personal favoritism, nepotism, and seat-of-the-pants decision making, i.e., they emulate the norms of professionalized administration, whether public or private.

Third, the presupposition that the private sector is disciplined by the market while the public sector escapes it hides important truths. For one thing, perfect competition among firms is explained elegantly in economics texts but is not necessarily discovered in the real business world. I am referring not merely to oligopolies or ineffective competition but to that sector of private enterprise disciplined by the enemy, government regulatory bureaucracies.

Furthermore, to suggest that government bureaus are unexposed to a disciplining environment is to confess ignorance about the nature of bureaucracy. Agencies continuously face turf battles, historical rivalries, budget competition, press scrutiny, legislative and group attacks from every side, and — in the 1980s — a concerted move to cut back most programs. In short, the bureaucratic environment contains plenty of performance-demanding harshness too, although it is not readily reducible to diagramed curves or mathematical expression.

A final point is that comparisons between the two sectors run into inevitable "apples versus oranges" problems. Public bureaucracy is not created to perform according to economic criteria alone. Government is given tasks that the private sector would not touch or has abandoned. Also, agencies must not only be economical and efficient but must carry out statutes, observe due process, follow election returns, involve citizens, and symbolize open and honest government. Thus, to compare them with private businesses on the basis of cost-effective achievement of program objectives alone is to stack the argument in advance in favor of business.

Far be it from me, however, to hide behind the "public" nature of public administration in defending bureaucracy against the charge of incompetence. Let us turn now to the available empirical studies that shed light on whether government bureaucracy is in fact a comparative bungler.

We begin with the unglamorous example of garbage collection. It is performed by both sectors, and comparative studies have been done. E.S. Savas contends that municipal refuse collection is more expensive per production unit than when collection is by private hauler. He calculates that in 1968-69 the New York City Department of Sanitation's costs were $39.71 per ton of garbage, while those for the city's private collection firms averaged $17.28.[38] A very different conclusion is arrived at by William Pier and associates, who compared private and public refuse collection efficiency in Montana. From service and cost data gathered from 34 public and 29 private haulers, production functions were estimated for the two sectors. Pier and his co-authors found "greater governmental than private efficiency for garbage collection in Montana for all but very small communities." Moreover, only the municipally provided service was ever offered twice per week.[39]

Cost comparisons have also been made between private and public hospitals. Again the results are mixed. Cotton Lindsay calculated that from 1969 to 1973 per diem patient costs in Veterans Administration hospitals were nearly half those in proprietary hospitals. The figures for 1973 were $49.09 for VA institutions and $82.87 for others.[40] Yet in a study of 338 inpatient psychiatric departments based on 1969 data, Hrebiniak and Alutto calculated higher costs for government than nongovernment hospitals, although VA daily costs were only insignificantly higher (see table 3.1).[41]

TABLE 3.1. COSTS OF GOVERNMENT AND NONGOVERNMENT HOSPITALS

	City-County Hospitals	VA Hospitals	Proprietary Hospitals	Nonprofit Hospitals
Cost per patient day	$ 33.60	$ 23.91	$ 22.10	$ 23.00
Cost per discharge	939.00	917.00	407.00	544.00

On the quality of service rendered in private versus public hospitals, a study by Noralou Roos and associates showed that proprietary hospitals perform relatively well in the category of small institutions, while among bigger hospitals government facilities tend to be just as good. (See table 3.2 for 1970 data on institutions of 500 beds and more.)[42]

TABLE 3.2. QUALITY OF SERVICES IN PRIVATE AND PUBLIC HOSPITALS

	State and Local Hospitals	Not-for-Profit Hospitals
Staff per patient day	2.91	2.92
Expenses per patient day ($)	31.73	32.03
Plant assets per bed ($000)	18.87	26.81
Mean number general services	16.34	16.01
Percent hospitals:		
Accredited	97	100
Certified for Medicare	97	99
Approved residency	95	89
Approved cancer program	69	64

Some comparative studies have been made on transportation. Peter Pashigian found that publicly owned urban mass transit systems are generally less profitable than private.[43] In an overseas example, David Davies discovered that the privately owned interstate airline in Australia was more efficient than the government airline, in terms of both load carried and revenue earned per employee.[44] As for a limited, comparative test of the performance of the U.S. Postal Service and the private United Parcel Service, one newspaper sent four sets of matched parcels by both carriers to reporters living 50 miles or more distant. Delivery safety and cost were almost identical, but Uncle Sam delivered earlier by 1 to 24 hours.[45]

With respect to utilities, John Fisher maintains that power operating costs per kilowatt hour for the Tennessee Valley Authority system are less than half the average for the nation's private utilities in producing, transmitting, and distributing electricity. TVA costs are also said to be lower for customer accounting and collection, sales promotion, research, administration, and depreciation.[46] In another utility study, Sam Peltzman determined that mean residential electricity prices charged by government utilities serving 74 cities were substantially lower than those levied by private utilities serving 71 cities. The difference ranged from 9 to 14 percent, depending on service class. In the same study Peltzman also found that liquor prices in state liquor stores were 4 to 11 percent cheaper than those charged by private retailers in "open" states, depending on the type of spirit.[47]

As for the insurance industry, it has been pointed out that for every two dollars of benefits paid by private insurers, they spend about one dollar for dividends, taxes, and the costs of administration, advertising, and sales. Although comparisons to Social Security are not fair in many ways, it seems remarkable that in 1972 total administrative costs of the Old Age, Survivors, and Disability Insurance program were a mere 1.8 percent of benefits paid.[48]

In addition to these common-activity comparisons, studies have been made of other aspects of private versus public sector performance. One of these has been the proportion of overhead or supportive personnel in organizations. Critics expect public bureaucracy to be relatively "top heavy" and hence supposedly less efficient.

Eugene Haas and his co-authors compared 30 business, financial, manufacturing, governmental, political, educational, and other organizations. My reanalysis of their data shows that aggregatively for all 30 organizations, approximately one-fourth of employed personnel were engaged in supportive activity. Breaking these down by sector reveals that, contrary to common expectations, government was relatively slim on the upper body, not overweight —only 12 percent of the staff were in supportive activities, compared to 27-28 percent for private organizations.[49]

A somewhat parallel study was conducted by Lorraine Prinsky of 575 institutions of higher education. Using Office of Education data, she calculated ratios of administrative personnel, defined as all individuals not doing teaching or research, to staff engaged in those pursuits. Means of these ratios by educational sector once again portray relatively lean public organizations. Her ratios were 1.003 for public colleges and universities, 1.433 for church-related institutions, and 1.542 for other private schools.[50]

Attempts to measure productivity in government have been made in recent years. An analysis by the Office of Personnel Management of productivity trends in the federal government was published in 1980 that covered 65 percent of the federal work force. It showed a 17.4 percent increase in output per employee year between 1967 and 1978, with an average annual increase of 1.4 percent. This annual rate is somewhat higher than the increase experienced by the private sector during this time, although bases for computation differ. Moreover, while federal productivity grew steadily each year, during part of this period the private economy's productivity declined over several quarters.[51] In some functional areas the annual federal percentage increase was particularly impressive: communication, 10.1; general support services, 3.9; library services, 5.3; loans and grants, 4.2; personnel investigations, 3.6; records management, 3.1; and social services and benefits, 2.8.[52] The Postal Service also has some notable statistics along this line: It took 741,000 employees to deliver 85 billion pieces of mail in 1970; a decade later, 667,000 handled 106 billion pieces. This constitutes a 34 percent increase in gross productivity.[53]

Innovation is of course linked to productivity, and some attention has been given to the issue of whether private or public organizations are more innovative. In addressing this question, David Roessner cites a number of studies and concludes that while we do not know enough to arrive at firm conclusions, there is "reason to doubt the validity of hypotheses that the public sector is inherently immune to efforts to increase innovative behavior there." He notes, for example, that studies of technology diffusion among hospitals show that whereas state and local government institutions have fewer intensive care units, they more frequently possess renal dialysis and burn units. Roessner also points to a study in our familiar field of garbage collection that reveals that technology diffusion rates in the public sector are not always much different than, let alone slower than, those in the private sector (see table 3.3).[54]

Case studies of behavior in bureaucracies have likewise come up with interesting findings with respect to the innovativeness of public organizations. In Peter Blau's well-known study of a state employment agency and federal enforcement agency, it was concluded that bureaucrats are less resistant to change than factory workers. While chronic resisters in both settings are a minority of personally insecure individuals, Blau reasons, change in private bureaucracy frightens such persons by threatening their jobs, but does not intimidate civil servants so much because of their job security. Blau found in the two

TABLE 3.3. TECHNOLOGY DIFFUSION RATES, GARBAGE COLLECTION

Solid-Waste Technology	Extent of Diffusion as of 1975	Years Taken to Reach this Extent	
		By Public Sector	By Private Sector
Packer trucks	40%	27	28
Container trucks	20	18	20
One-man crews	10	13	21
Transfer stations	10	20	14

agencies he studied that bureaucratic conditions actually generate favorable attitudes toward change. This is done by removing job irritants, enlarging opportunities, supporting ideological beliefs, and making jobs more interesting while not increasing workload. "Most officials in the government agencies studied here," he states, "were favorably disposed toward change."[55]

In another relevant case study, Louis Bragaw examined the U.S. Coast Guard from the standpoint of whether that agency received stimuli for innovation down through its history. Bragaw was particularly interested in determining whether the coast guard was affected in its performance by factors analogous to pressures of the marketplace on the private firm. He discovered that indeed several innovations occurred, such as replacement of earlier revenue and lighthouse functions, development of the Loran navigation system, and establishment of a marine environmental protection program. Bragaw explains this innovative behavior in terms of response to threats that developed from time to time against the agency, for example absorption attempts by the navy, fiscal starvation following wars, and moves to liquidate or control the agency. Bragaw regards these threats as a "hidden stimulus" somewhat comparable to the effects of economic competition.[56]

To summarize, available comparative data on the efficiency, costs, and quality of services in refuse collection, hospitals, transportation, utilities, and insurance show that whereas at some times business seems superior, at other times government appears to perform better. In still other instances the two sectors do about equally. Hence the results of our survey are mixed but by no means convincingly supportive of the common contention that the private sector always functions better, even according to economic criteria. Moreover, evidence is available to show, perhaps surprisingly to some, that governmental bureaucracy may be less top heavy than private, is capable of impressive productivity gains, and can be just as innovative as private bureaucracy.

These comments may sound heretical to probusiness conservatives and those who believe only the profit motive and market mechanism can produce effective collective action in a society. Although certainly a government agency cannot necessarily outperform a private firm, or even do as well in all instances, we are nonetheless in a position to insist that the deductive arguments that condemn bureaucracy to automatic inferiority are awash in gross oversimplification, unwarranted assumptions, and a lack of evidence.

A commentator on this subject, John Fisher, is willing to go farther. He believes that despite differences in incentives between business and government, "the initiative, ingenuity, and inventiveness which is generated in private business is as often found in government." Profit, in his eyes, is a greatly overrated incentive with respect to individual behavior, with businessmen and bureaucrats driven by essentially the same sets of motivations. Claimed advantages of business are to him "fictitious," with their widespread acceptance due chiefly to "individual economic advantage and to fulsome ballyhoo carried out over a long period of years."[57]

AMERICAN BUREAUCRACY COMPARED

This chapter has had a *comparative* focus: We have compared bureaucracies with each other, we have compared their treatment of different groups, we have compared private and public bureaucracy. Now we briefly compare American bureaucracy to that of other nations, the traditional subject matter of "comparative administration."[58]

The point to be made here is simply that, however satisfactory or unsatisfactory American bureaucratic performance is to us in the United States, it is superior to that found in the vast majority of countries of the world. Some national bureaucracies may be roughly the same in quality of overall performance, but they are few in number.

To Americans who have traveled and lived abroad this statement will come as no surprise. In many parts of the world it seems painfully difficult to perform even the simplest chores involving government functionaries. Passing customs, applying for permits, securing approvals, paying stamp taxes, and even making routine appointments can seem incredibly arduous and time-consuming. Part of this perception is lack of familiarity with foreign habits and language. Part is due also, however, to a syndrome of behaviors stemming from the inadequate resources and differing cultural attitudes toward administration found in many countries.

Fred Riggs has generalized that bureaucracies in less developed countries are characterized by patronage, overcentralization, nonenforcement of rules, inequitable treatment of clients, political dominance, corruption, waste, and inefficiency.[59] The negative language of these descriptors itself implies a strong condemnation of bureaucracy in such nations. Given the very different cultural and political systems of the world, such a pejorative judgment may be too harshly ethnocentric.

Nonetheless, *Americans* find such bureaucracies woefully inadequate. Advere comparison with the United States is the point. Even those professors who at home castigate American bureaucracy most emphatically would deeply miss, I wager, U.S. standards of bureaucratic performance when they traveled abroad. Certainly most Third World governments perceive themselves as weak with respect to administrative performance. In fact, bureaucratic short-

TABLE 3.4. PERCEPTIONS OF ADMINISTRATION
REFLECTED IN FIVE-NATION SURVEY

Suppose there were some question that you had to take to a government office — for example, a tax question or housing regulation. Do you think you would be given equal treatment — I mean, would you be treated as well as anyone else?

	United States	United Kingdom	West Germany	Italy	Mexico
Expect equal treatment	83%	83%	65%	53%	42%
Don't expect it	9	7	9	13	50
Depends	4	6	19	17	5
Other, don't know	4	2	7	17	3

If you explained your point of view to the officials, what effect do you think it would have? Would they give your point of view serious consideration, would they pay only a little attention, or would they ignore what you had to say?

	United States	United Kingdom	West Germany	Italy	Mexico
Serious consideration	48%	59%	53%	35%	14%
A little attention	31	22	18	15	48
Ignore what's said	6	5	5	11	27
Depends	11	10	15	21	6
Other, don't know	4	2	9	18	3

comings are almost always seen as a chief obstacle to economic development and a fruitful target for technical assistance in public administration. This assistance is often American.

What about comparisons of American bureaucracy to that of other "developed" countries, such as those of Western Europe, the British Isles, Canada, and the industrialized Pacific powers? Here contrasts in overall performance quality may be less vivid. Yet, despite a paucity of truly comparative studies, we have some basis for conclusions.

Some bureaucracies of Europe (e.g., those of France and Germany) have distinguished historical origins and have served as enormously influential models to governments all over the world. Yet their contemporary counterparts are often regarded as relatively impersonal and officious. In a study of the French social security system, Catrice-Lorey found administrators losing sight of the public at all levels.[60] Michel Crozier's examination of French bureaucracy depicts a near-nightmare of rigidity and overcentralization.[61] An essay by Wallace Sayre comparing British and American administration found the civil servants of Whitehall to be relatively elitist, secretive, and conservative. The American bureaucrat was portrayed as relatively representative, innovative, and energetic.[62] These studies are not systematic and may be subject to the selective observation that plagues relatively impressionistic critiques of American bureaucracy. What more rigorous studies are available?

Amazingly enough, despite three decades of research in comparative administration, there is not much. We do have some public opinion surveys conducted in various countries. Almond and Verba's five-nation study, done in 1959-60, involved approximately a thousand structured interviews in each country. In the interviewing two pertinent questions were put (see table 3.4 on page 56); in them the United States compares well but is not always rated the best.[63]

TABLE 3.5. RESPONSES TO SIMILAR QUESTIONS
ASKED IN DETROIT AND DELHI

How many government officials would you say are probably corrupt?

	Detroit	Delhi (Urban)	Delhi (Rural)
A majority ⎫	13%	42%	48%
About half ⎭		17	9
Just a few	71	19	16
None	7	7	12
Other, don't know	9	15	16

TABLE 3.5. *(Continued)*

Is political pull important in whether the government will help a private
citizen?

	Detroit	Delhi (Urban)	Delhi (Rural)
It plays an important part	41%	54%	70%
It plays some part	28	6	5
Depends	4	3	2
No	15	7	11
Other, don't know	12	30	12

In addition to a coordinated multination study, comparative data are available from similar questions asked independently in different countries. Samuel Eldersveld repeated the basic wording of certain survey questions in the Delhi State of India that had been asked in Detroit a decade earlier. Two such questions appear in table 3.5 above on pages 57-58.[64]

In 1967, in behalf of research being conducted by Verba and Nie, a national sample of 2,549 Americans was asked, *"How good a job do you think the police do in protecting the lives and property of the people around here?"*[65] Recently Otwin Marenin reported a survey in which 784 respondents in Nigeria were asked almost the same question: *"Generally speaking, how good a job would you say the police are doing in maintaining law and order in this community?"*[66] The results of the two surveys are shown in table 3.6.

TABLE 3.6. RESPONSES TO SIMILAR QUESTIONS
ASKED IN U.S. AND NIGERIA

	U.S.		Nigeria
Very good	44%	Excellent	5%
Fairly good	41	Good	38
Fairly poor	7	Fair	44
Very poor	6	Poor	13
Don't know	2	No answer	1

Some systematic comparative evidence is available beyond survey results. This concerns postal service, an activity whose universal nature makes it unusually susceptible to international comparisons. Whereas in 1981 the postage for a first-class letter in the United States was 18 cents, in most countries of Europe it was 24 to 30 cents (currencies converted at current exchange rates). In the United States approximately 157,000 pieces of mail are processed per employee per work year; in Japan this figure is 108,000; in Canada it is 103,000; and in Russia, West Germany, France, and Britain, it is 69,000, 63,000, 62,000, and 59,000, respectively.[67] A statistical study done by Lee Sigelman in which 68 nations were ranked with respect to postal productivity placed the United States sixth most productive.[68] A survey by a U.S. magazine of the postal performance encountered by its various foreign bureaus came to the conclusion that many national systems are frightful in quality, with the American post office receiving a "satisfactory rating" by comparison.[69]

Some years ago I compared the postal systems of the United States and Costa Rica. The small Central American nation's postal productivity was computed at 64,000 pieces per employee per work year, probably high by Latin American standards. Aside from overall size and productivity level, three areas of dramatic contrast emerged between the American and Costa Rican systems.

First, postal expenditures in Costa Rica are minuscule by comparison. In 1972 postal spending per capita was $46 in the United States but 87 *cents* in Costa Rica; expenditures per square mile of national territory were $2,625 versus $82. Second, delivery took two to three times longer in the smaller country. For 53 first-class test mailings the mean elapsed time prior to delivery was 1.22 days in the United States and 3.40 days in Costa Rica, even though the average distance covered in Costa Rica was less than one-fourth as great. Similar tests on 42 special delivery postings yielded comparative times of 20.2 and 39.5 hours with even a greater distance differential involved.[70]

The third contrast uncovered concerns behavior of postal clerks. This was studied comparatively by sending confederates into post offices in both countries to play the role of normal customers, as the U.S. Postal Service did at a later date in the contracted studies mentioned earlier. Somewhat lower levels of courtesy were noted by the confederates in Costa Rica, especially toward a relatively uneducated youth. Clerks in both countries tended to be casual in returning previously posted letters, constantly violating official rules to do so. When the confederates deliberately contested announced rates of postage, American clerks frequently explained the error or rechecked it, while Costa Rican officials tended either to reject the claim out of hand or accept the incorrect tariff as valid.[71]

Our point in this section has merely been that, despite Americans' own negative image of their own bureaucracy, impressionistic experience and the systematic data available tell us that it performs better than the vast majority of the 150-odd national bureaucracies on earth. These data include opinion polls that make U.S. bureaucracy look quite good compared to West European bureaucracies and very good compared to those of the Third World. Comparative postal data indicate that the U.S. Postal Service is one of the best, if not the best, in terms of productivity, speed, and courtesy. As an American I say this not out of inflated national pride but from a desire to encourage my fellow countrymen to recognize how fortunate we are, bureaucracy-wise.

CHAPTER 4

GREAT (BUT IMPOSSIBLE) EXPECTATIONS

Despite Vietnam, inflation, recession, and an inability to cure cancer, Americans retain a basic faith in rational action, technological achievement, and human progress. Part of our heritage is to believe in the future and have faith in our ability to achieve almost anything if we try hard enough. In the 1930s Americans made a collective decision to depend on government as the central steering mechanism of our society. Our traditional optimism about achieving goals, once held at primarily an individual and private action level, was now applied to the public sector as well. In the 1960s yet another collective decision was made: to assign all important social problems to the federal government for solution. Americans placed such responsibility not casually or merely for the record; we actually expected the problems to be removed. When they were not, something was "wrong." As the implementation arm of government, public bureaucracy was seen as a direct cause for failure and hence a major part of what was "wrong." The bureaucrats were either falling down on the job or deliberately committing sabotage, it appeared. This logic seemed particularly irrefutable in light of the fact that bureaucratic administration's reputed core advantages, rational action and technical knowledge, were at the heart of the faith that led to America's optimism in the first place.

Bureaucracy was, in short, set up for "failure." This was done in four specific ways, each of which is explored in this chapter. First, bureaucracy was given inconsistent, contradictory, and thus unachievable goals. Second, its capacities were undermined by a tendency that emerged contemporaneously with government's assignment of new responsibilities, a disengaged form of bureaucracy that may be called "administration by proxy." Third, we determined to evaluate bureaucracy not in terms of its own actions but the societal effects of its actions, a far different matter. Fourth, we misrepresented the role of bureaucracy with respect to social change, both by overselling and underselling its potentialities in this area.

No-Win Situations and Red Tape

The business consultant Peter Drucker has written that public administration

seriously harms itself by committing six deadly sins. Two of these are sufficiently important to repeat here. The first sin is to administer a program with a
lofty but vague objective, which then makes specific evaluation of focused
work impossible. The second transgression is to attempt many things at once.
Drucker illustrates these errors with two programs, Head Start and the Tennessee Valley Authority. Both had lofty objectives and multiple purposes.
Those Head Start projects that "failed" tried to help youngsters in innumerable but diffuse ways. Those that "succeeded," Drucker says, decided on one
overriding priority, namely, teaching children to read numbers and letters. As
for TVA, under its first chairman the Authority tried to carry out all potential
missions, could not do so, and was thus considered a "failure." Under David
Lilienthal, however, power production was singled out as the prime objective,
with the consequence that the organization could later be hailed a "success."[1]

Bureaucracy itself may commit these sins, but they are also visited upon it
by others. Statutory mandates to agencies are usually the result of legislative
compromise. This means they are often deliberately phrased in vague or ambi-
valent language so as to satisfy competing interests. In fact, a forthright policy
mandate may be intentionally accompanied by cumbersome methods of exe-
cution for the express purpose of curbing its realization. Even if agency goals
are clear initially, they almost inevitably become multiple as statutes are
amended, political leadership rotates, and hidden agendas emerge inside and
outside the organization. Whoever is most at fault, the public agency too often
ends up with confusing and diverse goals nested in a lofty but meaningless
ideological mission and frequently in conflict with one another. Sometimes expectations are even directly contradictory. Regulatory bodies must both re-
strain and promote the industries they regulate, agricultural bureaucracies are
to expand farm productivity while keeping commodity prices high, prisons
should confine convicts securely and cheaply in close quarters but rehabilitate
their psyches. No matter what is done, a failing record can be constructed by
any critic who wishes to do so.

The private sector is very different in this respect. The problem is mini-
mized by widespread agreement, despite widely differing perspectives and interests in various parts of the organization, on the central importance of certain profit or sales indicators. Measurement of these indicators is precise and
all participants essentially agree on their meaning. A dramatized "bottom line"
overshadows all other considerations. In government, achievement is hard to
measure, overriding end-product goals are seldom operative, and progress toward confused or conflicting objectives can be variously interpreted.

James Q. Wilson observes that "the bureaucracy problem" is one precisely
because it is not *one*—that is, it is several. He regards these problems as ac-

countability, equity, efficiency, responsiveness, and fiscal integrity. Each mobilizes a different constituency, Wilson points out, and furthermore the incompatibility of solutions to these problems means that steps taken to satisfy one dissatisfy another (or several others).

> Obviously the more a bureaucracy is responsive to its clients—whether those clients are organized by radicals into Mothers for Adequate Welfare or represented by Congressmen anxious to please constituents—the less it can be accountable to presidential directives. Similarly, the more equity, the less responsiveness. And a preoccupation with fiscal integrity can make the kind of program budgeting required by enthusiasts of efficiency difficult, if not impossible.[2]

The problem of contradictory goals is bad enough inside public bureaucracy. Officials of each department are at a loss as to why their perception of what should be done is not accepted by others. But, in relations between bureaucracy and the outside world, the frustration is perhaps worse—at least the contradictions are more mystifying because they are harder for an outsider to understand. The reaction is the cry of "red tape!"

One of the most enduring and universal rejection symbols in the English language, red tape refers historically to the narrow ribbons used at one time in England and America to tie up packets of legal and government documents. Popularized in the nineteenth century by Sidney Smith, Thomas Carlyle, and Herbert Spencer, the term came to refer to all government with which one is disgusted. It is a classic "condensation" symbol in that it incorporates a vast array of subjectively held feelings and expresses them succinctly in a way to which all can relate on an emotional plane. The very vagueness of its meaning enhances its symbolic value. The mental image projected of endless lengths of ribbon lends itself nicely to referring to any conceivable kind of excess, with the cartoonist's rendering of Uncle Sam bound in yards of red-colored tape a typical pictorialization.[3]

The symbol of red tape is functional to the frustrated observer of bureaucracy in that it suggests that what is disliked has its origins in the badness of bureaucracy and not in the observer or in the incompatibility of legitimate goals. Although Alvin Gouldner argues that perceivers of red tape tend to be resentful conservatives,[4] my experience is that persons of all political persuasions find the concept comforting. Let us consider some of the specific goal conflicts that give rise to the symbol's popularity.

One common trigger for the symbol's use is frustration over what are regarded as procedural delays. Waits, for whatever reason, are irritating. The

traversing of numerous steps in achieving a personal objective that one brings
to a government office is regarded as an imposition of unneeded complexity
and obstruction. Yet the bureaucratic outsider, by definition, cannot know
what is required within that office to achieve the objective. Paul Appleby
quotes a manager of his acquaintance as describing red tape as "that part of
my business you don't know anything about."[5] The delays are unadorned "inefficiency" to the outsider, but from an inside perspective, they may constitute
unavoidable steps to assure accountability by compiling a written record, as a
basis for appeal. Also, delays could serve such values as: legality by checking
for conformity to regulations; fairness and equity by handling clients on a
first-come, first-served basis; or efficiency by "clearing" the action with another agency where failure to do so would result in a duplication of effort.

The values embodied in delays and procedural complexity may also represent substantive policy considerations. This point is illustrated by comments
made in the 1979 debate over President Carter's Energy Mobilization Board,
whose powers were to include an ability to "cut red tape" to launch, quickly,
critically needed energy supply projects. To some observers, this special power was eminently sensible; to others, it downgraded policies equivalent in importance to energy independence. Amory Lovins stated the issue this way:

> Does "red tape" mean the procedural defects everyone wants fixed—
> dilatory schedules, unconsolidated disparate hearings, uncoordinated
> agencies, and impact statements padded to disguise weakness with
> bulk? Or is "red tape" a code phrase for the painstakingly crafted sub-
> stantive laws governing clean air and water, strip-mining, toxic sub-
> stances, endangered species, and advance assessment of alternatives
> —or for the judicial review and public participation that give those
> laws practical effect?[6]

A second stimulus for outcries of red tape is government reporting requirements. In his book on red tape, Herbert Kaufman points out that the fill-
ing out of informational forms and reports for bureaucratic agencies is at the
core of the image. If they involve one's own effort, money, or anxiety, the reports are naturally castigated as irrelevant, needless, and burdensome. The
small businessman in particular feels aggrieved on this score, and in the 1972
hearings on "The Federal Paperwork Burden" congressional committees ex-
tracted no small amount of political payoff from this attitude. Waste, duplication, and invasion of privacy were among the ills portrayed, together with a
generalized concept of massive, oppressive government stemming from the
sheer volume of reports.[7]

Such information filing *is* a waste of the businessman-citizen's time and money. To him or her there is no gain whatever in expending the effort required, except to stay clear of trouble. In fact *no* defensible reason of any kind for collecting the information is usually apparent. Furthermore, the reporting individual often feels insulted by the standardized nature of forms; they never fully fit the peculiarities of the citizen's own case, an incongruence that may be regarded, deep down, as a public violation of one's private sphere. Matters may be made worse by information verification requirements, which by their nature question personal integrity.[8]

Yet the reason for the forms and reports in the first place is to carry out mandated public policy goals, each of which is eminently worthwhle. Affirmative action statistics are gathered to promote equal opportunity. Information on a businessman's payroll and employment is essential to operate an unemployment compensation program. Efforts to desegregate schools get nowhere without voluminous reports on pupil enrollments and demographics. Improvement of any aspect of the quality of life through collective action requires information for the development of plans. But in every instance the reasons for each report are intimately bound up in the details of the respective program — and are therefore not easily explainable and usually of no interest to the average layperson. To the citizen, the only logical goal is to get the government "off my back." This is a perfectly laudable end but it must compete with others.

Still another goal conflict arena is categorization of clients and the application of rules. As mentioned, critics of bureaucracy's service delivery performance are dismayed by the fact that individual clients with individual problems are treated by an agency as a "case." "A person is far too complex to be effectively processed by a bureaucracy," it has been argued.[9] From the client's standpoint this is certainly so. He or she wants to be treated as an individual because he or she *is* an individual. Moreover, the goal of personalized treatment is inherently laudable from any external observer's point of view, for it constitutes ultimate fulfillment of the basic notion of "service."

But other goals get in the way, particularly efficiency and equity. Categorical action by those informed on the details of eligibility is the only way conceivable that masses of people can receive services on an equal basis. In public welfare, for example, farflung programs of public assistance involving millions of people and being handled in thousands of offices around the country would, without strict eligibility requirements, become a chaotic nightmare of favoritism and bickering. I doubt that even the most vociferous critics of treating people as "cases" would favor returning to earlier welfare systems where eligibility was not a factor, such as private charity's Christmas basket or the party machine's scuttle of coal.

Even some critics of bureaucracy concede the point. Michael Hill notes that regularized rules provide predictability of agency actions, protect clients against arbitrary denial of benefits, and facilitate as well as inhibit the rendering of service. "Is it better to be confronted by polite and sympathetic officials with a great deal of power over one," he asks, "or by rude and rigid ones who have no alternative but to provide a statutorily prescribed service if you qualify for it?"[10]

Charles Perrow goes farther and points out that the very rules disparaged as "red tape" permit the organization to be human rather than mechanized, heterogeneous rather than uniform, and flexible rather than isolated and unchanging. Rules nevertheless irritate social scientists, Perrow notes, for, granted their advantages, "rules are still a bore. We would all prefer to be free of them, or so it would seem. Actually, only *some* rules are bores. The good, effective rules are rarely noticed; the bad ones stand out."[11]

These highly visible "bad" rules moreover, are often so identified precisely because their intended purpose is eclipsed by another norm that seems to make more sense at the moment. We were all outraged, for example, when as a military veteran New York City's imprisoned "Son of Sam" killer seemed eligible for VA benefits.[12] We are even more outraged when *our* benefits are jeopardized. The offending rule or procedure is instantly transformed into one more manifestation of onerous "red tape." No interest whatever exists on our part in checking out the net merits of the situation. Making this point in terms of bureaucratic efficiency, Blau and Meyer write:

> Think of the last time you accused some officials of being so entangled in red tape that they could not work effectively. Did it happen after you had made a careful investigation and obtained evidence that given operating methods were disadvantageous *for the bureaucracy*? More likely, it was *you* who felt disadvantaged by a bureaucratic decision, and you gave vent to your powerless anger by leveling the accusation without knowing whether inefficiency was involved or not. We all do this—it makes us feel better.[13]

A final area in which denunciation of bureaucracy is inevitable is the application of technology to service delivery. Most citizens, as taxpayers, become angered by rising government budgets and are eager to "cut out" waste and "streamline" the bureaucracy. An obvious means for reduction of costs is the use of computer and automation technology. Yet in pursuit of this desired goal we find ourselves coping with nine-digit Zip codes, form letters written by word processors, and data processing cards that caution us not to "fold, spindle, or mutilate." Efficiency is purchased at the price of depersonalization — which goal should bureaucracy seek? The retention of face-to-face contact with the bureaucrat for whom we must wait to see is rejected as the "red tape" of laborious, old-fashioned procedures; the installation of incredibly efficient computers becomes the "red tape" of entering our Social Security number on a data-input form.

The dilemma is posed nicely by academic attacks on bureaucracy from two polar positions. On the one hand, Michael Inbar castigates "clerical" bureaucracy for committing human errors and for showing disdain toward supplicating clients. He urges that it be replaced by an automated, computerized bureaucracy where most decision making is accomplished by machine. Not worried about any coldness of manner the machine may show, Inbar says a computerized system would "make little difference in terms of feelings of rigidity and impersonality of treatment." To the contrary, he says, the logic of the system "equalizes the treatment of the powerful and the powerless."[14]

Meanwhile, from the opposite pole, Benjamin Singer attacks "incommunicado social machines." These are described as large-scale organizations that do not listen to people but only tell them what to do. The information-processing revolution has enabled bureaucracies to communicate extremely well but in one direction only, according to Singer. "As *their* ability to communicate with us increases, *ours* diminishes and our feeling of legitimacy in *attempting* [to communicate] decreases," he warns.[15] The two viewpoints beg the question: Does talking to computers mean more power or less power to the "suppressed" client of bureaucracy?

So, as we see, bureaucracy cannot win. It responds not to market demand but to political process, which means it must always be judged by multiple and inconsistent standards. Hence it must inevitably dissatisfy at least somebody. Even though these frustrations and irritations are extremely varied and stem from disparate origins, they are conveniently denounced as "red tape." Uncle Sam will always be bound in this nineteenth-century ribbon.

ADMINISTRATION BY PROXY

Another way in which bureaucracy is set up for "failure" is to hobble it by demobilizing its power, resources, and operations. By this I am referring to the effects on federal, state, and local bureaucracies of this country created by heavy reliance on indirect means of administration through grants, loans, and contracts.

Named "administration by proxy" by Christopher Hood,[16] these administrative mechanisms seem harmless unto themselves. But when employed massively, as has been the case in American bureaucracy, they can detract from performance. In fact it is quite remarkable that U.S. public administration performs as well as it does in view of the tendency.

Administration by proxy is nothing new. It was commonplace in ancient times, as in the "farming out" of tax collection. Also, it is by no means restricted to the United States. In this country it has grown at a considerable rate in recent decades largely as a consequence of attempts to remold the structure of American federalism in the direction of policy nationalization through federal grants. Also contributing to the tendency has been government's determination to exploit the knowledge and productive base of American capitalism while retaining its private structure, via contracting out to it. Still another underlying factor has been the desire to amplify the effects of federal expenditures as much as possible, for example through loan guarantees.

No one to my knowledge has attempted to estimate the proportion of American public administration accomplished by proxy, but it is no doubt very sizable. In recent years federal grants to state and local governments constituted fully one-fourth of spending at those levels. In 1977 approximately 40 percent of municipal revenues came from intergovernmental sources. The comparable figure for county governments was 45 percent, townships 30 percent, school districts 50 percent, and special districts 40 percent.[17] Probably about four times as many employees are on federally supported payrolls as work directly for Uncle Sam, it has been estimated, and over half of federal expenditures for goods and services are made to private contractors. It is notable that the cost of the federal government's contracted work force actually exceeds that of the directly employed civilian federal work force (by nearly $20 billion in 1980). With respect to functional areas involved, most federal research, weapons development, and facility construction are contracted out, and contracts are often let for such activities as long-range planning, provision of social services, institutional care, financial processing and recordkeeping, facility management, dissemination of information, and maintenance and security of offices.

In the realm of federal credit, hundreds of loan and loan guarantee programs exist and play very prominent parts in agriculture, housing, urban redevelopment, small business, education, and export expansion policy. During the 1970s, outstanding federal credit to borrowers and guarantors roughly tripled, amounting to about the size of the federal budget itself. Frederick C. Mosher estimates that as a result of the scope and extent of these and other methods of indirect administration, the proportion of federal expenditures actually allotted to direct performance of federal domestic activities amounts to only 5 to 7 percent.[18]

American public administration suffers many handicaps as a result of such massive administration by proxy. First, its complexity is vastly increased. Governmental bureaucracy does not perform by means of its own readily identifiable institutions but through hundreds of thousands of quasi-public and private organizations. Hence even understanding the implementation process in a given policy area is difficult, let alone establishing who is accountable. "Some scholars have extolled complexity in public administration and legislation," says Mosher; "it is a challenge, it is fun. But it is at least possible that complexity may grow beyond the bounds of the most brilliant minds. I suspect that it already has."[19]

Second, the task of controlling and coordinating resources is made much more difficult. The controls inherent in the operations of "in-house," direct administration—exercised via formal lines of authority and established channels of communication—are absent or reduced in effectiveness. Integration of collective effort depends on a loosely coupled process of negotiation, bargaining, and collaboration between autonomous organizations. Multiple sets of decision and procedural rules are in effect. Budgeting loses its significance as a means of managing the allocation of resources. The number of groups interested in "getting a piece of the action" is large and eminently expandable. Operational interdependencies are great in complexity and degree, yet the levels of mutual interest and reciprocal acceptance available to sustain them are often low. Enormous time is sometimes necessary to begin relatively simple undertakings, with the potential number of "veto" points greatly proliferated. Integration difficulties are compounded further by attempts to introduce order to chaos by creating intermediary coordinating agencies, such as contract review boards, impact review units, and regional planning commissions. These organizations add further to the layers and the many steps required for joint approval.

All of this was made vividly clear by Pressman and Wildavsky's famous study of federally financed public works projects in Oakland, *Implementation*. The authors found that the Oakland plans—which were accepted in principle by all concerned—required some seventy separate agreements among the many parties involved in order to be carried out. Even with an 80 percent probability of consensus on each matter, Pressman and Wildavsky calculated that the mathematical chances of completion of all necessary clearances were about a million to one. In any case, lengthy delays were inevitable as interorganizational bargainers took time to prepare their respective policy positions and jockey for advantage. The study led its authors to speculate that the relative predictability of internal coordination within a single organization places such conventional features of administration as multiple and advanced clearances and standard operating procedures—usually denounced as "bureaucratic"—in a quite different light.[20]

A third problem is that, as a result of indirect administration, many federal agencies nearly constitute what might be thought of as "empty shell" bureaucracies, whose main purpose is to receive bids and applications, write checks, and monitor the activities of others. Good examples are the Departments of Education, Energy, and Housing and Urban Development, NASA and the procurement agencies of the military, the National Science Foundation and other research funders, credit agencies like the Farm Credit and Small Business Administrations, and special-purpose grantors such as the Economic Development Administration and Urban Mass Transportation Administration.

These "nonadministering" bureaucracies, even though they perform well considering the circumstances, encounter special handicaps. As any patrons, they always face more supplicants than can be satisfied by the amount of largess to be distributed. Thus, their actions inevitably create disgruntled groups who can become potential enemies. Also, such agencies suffer from possessing only limited control over program results. Yet such influential people as congressmen, the press, and GAO auditors hold them responsible, nevertheless, for cost overruns, vacuous think-tank reports, and Golden Fleece awards. Finally, agencies that administer primarily by proxy are particularly dispensable when budget-cutting time comes, for their business is itself to hand out money, not directly manage services that voters will insist on continuing to receive.

A fourth problem is that bureaucracies on the receiving end of federal grants—that is, agencies of state and local governments—encounter intensified political difficulties of their own. Valuable time and resources must be spent on dogged grantsmanship rather than rendering needed services. Once grants are received, the costs of keeping the necessary records, filing the periodic reports, and complying with the attached "strings" must be borne. Even more important, the availability of grant money in only certain policy areas skews agency programs in favor of political preferences outside the region or community. Agencies find themselves responding not fully to their immediate constituencies but instead being forced by the lure of dollars into partial noncongruency with their own political base. That "natural" base then erodes.

The extent to which municipal bureaucracies in particular have become subject to external influences is understood by the results of a study by Lovell and Tobin of federal and state mandates. These are obligatory instructions handed down to "lower" governments by regulation or legislation. The authors identified no less than 1,260 federal mandates, most of which are associated with grants. In addition they found 3,415 mandates imposed on local government by just five states, with California issuing some 1,500 alone. These requirements cover both the nature of programs and the way they are run, dealing with such matters as personnel, finance, and evaluation. Conformity to the mandates often costs considerable money, and that is usually not provided by grants. Lovell and Tobin believe that this feature of contemporary intergovernmental administration not only gives local governments more to do while reducing their autonomy, but carries the danger of "dysfunctionally constraining implementation initiative and ingenuity."[21]

The substitution of block grants for narrowly based categorical grants may lead to some increased flexibility and autonomy. Yet at the same time, the accompanying reductions being made in total flows of assistance from Washington means that municipalities are also being forced both to cut services back and search for more local revenue. They are not in a strong position to do this after years of dependency on external funding and consequent deterioration of their community political base. In addition, local bureaucracies are forced to compete with each other for scarce block-grant dollars at the state level.

If past experience is a guide, recipients of block grants may also continue to experience frustrations in dealing with the "feds," despite the best of intentions in Washington. Upon examining the implementation of two earlier block-grant programs, the Comprehensive Employment and Training Act (CETA) and the Community Development Block Grant (CDBG), Walter Williams concluded that the increasingly open funding process caused its own problems. Grantor agencies seemed to feel a greater need than ever to protect themselves against charges of failure, and thus they overemphasized compliance to operational regulations and stressed negative veto powers. Recipient agencies resented the restrictive attitudes, as did their own local constituencies. Meanwhile, intermediary federal field officials felt bypassed. Williams reports that the outcome was an overwhelming sense of futility and impotence on the part of all concerned.[22]

In short, American bureaucracy, as capable as it is, could doubtless do even better if administration by proxy were reduced. That is at least one objective of the Reagan administration's New Federalism. Yet asking for the dismantlement of systems with decades or more of momentum and countless immediate beneficiaries may be to ask for the impossible. Perhaps all we can hope for is a continuous effort to minimize the harm by adjustments here and there. At the same time, though, we can keep in mind that the problems of proxy administration are not inherent to public bureaucracy as a generic concept, but constitute an additional hindrance to it in our own society.

Solve Those Problems!

American bureaucracy not only faces no-win situations and proxy impediments, it is expected to "solve problems." You may say, Can this be too much to ask? Why else would bureaucracies exist? Indeed, we might logically conclude that if bureaucracies do *not* solve problems, they must be guilty of the sins attributed to them after all!

The point is that identification of a "problem" is no guarantee whatever that a solution exists to that perceived problem. To demand correction of what is regarded as "bad" is, in some cases, reasonable; in others, it is expecting the impossible. But when impossible situations arise, concerned citizens and groups do not politely give up on problem solving. Instead, they seek enemies and scapegoats, one of which is bureaucracy.

What is a "problem"? It is something we do not like—a pain, difficulty, noxiant, conundrum, disruption, disaster, or whatever, all of which are *subjectively* defined. This is easy to lose sight of, because others who have already defined *their* problems assume they are "real." Yet one person's problem may be another's amusement, such as massage parlors, the smoking of pot, or the presence of Harold Robbins' novels in the public library.

In the study of politics we become aware of how politicians and interest groups attempt to influence the definition of problems. To them the objective is to achieve widespread perception that a "problem" exists. Then, in the language of Cobb and Elder, it can be "manufactured" into an issue and eventually placed on the "agenda" of the political community.[23] This step is of great benefit to the political actors involved, for it permits them to establish a distinctive public policy image as "standing" for something. The image then attracts media attention. Publicity begets publicity, and eventually a perception emerges that "something must be done." That "something" usually means government action, and—if enough pressure is generated—a law is passed. At this point the facile process of wishful thinking, media amplification, and legislative condemnation no longer runs free, however. The harsh realities of actually doing something in terms of altering human behavior or intervening in the natural environment are encountered, both of which may have prohibitive costs or be downright impossible. Nonetheless, it is at this point that bureaucracy enters the picture in terms of being responsible for achieving the desired modification of man or nature. And, if it cannot be done, bureaucracy is blamed. As James Q. Wilson has written,

> If enough people don't like something, it becomes a problem; if the
> intellectuals agree with them, it becomes a crisis; any crisis must be
> solved; if it must be solved, then it can be solved—and creating a new

organization is the way to do it. If the organization fails to solve the problem (and when the problem is a fundamental one, it will almost surely fail), then the reason is "politics," or "mismanagement," or "incompetent people," or "meddling," or "socialism," or "inertia."[24]

I do not wish to sound callous or flippant here. I personally agree with many of my fellow citizens that alcoholism, street crime, drug abuse, discrimination, poverty, pollution, inflation, and teenage pregnancies should be regarded as "problems." Also we should not eschew the idealistic state of mind in which anger aroused by defining a problem is transformed into insistence that something be done. Rather, it is that humankind's remarkable collective achievements in some areas should not lead us to expect the same success everywhere. President Kennedy's successful call to put a man on the moon and bring him back alive within the decade is not a realistic model of bureaucratic action in most fields.

Several reasons merge subtly to cause us to overestimate the capabilities of public bureaucracy. Candidates seeking office and interest groups seeking influence have everything to gain and little to lose in promising to "get crime off the streets" or "clean up the rivers." Then, too, officials at visible levels of power are motivated to promise grandiose results in order to get legislation passed or secure appropriations.

But more than "mere politics" is involved. We identify action by government with action by the nation. Thus patriotism itself seems to demand an optimistic outlook. This particularly is so in a nation that regards itself as the most successful in history. Moreover, specific incidents in American history, such as building the Panama Canal, combating the Great Depression, and fighting World Wars I and II—not to mention going to the moon—seem to provide confirming evidence that sufficient resolve and money can accomplish anything. If bureaucracy "worked" then, it should work now—on inflation, unemployment, crime, and cancer.

But reflect for a moment on what "solving" the great social problems of the day calls for. First, it often means achieving what other sectors of the society could not achieve. When parents are unable to give their children sex education, public schools end up trying. When the community's economic viability breaks down, welfare departments are expected to step into the breach. When oil companies cannot give us energy independence, the Department of Energy is given the task. When market shifts or automation throw people out of work, the U.S. Employment Service is expected to find them jobs. Regarded as occupying a standby position and holding a final-recourse responsibility, government takes on jobs others cannot do and is blamed when they are not done.

Second, "solutions" to problems such as poverty, racism, crime, drug abuse, infant mortality, heart disease, automobile deaths, and workplace safety call for modifications of deeply rooted human behaviors. Long held, deeply ingrained habits of countless millions of individuals are involved. Chains of causation are infinitely complex and elude even the most crude tracing by the best of scientists. Not all the data, money, or even direct control of daily lives imaginable could do more than modestly alter the statistics of incidence in many problem areas. Making this point for the field of health policy, Aaron Wildavsky says:

> Only when one focuses, clear-eyed and in literal detail, on the centrality and depth of the behavioral changes necessary to improve health does the immensity of the task become apparent. We are not talking about peripheral or infrequent aspects of human behavior but about some of the most basic and often experienced aspects of life: what one eats, how often and how much; how long, how regularly, and how peacefully one sleeps; whether one smokes or drinks and how much; even the whole question of personality. Health, then, . . . is a product of innumerable decisions made every day by millions of people. To oversee these decisions would call for a larger bureaucracy than anyone has yet conceived and methods of surveillance bigger than big brother. The seat-belt buzzer that screeches at us if we do not modify one small bit of behavior would be but a mild harbinger of the restraints necessary to change bad health habits.[25]

A third point relates to the time scale needed to solve some contemporary problems. In many areas the needed attitudinal change on a mass basis would require decades, generations, or even longer. Most appropriations chairmen, budget examiners, program evaluators, and investigative reporters will not wait that long. Nor should they have to. Bureaucracies should be evaluated within a reasonable time frame, which means judging them when they tackle the more manageable parts of the public agenda.

A related problem having to do with time is prediction of future events, an exercise constantly engaged in by those justifying policy. They must "show" what good things will result from new policies. Unfortunately, because of the complexities of human behavior, prediction is nearly impossible in the social realm. But those doing the predicting do not concede their crystal-ball pretentiousness; instead, they blame bureaucracy for "failing" to achieve the outcome that had been forecast. Moreover, if unintended aftershocks are set off by the planned interventions, as is often the case, public bureaucracy is usually expected to pick up the pieces. "The more we do," writes Wildavsky, "the more there is for us to do, as each program bumps into others and sets off consequences all down the line. In this way past solutions, if they are large enough, turn into future problems. And who is to deal with such problems? Naturally, those people paid to work at it full time; namely, the bureaucracy."[26]

Finally, solving problems usually means altering the *external* environment—the world "out there." This point seems obvious enough, yet it has an implication of fundamental importance for our judgment of bureaucracy. Business firms and many other private organizations are often evaluated for the quality of the product they make themselves, as in a factory, or the service they render on an immediate basis, as in a restaurant. The subject of evaluative decision is tangible, self-contained, and traceable to prior action. Governmental administration, however, is often evaluated for the eventual effects of its activities. We look not so much at what bureaucracy does as at the aftermath of what it does, which means allowing many uncontrolled variables and intervening events to influence what is judged.

For example, we evaluate a police department on the safety of city streets, not the quality of its personnel or equipment; yet the Mafia may move to town, or citizens may be unwise enough to jog in the park at 2 A.M. We evaluate public schools on the basis of standardized test scores and admission rates into college, not on efforts to provide first-rate instruction; yet culturally impoverished children may be extremely hard to teach, and hiring the best teachers may be impossible at the salaries set by the school board. We assess prisons on recidivism rates and the frequency of riots, not how well they are managed; yet the overcrowding of facilities and televised coverage of prison riots elsewhere may have an irresistible effect on what happens. Outcomes, not efforts, are what count. Bureaucracy is expected not only to be perfect, but to perfect society.

The foregoing analysis of the fruitlessness of expecting complete solutions from bureaucracy should not leave the impression that little is done. Poverty has not been eliminated in America, but the percentage of Americans below the official poverty line has been more than halved. Also, tremendous strides have been made in providing minimal health care to all citizens, improving levels of nutrition, and reducing the incidence of communicable disease. These achievements are nothing short of remarkable for a continent-sized country. Moreover, all of them were accomplished by or with the help of public bureaucracy. More important, regardless of aggregate statistics or trends, the lives of millions of Americans are individually touched, on a daily basis, by public programs. Each job placement through the Employment Service and each stomach filled by food stamps has profound, immediate importance for the person involved. Macrocosmic social change may occur incrementally, but the single units of change constituting it may be drastic, not "marginal," to the persons involved.

Observers have argued that we underestimate the achievements of public programs because of the nature of modern public policy analysis. This young "science" was not around in the New Deal, and perhaps even that legendary set of bureaucratic accomplishments could not have survived very rigorous "program evaluation." The field's preoccupation with rationality and efficiency may itself foster unwarranted skepticism. Mark Moore, for example, believes that social science plays a "spoiler's role" in policy analysis. "Because conservative rules of evidence make it hard to conclude that a policy's desired effect actually has occurred, evaluations of governmental programs nearly always fail to show any effect."[27] Along the same lines, Levitan and Taggart condemn analysts for adopting a null hypothesis of assumed failure and then demanding proof of any significant success. Instead, they argue, success should be assumed and failure proved, an approach that would have notably more positive results. Also Levitan and Taggart criticize evaluators for comparing implemented, "real" programs to hypothetical, ideal ones, concentrating on negative secondary effects rather than positive ones, and focusing on economic efficiencies rather than net social gains.[28]

Without attempting to settle here the internal debates going on in the policy analysis field, let me merely point out that matters more deep-seated than conservative rules of evidence and null hypotheses of failure are behind our condemnation of the achievements of government. The reasons why we overestimate expectations and underestimate attainments with respect to bureaucracy are not technical issues of research design or even the internal biases of a field. They have to do with fundamental misinterpretations of public bureaucracy.

Bureaucracy and Social Change

Bureaucracy may be expected to "solve those problems," but it is generally not expected to foster social change. Most critics of bureaucracy consider bureaucracy antipathetic to social change. Also, its few sympathizers tend to play down any positive relationship. Yet Peter Savage once noted that both campus radicals and racial segregationists fulminate against "bureaucrats," even though one group advocates radical social change and the other stands for the status quo or even reaction.[29] The issue must be more complicated than it appears.

Those who view bureaucracy as antithetical to social change make the argument on deductive grounds. The sociologist Richard LaPiere, for example, argues flatly that creative and innovative people are not attracted to employment in bureaucracies. Those who become bureaucrats are security minded, preferring to obey the rules faithfully and not take risks. Also, LaPiere contends that the monopolistic nature of bureaucracy prevents it from sensing the need to innovate. Mature bureaucracies are, he claims, isolated, self-validating systems concerned only with their own maintenance. To promote stability they even develop defense mechanisms against change, such as committee decision making and "passing the buck" behavior.[30]

In the field of public administration the position that bureaucracy and social change are contradictory is most vividly expressed in the "new public administration" literature. This came out of the antiestablishment rebellion that swept the field (and all social sciences) in the late 1960s and early '70s. George Frederickson, speaking for this orientation, contends that "traditional bureaucracy has a demonstrated capacity for stability, indeed, ultrastability."[31] This means, according to Frederickson, that it protects established interests and perpetuates existing social injustices. Instead, he argues in the new public administration vein, bureaucracy should play an open advocacy role in pursuing social equity and responsiveness to citizens. Bureaucrats should not follow the dictates of elected representatives under the guise of neutrality but actively assist and involve the urban poor and racial minorities. Interestingly enough, Frederickson and his fellow new public administrationists do not propose abandoning administration as an instrument of collective action. Rather, they call for its modification through neighborhood decentralization, situational authority, temporary work teams, client representation, and matrix organization.[32]

The reactions within orthodox public administration to this challenge have been fascinating to watch. While many have agreed the field was inflicted with an excessively promanagement perspective (and general stodginess as well) and thus needed a strong rebuke, others have lashed out with counterattacks. Among the most prominent opponents has been Victor Thompson. As mentioned in chapter 1, Thompson contends that helping the downtrodden outside the channels of democratic control constitutes outright theft. Administration in a democracy is "owned" by all the people, he says, and to give special access and privilege to certain subgroups is "a brazen attempt to 'steal' the popular sovereignty."[33]

Another critic, Richard Simpson, believes the thievery has already begun. He interprets the activism beginning in the 1960s as embarking bureaucracy on nothing short of ventures in irrationalism. Bureaucracy, he says, should instead be the stronghold of rationalism. Simpson is disturbed that bureaucracy has not fought off activist campaigns but actually institutionalized them. Thus, antiestablishment movements did not destroy or even bypass bureaucracy, but involved it and made it their own.[34]

The great synthesizer of American public administration, Dwight Waldo, has taken a position that seems to straddle the field's warring factions. He sees bureaucracy as inimical to social change in some ways and not so in other ways. On the one hand, Waldo reminds us of the supposed timidity and lack of imagination among bureaucrats, plus what he regards as the flywheel or ballast function of bureaucracy. "Its indispensable function is to provide the element of predictability, stability, and continuity which, if missing, would result in imbalance and might lead to chaos or catastrophe." On the other hand, Waldo believes bureaucracy is an important force for change in society. It has had a central role in fostering the development of revolutionary technologies such as computers. He points out, moreover, that the present era in which bureaucracy has flourished has by no means been static. "The era of large bureaucracies is *par excellence* the era of rapid change in nearly every dimension."[35]

In reflecting on these various ideas regarding the interrelationship of public bureaucracy and social change, several things seem clear. First, government agencies *are* a part of the "establishment." There is no doubt of that. They are created by, and act in behalf of, established authority. They are not in any sense "neutral" but instead advocate and perpetuate policy points of view acceded to by established authority. They are, in addition, irrefutably political animals, operating within a sanctioned political turf. They are "public" in the broadest sense.

The point is, however, that public bureaucracies cannot stray far from their own territory. They cannot blithely man the barricades when a revolutionary fervor pervades the nation's campuses and small-circulation journals. Like all organizations, bureaucracies are context-bound: They are energized by their political environments but at the same time cannot move beyond them —at least not very far—without committing suicide. Hence, we might expect some government agencies to "advocate change," but only within the confines of what "advocacy" and "change" are accepted to mean in their respective political arenas.

Stereotyped views of public bureaucracy to the contrary, the meaning of such words as "advocacy" and "change" varies greatly among individual administrative institutions. To the Department of Commerce, advocating change means improving the productivity of American industry and advancing U.S. exports overseas. To the Department of Defense, championing change means rearming an alarmingly weak military establishment and closing the security gap open to the Russians. To the local police department, it is conducting an all-out war on crime and perhaps at the same time running a campaign to improve departmental communication with ethnic groups.

But these are not "radical" activities, at least to most adherents of the new public administration. These "changes" would be regarded as mere examples of bureaucratic advancement of the status quo. I personally disagree, and feel a right to do so because definitions of "social change," just like "social problems," are subjective in nature.

What is important for understanding contemporary public administration, though, is that even the kind of "change" called for by militant activists is advocated by bureaucracy. The Equal Employment Opportunity Commission and Civil Rights Commission, not to mention Justice's Civil Rights Division and countless equal employment and affirmative action offices around the country, determinedly advance the centerpiece cause of the 1960s, the civil rights movement. The Environmental Protection Agency, Consumer Product Safety Commission, Occupational Safety and Health Administration, and Legal Services Corporation also pursue what might be thought of as liberal causes. Advocacy bureaus representing causes of an earlier era are the Food and Drug Administration, National Labor Relations Board, and Farm Security Administration. In each successive reform wave, one might even conclude that political activism usually gives birth to bureaucracy. This is not "irrationalism," as Simpson charges, but simply system responses to political cues within the society that could not be ignored. Even activists expressing a natural distaste for bureaucracy find themselves advocating creation of bureaucracy as the crowning achievement of their own agitational efforts.

Hence bureaucracy is not merely "for stability" and "against change"; it is *for* all kinds of things, such as increased productivity, more missiles, reduced crime, more employment of blacks, cleaner air, safer products and plants, and so on. As for what bureaucracy opposes, it is against the opposites of all of these, namely, declining productivity, rising crime rates, worsening pollution, reducing opportunities for blacks, and so on. All of this is "change" but what counts is not the abstract category but particular changes and whom they help or hurt. And on such changes bureaucracy is no monolith, but an incredible plurality of institutionalized viewpoints and political interests. To associate it wholesale with social stability is to engage in conceptual game-playing, in which facile associations of bureaucracy with "continuity" and unfounded assumptions of bureaucratic "timidity" are parlayed by intellectual sleight-of-hand into irrefutable truths.

The reason people get away with such loose talk on the subject of social change and bureaucracy is that both terms are already normatively loaded, with opposite valences. "Social change" stands for whatever *we* want to happen. "Bureaucracy" symbolizes obstruction and recalcitrance in reaching goals. Hence the two terms are inevitably counterposed, but this says nothing about the concrete relationships between the two phenomena named.

If we are a little more honest with these words, we realize that bureaucracy is essential to most social change, whether it is "our" kind or not. In fact, it is difficult to think of any large-scale, planned change in the social realm that would *not* require the efforts of bureaucratic organizations. This is true whether we are desegregating schools by busing, building a highway that revolutionizes an isolated valley, or operating a food stamp program that raises the possibility of having an entire national population reach nutritional minimums, perhaps for the first time in world history. The reason bureaucracy is indispensable is that it only provides the necessary mobilized resources in a form that can be utilized over sustained periods of time to achieve complex tasks requiring high levels of knowledge and coordination. This is precisely why radical movements become institutionalized bureaucracies once the fight is won. Also, this is why Waldo feels compelled to note how bureaucracy has accompanied the unfolding of the most turbulent century in human history. Even Richard LaPiere, who equates bureaucracy with the status quo, concedes that bureaucracy has at times laid the groundwork for momentous social change. In fact, he cites the bureaucratization of police forces—as first exemplified by Sir Robert Peel's "bobbies"—as contributing momentously to social change. This single step yielded far-reaching social change of the most revolutionary kind, for it permitted people for the first time to move about their communities freely, liberating them from constant fear of violent attack.[36]

The indispensability of bureaucracy to large-scale, planned societal change is not even an issue in the less developed countries. There, thinking on the subject is not in terms of such code words as social change and bureaucracy, but another verbal symbol, "development." By this is meant accelerated and planned moves toward industrialization and furtherance of human welfare, *under government direction.* Hence, the all-important role of bureaucracy is implicitly understood. Public administration is, in fact, considered a vital contributor to development, along with capital and technology. One could scarcely find a government in the Third World that did not contain a central planning organization, numerous development authorities, and a series of government corporations, all engaged in spurring economic growth and social improvement. Most Third World governments rely on public enterprises for aspects of economic production as well.

The perceived problem of "bureaucracy" in the developing countries is not that public administration opposes social change but that it is not itself well enough developed and financed to push changes more quickly. When some years ago I argued that the socioeconomic transformation of Puerto Rico that occurred in the 1950s could be traced to a union forged in the 1940s between effective political power and energetic public bureaucracy, [37] I was denounced by certain antiregime Puerto Ricans. But their complaint was over my implicit endorsement of the 1940s' program, not my analysis of the contribution of administration to it. In most countries of the world those who regard themselves as advocating radical social change perceive bureaucracy as essential to its achievement, not as an obstacle to be overcome.

CHAPTER 5

BUREAUCRATS AS ORDINARY PEOPLE

We now turn attention from bureaucracies to the bureaucrats employed in them. Our purpose in doing so is simple, namely, to demonstrate how these men and women are ordinary people. A visitor from another planet would be amazed that the point needs any attention. Yet it does, for the generalized hostility felt toward bureaucracy as an abstraction is transferred to its employees, again as an abstraction. We may know intellectually that the individuals we talk with across reception counters and in government offices are not all lazy, incompetent, arrogant, and power-hungry. Yet when the occasional unpleasant run-in with bureaucracy occurs, we are ready at once to curse at stereotypes.

This habit of mind is perfectly understandable and certainly forgivable as a means of coping with the daily chores of living in a modern society. Yet stereotyped thinking is perpetuated by those who have a responsibility to be more exacting, the professional students of bureaucracy. They invent such concepts as the "bureaucratic personality" or "bureaucratic mentality" to serve as central components of antibureaucracy theories. One writer even claims that "bureaucracy gives birth to a new species of inhuman beings." Any notion that "bureaucrats are people like us" is a "misunderstanding," he says; instead, they constitute "a new personality type, headless and soulless."[1]

This chapter begins with consideration of personal, occupational, and attitudinal attributes of government bureaucrats, comparing these to the population at large. Then it explores job-related attitudes and personality characteristics in the light of notions of a fixed "bureaucratic mentality." Next, data on work attitudes and job satisfaction are examined to determine whether bureaucracy is as dismal a workplace as is often said. Finally, consideration is given to the public reputation of the bureaucrat and what that seems to mean in terms of antibureaucracy sentiment in this country.

WHO ARE THE BUREAUCRATS?

One way to strip the bureaucrat of his or her supposed distinctiveness is simply to note how many bureaucrats there are. The club of bureaucrats is not exclusive enough to be very ominous. A sizable proportion of Americans belong, in fact more than one out of six employed persons. The overall figures, rounded off, are that the federal government employs 5 million (3 civilian, 2 military), state governments 4 million, and local governments 9 million. This adds up to 18 million people.

Besides their vast numbers, another feature of bureaucrats that places them on a fairly ordinary and nonawesome plane is what they do. They do not simply shuffle papers, attend meetings, and telephone laconically with no hands. Nor do they just give orders; managers in government are a distinct minority of the whole. What bureaucrats do is nothing less than the myriad of highly specialized tasks performed in a modern technological society—the matter is both that complex and that simple. "The popular impression of a civil servant is like an outdated photograph," John Weaver writes. "It was taken before the technological revolution, and has as little relationship to today's government worker as one of his baby pictures."[2] Bureaucrats operate bridges, investigate crimes, manage forests, program computers, arbitrate labor disputes, counsel teenagers, calculate cost-benefit ratios, operate sea-rescue cutters, run libraries, examine patent applications, inspect meat, negotiate contracts, and so on and so forth. The list could fill the rest of this book. Occupational directories and job classification handbooks put out by government personnel agencies run to the hundreds of pages. The point is simply that *bur*eaucrats don't "bur"—there is no common occupational activity they all perform. These men and women do almost everything, which means that even at face value generalizations about their nature or behavior are strongly suspect.

Thirty years ago Norton Long shocked an earlier generation of antibureaucracy critics with the argument that the federal civil service importantly supplements the U.S. Congress as an instrument of representation. One of the several intertwined themes of his argument was that recruitment into the American civil service is relatively open. Unlike the case in many countries, entrants come from all social levels, groups, and regions of the nation. This means that the federal bureaucracy substantially mirrors the makeup of the U.S. population, and certainly does so more faithfully than the national legislature.

If one rejects the view that election is the *sine qua non* of representation, the bureaucracy now has a very real claim to be considered much more representative of the American people in its composition than the Congress. This is not merely the case with respect to the class structure of the country but, equally significantly, with respect to the learned groups, skills, economic interests, races, nationalities, and religions.

The rich diversity that makes up the United States is better represented in its civil service than anywhere else.[3]

Such representation cannot replace formal organs of representative government, of course. Yet it means avoidance of a class-oriented administration or bureaucracy dominated by a particular region; both problems are found in not a few countries. Also, at the least, compositional mirroring means that bureaucrats are "ordinary" people in the sense of being typical in many ways. Indeed, empirical studies have shown that American civil servants are substantially like employed persons in other fields along such dimensions as educational level, social status, income, religion, and even party affiliation. Although the data (for 1975) in table 5.1 are drawn from a small sample, they typify what is generally found in comparisons of bureaucrats to the general public.[4]

TABLE 5.1. SAMPLE PROFILE OF THE PUBLIC AND PUBLIC EMPLOYEES

	All Respondents (N = 1490)	Respondents Employed In Public Administration (N = 96)
Education (years):	11.7	12.5
Father's education	9.0	9.0
Mother's education	9.5	9.8
Religion (percent):		
Protestant	66	68
Catholic	24	26
Other	10	6
Income (percent):		
Under $5,000	20	19
$5,000-9,999	24	21
$10,000-19,999	39	52
Over $20,000	17	12
Party identification (percent):		
Democrat	55	52
Independent	14	14
Republican	31	34

These data show bureaucrats to be discernibly different only in that they are more intermediate with respect to income, which is understandable in a largely salaried, middle-class institution like bureaucracy. A demographic variable not given in the data is race, which of course is of central importance in any test of representativeness. A study conducted as long ago as 1960 noted that whereas 11 percent of the general employed public was nonwhite, 21 percent of federal employees were nonwhite.[5] Since that time, the proportion of blacks and other minorities in federal employment has continued to remain well above their percentages in the general population. The same is true in state and local governments, where 20 percent of personnel were of minority status in 1975. Women remain underrepresented in all levels of government, constituting about 34 percent of federal employment and 38 percent of state and local.[6]

On the basis of total employment numbers, then, bureaucrats are not that much different from other people except that they are disproportionately male and nonwhite. In surveying data from several studies, Kenneth Meier finds that "in terms of father's occupation, education, age, and income one can conclude that the U.S. civil service does indeed mirror the American people as a whole."[7]

But the question of the representativeness of American bureaucracy does not end there. The issue addressed by minority interest groups and governments' affirmative action efforts is gross imbalance with respect to relative *levels of responsibility* within administration. And disproportionalities are unquestionably there: Blacks and women are relatively numerous in lower pay scales but are definitely underrepresented at upper levels. A recent study shows that black employees in state and local governments exceed the proportions of their presence in the populations of 30 states, but that in only one, Pennsylvania, is their median salary above that of their white colleagues.[8] This kind of misrepresentation is slowly diminishing but—unfortunate as it is—will probably take some time to be fully eliminated; in any case, the record of many bureaucracies—especially the federal—is not bad at all compared to the private sector in promoting equal employment opportunity.

On other variables, meanwhile, upper-level bureaucrats are often quite representative. Meier discovered this to be the case for region of birth and size of community of birth, but not for educational level. He also notes that higher federal civil servants are substantially more representative than federal political executives with respect to father's occupation. On this last criterion, federal senior officials are also far more representative than their counterparts in Britain, Denmark, France, Turkey, and India.[9]

This kind of proportionate mirroring, sometimes called "passive" representation in literature on the subject, is of course very important to minorities and women for symbolic and economic reasons. Another phenomenon sometimes discussed along this line is "active" representation, or behavior in office by members of socioeconomic subgroups that serves the self-interest of those groups. Interestingly enough, data available at present suggest that once in a government job, female and minority bureaucrats conduct themselves no differently from other bureaucrats. Frank Thompson, in a study of minority personnel officers, noted that the individual's race was not the most important factor in predicting their receptivity to hiring other nonwhites.[10] In another study, Meier and Nigro discovered that demographic characteristics of higher federal civil servants account statistically for less variance in their policy views than the agency in which they work.[11] The agency positions in which bureaucrats "sit" have much to do with where they "stand," as the old saw goes—and certainly more to do with it than their race or gender.

The broader issue of whether bureaucrats as a total group have distinctive policy views or political preferences is sometimes raised. If generalized biases exist, this would be of great importance in view of discretionary choices exercised by bureaucrats within the administrative state. Indeed, political conservatives have at times charged that bureaucrats invariably vote for Democrats so as to perpetuate a philosophy of "big government" that will protect their jobs. Such reasoning probably helped delay passage of the Twenty-third Amendment, which secured the presidential vote for District of Columbia residents. At the other end of the political spectrum, some Marxists assert that the higher civil servants of the capitalist state perform as ideological disciples of capitalism in order to promote maintenance of existing economic structures.[12]

TABLE 5.2. POLITICAL AND POLICY VIEWS OF PUBLIC EMPLOYEES

	General Public	Government Employees
Political Views (1975):		
Extreme liberal	3%	6%
Liberal	13	13
Slightly liberal	14	10
Moderate	40	35
Slightly conservative	17	17
Conservative	11	12
Extreme conservative	3	8
Policy Views (1972):		
Withdraw from Vietnam	44	48
Trade with communists	64	83
Increase taxes on rich	53	60
Legalize marijuana	24	22
Protect the accused	43	51
Help racial minorities	44	51

What we actually find empirically is that once again bureaucrats are fairly ordinary people. Surveys show that their expressed opinions on questions of the day are similar to those of the general public. The data that are given in table 5.2 on page 86 show bureaucrats to be somewhat more liberal on certain policy issues current in 1972, but otherwise not much different from the overall population.[13]

Another set of survey results available for comparison purposes suggests that bureaucrats may be closer to the general public in their political opinions than are politicians themselves. This kind of representation could again support the contentions of Norton Long. In 1957-58 Herbert McClosky obtained survey data from a national sample of the general population and also from more than 3,000 delegates and alternates to the national 1956 conventions of both parties. In these surveys identical questions were asked in which degree of commitment to various values associated with a democratic polity were tested. In 1969-70 some of the same questions were repeated by Bob Wynia in a survey of about 400 federal executives attending training seminars. Four of the statements reacted to in common by the three samples are shown in table 5.3.[14]

TABLE 5.3. DEGREE OF AGREEMENT WITH ANTIDEMOCRATIC STATEMENTS

	Percentage Agreement		
	General Public	Convention Delegates	Federal Executives
There are times when it almost seems better for the people to take the law into their own hands rather than wait for the machinery of government to act.	27	13	32
To bring about great changes for the benefit of mankind often requires cruelty and even ruthlessness.	31	19	27
The true American way of life is disappearing so fast that we may have to use force to save it.	35	13	19
We have to teach children that all men are created equal but almost everyone knows that some are better than others.	58	55	38

We note that in the first three statements the sample of executives was closer to the general public in viewpoint than were the convention delegates. It is important to note also that a distinct minority of executives agreed with these deliberately antidemocratic statements. Another interesting point is that among the three samples, bureaucrats were the least patient with the machinery of government, i.e., themselves.

Who, then, are the bureaucrats? They are a great bunch of us, in the first place. In the second place they are not generalizable in terms of occupational activity. Third, bureaucrats are representative of the public at large in terms of education, social status, religion, income, and party affiliation. Minority bureaucrats are disproportionately present in overall numbers but do not hold their fair share of high-level jobs. Women are underrepresented on both counts, although this is changing. Finally, bureaucrats and the rest of us have similar political and policy views. Charles Hyneman wrote more more than three decades ago,

> The officials and employees of the federal government are typical American citizens. They are just as devoted to our ideal of government by the people and just as loyal to our form of government as the farmers of Indiana; they would be as reluctant to leave their homes in the evening and join in a conspiracy against the people as the bankers of Iowa, or the lumbermen of Minnesota.[15]

The "Bureaucratic Mentality"

One may reply to Hyneman by saying that certainly these ordinary Americans do not leave their homes at night to join conspiracies, but on arriving at the office the next morning, something even worse happens. They become transformed into petty tyrants. This argument has been taken very seriously in academic circles for some forty years and should be examined closely. The contention is formidable: The structure of bureaucracy itself produces a distinctive mentality or personality on the part of its full-time, appointed staff. Whether by self-selection in entering bureaucratic employment or by socialization once in it, the bureaucrat is deemed to possess a particular turn of mind and pattern of behavior. These attributes and behaviors are said to be quite nasty, at the least.

This school of analysis began with a famous article by Robert Merton, "Bureaucratic Structure and Personality," published in 1940. Merton argued that at least four principal traits of the bureaucratic personality are produced by the Weberian structure of bureaucratic organization. First, the specialized nature of bureaucratic work causes "an inadequate flexibility in the application of skills." This is said to occur because an extreme narrowness in scope of work does not allow the functionary to be capable of adapting to ever-changing conditions. Second, the need for reliability and discipline in bureaucratic output causes officials to overemphasize the importance of rules. They then forget the initial reason for the rules, and in a "displacement of goals" phenomenon, enforcement of the rules surpasses in importance in the bureaucrat's mind what the organization is trying ultimately to achieve. "An extreme product of this process of displacement of goals," Merton writes, "is the bureaucratic virtuoso, who never forgets a single rule binding his action and hence is unable to assist many of his clients." Third, the lengthy, career nature of the bureaucrat's position leads the official to be cautious, conservative, and protective of an entrenched position. Too much is at stake to take any chances with innovation or risk. Fourth, the general application of rules to individual cases creates an impersonal categorization mode of thinking that ignores the humanity and individuality of clients. "The personality pattern of the bureaucrat is nucleated about this norm of impersonality," Merton writes. Accompanying it is an arrogant and haughty manner, stemming from the formal authority with which the bureaucrat is vested, plus the lower-level official's psychological need to compensate for his inferior position inside the organization by exhibiting superiority to those outside it.[16]

Other theorists have elaborated on Merton's thesis. Bensman and Rosenberg, writing from a social-psychological perspective, believe the bureaucrat must slavishly remodel his or her personality to fit the employing organization's norms. This produces a loss of personal identity, which causes some bureaucrats to lose interest in their work and perform duties perfunctorily. In others it sets the stage for the substitution of organizational ties for their own personal relationships or, alternatively, identification of their individual egos with uncompromising adherence to the rules. To confuse matters a bit, Bensman and Rosenberg also deduce that a sense of powerlessness in the large and subdivided organization may lead to a blatant disregard of the rules, in a kind of rejectionist syndrome. Still another alleged reaction to perceived powerlessness is to redirect resentments against clients and subordinates, thus performing as a tyrant toward them while as a sycophant toward superiors.[17]

Ralph Hummel echoes much of this analysis in his depiction of the bureaucrat as suffering from a "truncated" ego caused by the supposedly debilitating effects of working within a framework of rules, hierarchy, and specialization. The bureaucrat is no longer a genuine human being but a dehumanized, psychological cripple. Relations between the official and the client become a "theater of war" between this dehumanized official and psychologically normal outsiders. "In brief," says Hummel, "the way bureaucrats relate to clients is analogous to the way people in one country relate to people from an entirely different country."[18]

Moreover, the structure of civil service protection afforded the official is said to make an unfortunate imprint on his or her personality. This is because, regardless of performance, the bureaucrat supposedly cannot be fired. This widely believed feature of government employment allegedly attracts persons who lack confidence, competence, drive, courage, and other such attributes. To illustrate this point of view, Charles Peters argues that "as we begin to climb the administrative ladder, a dominant personality type does emerge (or maybe it's that a certain element in civil servants' personalities comes to dominate as they climb the ladder), and an excess of caution is certainly one of its characteristics. . . . Civil servants are too often mother's little boys and daddy's little girls who have learned to expect security without having to earn it."[19]

Endless additional pieces of published writing could be cited on the bureaucratic mentality, inasmuch as it is a favorite theme not merely among professional critics of bureaucracy but among journalists, novelists, and writers of letters to the editor. Like the stereotype of bureaucracy, the image conveniently captures the many frustrations of those who work in or with large governmental organizations, a group that includes just about everyone that is of school age or over. Moreover, within the social sciences the notion has acquired its own momentum as an idea in vogue, and this momentum has scarcely slowed over four decades. To what extent, then, is the model verified empirically?

Perhaps the best-known empirical study, and partly for that reason one of the most controversial, is a project undertaken by Melvin Kohn. In it he attempted to measure the effects of employment in a bureaucracy, whether private or public. Kohn's interest extended to the employee's values, social orientation, and intellectual functioning. A national sample of 3,101 men employed in civilian occupations was surveyed by structured interview. The extent to which the respondents were employed in a bureaucratic milieu was identified by the respective organization's number of supervisory levels and number of employees, with more of each denoting more bureaucratization. Variables examined for the possible effects of bureaucratization were the extent to which an individual values conformity to external authority; the exhibited social orientations of an authoritarian, legalistic, and noninnovative nature; the scores on form perception and problem-solving intelligence tests; and analysis of the use of leisure time. With all this complexity in research design, Kohn's main finding was simple: Correlations of bureaucratization with these factors were notably small. Even more interesting, the directions of correlation *consistently contradicted* what the bureaucratic personality is supposed to be like![20]

Men who work in bureaucratic firms or organizations tend to value, not conformity, but self-direction. They are more open-minded, have more personally responsible standards of morality, and are more receptive to change than are men who work in nonbureaucratic organizations. They show great flexibility in dealing both with perceptual and ideational problems. They spend their leisure time in more intellectually demanding activities.

Kohn looked for mediating variables that might explain why bureaucrats are more self-directed. The only possible candidate seemed to be level of education; more bureaucratized organizations employ more educated individuals, who then display the orientations found. Another speculative thought by Kohn was that the nature of bureaucratic jobs may challenge independent and creative people. Supervision may be tighter with more layers of hierarchy, but protection is greater from arbitrary actions of superiors. In brief, "bureaucracy may hold a special attraction for self-directed, intellectually flexible men who are receptive to innovation and change."[21]

While the Kohn study involved bureaucrats in both the public and private sectors, other empirical studies have compared officials across the two sectors. James Guyot analyzed the results of personality tests administered to 100 business executives and 147 public managers. Guyot found the latter group to be significantly more motivated by achievement values than the former, but relatively less motivated by a desire for acceptance by colleagues. This conclusion does not square, obviously, with notions of an alienated and insecure bureaucrat. Also, Guyot noted that the groups were about equal in their orientations toward power. He concludes that "the opportunity to exercise power in a government bureau is no more enticing than it is in an executive suite in a business organization."[22]

In another business-government comparison, Julius Brown studied risk propensity and other personality characteristics between 63 business administrators and 84 public school administrators. In addition to utilizing a personality test and standard questionnaire, Brown employed a set of hypothetical gaming situations in which a decision was posed between two alternative choices. In the manner of the Prisoner's Dilemma game, one choice promised greater payoffs but at higher risk, while the alternative promised less but was safer. Brown found that, by a modest but significant degree, businessmen accepted more risk. Also, the business sample scored higher on achievement and initiative variables but was not statistically different with respect to self-assurance, decisiveness, intelligence, and supervisory ability.[23]

The bureaucratic mentality is supposed to generate arrogant, haughty, impersonal, and rule-bound behavior toward clients. What do available studies reveal on this score? In a study done by Meyers and McIntyre for the Department of Health, Education, and Welfare, more than 1,000 questionnaires completed by AFDC caseworkers in ten states were analyzed. One of the queries on the survey asked respondents to indicate whether they thought certain stereotypes of AFDC recipients applied to most, some, few, or hardly any of the clients they handled. The stereotypes presented for assessment were both negative and positive in connotation; they were, however, presented to respondents in mixed order and not labeled negative or positive. The results are shown in table 5.4.[24]

TABLE 5.4. CASEWORKERS' REACTIONS TO STEREOTYPES OF AFDC RECIPIENTS

	Most	Some	Few	Hardly Any
Negative stereotypes:				
Scheming	3%	21%	48%	26%
Immature	22	58	15	2
Immoral	6	33	40	18
Oversexed	3	13	34	46
Stupid	4	25	43	25
Dishonest	3	22	47	25
Positive stereotypes:				
Unfortunate	69	24	4	1
Decent	69	23	4	1
Maternal	53	36	6	2
Deserving	67	23	5	1
Conscientious	38	47	9	2

We see that substantial majorities of caseworkers associated the negative stereotypes with no more than a few of their clients (except for "immature") but identified the positive ones with most of them (except for "conscientious"). Also, Meyers and McIntyre asked several agree-disagree questions designed to elicit value orientations toward clients. Five of these, with levels of agreement, are shown in table 5.5.

While the response to the first statement indicates most caseworkers do not agree with relaxing the content of eligibility rules, the outcome of the sec-

TABLE 5.5. CASEWORKERS' VALUE ORIENTATIONS TOWARD CLIENTS

	Agreement with Statement
AFDC eligibility requirements now in effect should be made less strict.	40%
When a client's continuing eligibility is uncertain, the client should get the benefit of the doubt.	89
The AFDC client should have the right to refuse to let someone from the welfare department come into her house during the night.	89
Approve of organizations composed of welfare recipients who are trying to obtain more benefits for themselves.	67
The caseworker owes greater loyalty to the client than to the department.	51

ond suggests a flexible attitude on enforcement of those rules. To give the client "the benefit of the doubt" is hardly what Merton's rule-obsessed bureaucratic virtuoso would do. Preponderant majorities of caseworkers also expressed proclient attitudes about house visits and welfare rights groups. The fact that over half expressed more loyalty to the client than the department seems particularly notable.

A survey I conducted of social service workers also yields pertinent data. In 1977, in association with the exit-poll welfare interviewing described in chapter 2, I distributed a questionnaire to personnel inside the offices who dealt directly with clients. Primarily these were public assistance caseworkers, unemployment compensation examiners, and Social Security representatives. The questionnaire was returned directly and anonymously to me by mail; of 338 forms distributed, 244 were returned.[25]

The first question asked in this instrument was whether client benefit levels were thought to be too high, too low, or about right. The responses were 14, 38, and 45 percent, respectively.

Then a series of questions asked the respondents to indicate proportions of clients who seem "honest in their verbal statements concerning eligibility," "nervous when you first talk to them," "hostile to you or the system," and ready to "argue with you." The replies are shown in table 5.6 on page 94.

TABLE 5.6. SOCIAL SERVICE WORKERS' PERCEPTIONS OF CLIENTS

	Almost All	Majority	Some	Few	Almost None	No Answer
Honest	14%	64%	16%	4%	1%	0%
Nervous	6	27	42	21	4	1
Hostile	0	5	40	41	13	1
Argumentative	1	7	39	33	19	1

The questionnaire also listed, alphabetically, six possible responsibilities of an official who serves the public. Workers were asked to indicate the relative importance of each. The various concepts of responsibility are listed below in the order of number of citations received for being considered most important (with multiple answers from some respondents). In designing the question, the first, second, and fourth descriptions listed had been considered by the researcher as proclient and the remaining not so.

		Citations
1.	Meet client needs	144
2.	Treat clients courteously	126
3.	Process cases efficiently	114
4.	Alleviate human suffering	83
5.	Enforce the rules	77
6.	Protect the taxpayer	44

A final question asked workers to describe traits of two kinds of clients: those they currently deal with most of the time, and those they would *like* to deal with all of the time. The purpose of this query was to explore, open-endedly, any implicit condemnation of clients. Of those workers who did, in effect, seize this opportunity to criticize clients, most found fault with their demeanor or personal qualities rather than perceived obstructionist behavior. Most interestingly, a majority of answering respondents (52 percent) rejected outright this opportunity to condemn clients. They either had praiseworthy things to say about their clients or stated that it is impossible to generalize about clients.

In sum, the results of this survey suggest that more workers sympathetically endorse higher benefits for clients than the reverse; workers regard most clients to be honest but not hostile; client-oriented responsibilities are given more priority than department-oriented norms; and even when tapped indirectly, worker attitudes are quite proclient.

We discover, then, that the empirical evidence reviewed concerning the "bureaucratic mentality" is generally disconfirming rather than supportive. Bureaucrats are no less flexible, tolerant, and creative than other people — perhaps they are a little more so. Compared to business executives, bureaucrats may be less risk-prone but do not seem less motivated, assured, or decisive. Welfare bureaucrats, with their terrible reputation for being disrespectful to clients and overzealous in rule enforcement, entertain positive images of clients more often than negative ones, and exhibit flexible attitudes toward compliance with regulations. Also, welfare workers show high levels of respect, sympathy, and empathy with clients. If the bureaucratic mentality exists in the real world of bureaucracy, it has as yet not been found. One is struck here by parallels to another common stereotype, that of the "military mind," described by Fred Reed in this manner: "It exists: closed, narrow, explosive, combative, redolent of a hostility not associated with any discernible cause. Maybe these men really were dropped on their heads. The salient point about the military mind is that few officers have it."[26]

How Bad Is Work in Bureaucracy?

An associated criticism of bureaucracy as it affects bureaucrats concerns not what bureaucratic structure does to its staff members as they relate to others but how it hurts them personally. As mentioned in chapter 1, a long-standing theme in literature on the subject is that bureaucrats suffer unduly from being employed, often for their entire careers, in a large, hierarchical organization. "The individual bureaucrat cannot squirm out of the apparatus in which he is harnessed," Max Weber wrote near the turn of the century.[27] To many contemporary observers, this apparatus indeed chafes those strapped within it.

The analysis of Bensman and Rosenberg, discussed earlier, depicts the bureaucrat as having to adopt a false or artificial personality to succeed in bureaucratic employment. He (or she) is tightly associated with others, highly dependent on them, and anxious "to project those qualities which will be the most pleasing to others." Thus the bureaucrat adopts a synthetic personality in which he performs as a "poseur" rather than a sincere individual. Furthermore, as the bureaucrat sees others being equally deceptive, all interpersonal trust disappears. As a consequence the official feels socially and psychologically isolated, despite the closeness of working relationships. Exacerbating the situation is a sense of powerlessness, imposed on this isolation by the network of formal authority and pattern of fragmented, specialized activity. One of several potential outcomes is a craving to rise in rank at any cost; within the prevailing atmosphere of insincerity and distrust, the ambitious become

Machiavellian infighters capable of lies, betrayal, and ruthless tactics of intra-office conflict.[28]

Ralph Hummel contends that the bureaucrat's personality is "truncated," even "devastated." This supposedly occurs as appraisal of one's work is transferred from the self to the superior, individual uniqueness is denied by requirements to conform, and the individual comes to identify mastery of work with the specialized activities of the organization. As a result, the bureaucrat ends up being wholly integrated into the organization's dehumanized value system and left personally in a normless, purposeless state. "Thus, life in a bureaucracy," says Hummel, speaking in the voice of this unfortunate being, "has the effect of separating me from my ability to love people and of forcing me into the habit of associating affect only with process—things I do." Even in his private life the bureaucrat becomes unable to feel or experience human intimacy; bureaucracy "destroys the family" and leads to an emphasis on the "technical performance in sexual intercourse" instead of genuine love with the opposite sex.[29]

Frederick Thayer is another outspoken critic of bureaucracy as a mentally unhealthy environment. In his analysis, hierarchy as a structural feature of Weberian organization is singled out as a source of particularly vicious damage to the psyche. Said to have been invented by humankind some 6,000 years ago when the left side of the human brain became dominant, hierarchy created the need for an external God and a further need for legitimized political and organizational authority. A principal derivative of hierarchy is alienation, according to Thayer, which is regarded as embracing several forms of separation suffered by the individual. These are loss of control over decisions about work, similar noncontrol over what is produced, severance of authentic relations with co-workers (some of whom are mere extensions of machines like himself, while others constitute natural enemies), and finally, separation from oneself. This last form of alienation arises from a detachment of work activity from personal purpose. Bureaucracy, to Thayer, is truly "impersonal" in the sense that it denies our free and equal personhood and leaves us as nonpersons performing in roles, not as ourselves. Within bureaucracy, then, hierarchical structure condemns the roles of subordinates to a state of being ruled, obeying commands, and being repressed.[30]

Guy Benveniste provides yet another analysis of why working in bureaucracy is devastating. To him, the great problem is not alienation but fear. Bureaucrats face, at the same time, an increasingly uncertain world on the one hand and pressures from their organizations to act as if they could control or predict the future on the other. This tension is simply not resolvable to Benveniste, hence bureaucrats continually live in fear of being caught performing in error and thereby jeopardizing their careers. They respond by playing defensive games, which include minimizing and avoiding risks, inventing false risks, avoiding responsibility, stressing protective documentation, and deliberately doing nothing.[31]

Representing what is sometimes referred to as the "critical theory" school of administrative thought, Robert Denhardt believes our civilization has generally been overcome by an "organizational ethic." This value system stresses order instead of conflict; imposes authoritative structure rather than permits social change; and subjects the individual to unwitting acceptance of such inherent undesirables as discipline, regulation, and obedience. This means that individual expressiveness, independence of spirit, and human creativity are stifled if not destroyed. Furthermore, those living "in the shadow of organizations" (essentially everyone in modern society, but certainly employees of organizations) cannot discover their own meaning in life. They lack the opportunity to exercise free and meaningful choice, fail to achieve their own definitions of reality, lose a sense of personal moral responsibility, and even become wedded to a false organizational promise of immortality. And, sadly, human beings do not recognize these outrages because of the pervasiveness of organizational values. "This, then, is the problem with bureaucracy," writes Denhardt —"that in exchange for the benefits it brings, it exacts an enormous price in our lives."[32]

A final attack on the bureaucratic workplace that will be described is that of David Ewing. He argues that although American traditions enthusiastically celebrate civil liberties in the political and personal realms, "once a U.S. citizen steps through the plant or office door at 9 A.M., he or she is nearly rightless until 5 P.M., Monday through Friday." Even benign, enlightened, and well-intentioned bureaucracies in the private and public sectors tend to stultify employees, Ewing contends. The reason is that a managed system inevitably seeks to control, and this control almost inevitably undermines freedom inside the organization. "It is no wonder," says Ewing, "that employees may feel half-suffocated and long to cry out, the more so as the bureaucracy becomes more efficient and the supervisory control systems more advanced."[33]

The charges, then, are numerous and delivered with consternation and alarm, even bitterness. Bureaucracy is deemed a bad, even sick, place in which to work. The supposedly alienated, dehumanized, and repressed official is, at the least, deprived of having much fun on the job. More likely, he or she is beaten down, torn asunder, sexually crippled, stricken by fear, and incarcerated in a psychic prison whose bars are not even noticed. To sum this all up in eloquent literary style, Konrád's fictional character "the case worker" simply gives up:

In the meantime, my belly swells, my legs turn spindly, my mouth fills with gold, the hair on the back of my hands goes white, the perenniality of human failure grinds me and consumes me. I shuffle back and forth between tottering stacks of paper, I move eternally pending files from drawer to drawer and shelf to shelf, I turn into a cantankerous old bureaucrat who locks up his rubber stamp when he goes to the toilet, and refuses to lend anyone his book of regulations. I write my memos in a smaller and smaller hand on strips of paper cut out with my pocketknife. I cite my age and experience, time and time again I repeat the same anecdotes and words of advice, I get my clients mixed up, doze off more and more often while listening to them. I snap at them if they interrupt me or talk too much, I dismiss their complaints, and if any of them bursts into tears, I suck furiously on my cheap, foul-smelling cigar.[34]

Once again, as we did with the bureaucratic mentality concept, let us check these provocative theories and images against the bureaucrats themselves. Critical theorists may reject their views as inherently deluded, but at any rate let us hear what they say.

We begin with a study somewhat parallel to that of Kohn on the values of the organizational employee. In an extensive field study, Bonjean and Grimes interviewed at length some 332 independent businessmen, hourly workers, and salaried managers residing in a town of 11,000. In one aspect of the interview, these individuals were queried on the extent to which their personal work environment was bureaucratic in nature, as measured on scales that reflected varying amounts of authority, procedure, specialization, written rules, and impersonality. Also, the interviewees were given personality tests on the extent to which they experienced six kinds of alienation: powerlessness in the sense of feeling controlled by unfathomable forces, normlessness in terms of being unaware of clear standards, isolation from supportive social groups, anomia or generalized alienation from others, self-estrangement, and a sense of separation from society. Scores on these alienation dimensions were then correlated against the bureaucratization variables. The principal finding was, simply, "a relative absence of significant relationships." Of 101 intercorrelations examined, only 18 were statistically significant. Of these, only one concerned managers, namely, a positive association between extent of written rules and anomia.[35]

In another study, Moeller and Charters examined the relationship between bureaucratization and powerlessness in public schools. Twenty school systems in the St. Louis metropolitan area were rated by a panel of experts on extent of bureaucratization. Forty teachers from each district were then surveyed on their personal sense of power over such matters as choosing textbooks, exerting influence over policy, and selecting teaching partners. Contrary to expectations, teachers from more bureaucratic schools showed a *greater* sense of power than those from less bureaucratic institutions. Differences in mean scores were substantial and statistically significant.[36]

Recently Organ and Greene conducted research on aspects of bureaucratization and alienation in three corporate research and development divisions. They surveyed 247 senior scientists and engineers and their peers to see how such professionals were affected by "formalization" (i.e., the extent to which standard practices, policies, and position responsibilities were formally laid out for them). It was found that their sense of alienation, measured by a 5-point scale, was *inversely* related to formalization. The reason, the researchers suggest, is that formalization reduces role ambiguity, reinforces external norms, and clarifies professional contributions. In short, "by providing the professional with a greater scope and clearer context for self-expression in work, formalization may prevent self-estrangement."[37]

As in the research cited earlier on the bureaucratic mentality, some comparative studies have been made between business managers and public administrators with respect to workplace attitudes. If we regard government as more "bureaucratic" than business, one would expect more alienation in the public than in the private sector.

One study, conducted by J.B. Rhinehart and associates, examined job satisfaction scores within the conceptual framework of Maslow's Hierarchy of Needs. Managers and supervisors in the Veterans Administration's Department of Medicine and Surgery were compared with their counterparts in private health care. The latter group generally showed more need satisfaction at upper hierarchical levels, but at the level of unit chiefs, VA personnel registered higher scores on measures of esteem, autonomy, and self-actualization.[38]

Considerable private-public comparison has been done in the realm of job-related attitudes by Bruce Buchanan. In one study he conducted a survey of middle managers in four business firms and four federal agencies. Comparison between the two groups showed that business executives perceived the work situation as involving more, not fewer, structural restrictions in the form of rules, regulations, and formal procedures. The businessmen did, however, score higher on a job involvement scale that included such items as sense of pride and degree of job satisfaction. Another survey by Buchanan of managers in three industrial organizations and five federal agencies revealed a similar differentiation, with business respondents scoring higher on satisfaction with work, satisfaction with colleagues, and organizational commitment.[39]

A study by Hal Rainey of middle managers in five government agencies and four business firms in a midwestern state confirmed some of Buchanan's findings but not all of them. Rainey found that business executives tend to perceive more flexible personnel procedures; show greater interest in innovation; and demonstrate more satisfaction with supervision, co-workers, and promotion. The two groups were not statistically different as to work motivation, perceived role ambiguity and conflict, job involvement, and satisfaction with work.[40]

With respect to survey research conducted in the public sector alone, Stone and Stoker gathered questionnaire data from 479 employees of 39 local housing, community development, and community action agencies throughout the State of Maryland. Some of their questions on employee alienation and job dissatisfaction are given in table 5.7.[41]

TABLE 5.7. RESPONSES TO QUESTIONNAIRE ON
ALIENATION AND JOB DISSATISFACTION

	Strongly Agree	Agree	Not Sure	Dis- agree	Strongly Disagree
Employees like me do not have any say about what the agency does.	17%	25%	2%	42%	14%
There is little the typical employee can do to bring about change in this agency.	15	34	2	40	10
Employees like me can change things in the agency if we work at it.	12	54	3	26	4
Agency officials do not care much about what people like me think.	11	25	3	51	10
It is difficult to remain an idealist in this job.	20	54	2	22	2
There are many disappointments in a job like mine.	16	51	3	37	3
I often come home with a feeling of satisfaction about my job.	15	56	1	23	4

With respect to a sense of powerlessness, we note that 56 percent of those surveyed *disagreed* to one extent or another with the statement that "employees like me" have no say in agency operations. Also, although 50 percent disagreed to some extent with the notion that "the typical employee" can help to bring about change in the organization, two-thirds felt "employees like me" can do so. Also, it is noteworthy that 61 percent do not accept the idea that agency officials are uncaring about what "people like me" think.

On job satisfaction, Stone and Stoker found that while 74 percent agreed to some extent that idealism is out of place and 67 percent perceived disappointments in their job, 71 percent reported often coming home from work with a feeling of satisfaction. In another question, the investigators asked, *"Knowing what you know now, if you had it to do over again, how likely is it that you would choose your present occupation again?"* A response of "very likely" was given by 57 percent, "likely" by 24 percent, "somewhat likely" by 7 percent, "unlikely" by 5 percent, and "very unlikely" by 6 percent.

In a survey of federal employees conducted by Franklin Kilpatrick and associates some twenty years ago, extent of job satisfaction was measured by a question dealing not with retrospective career choice but future employment plans. More than 1,500 U.S. civil servants were asked, *"Do you plan to continue working for the federal government, or do you think you might leave it?"* The outcome is given in table 5.8, showing both general employees and certain subgroups within that category.[42]

TABLE 5.8. EXPRESSIONS OF JOB SATISFACTION, FEDERAL EMPLOYEES

	General Employees	Executives	Natural Scientists	Social Scientists	Engineers
Plan to continue	90%	95%	84%	79%	73%
Very sure	72	69	59	48	40
Fairly sure	16	25	23	30	29
Not sure	2	2	2	1	3
Plan to leave	7	3	10	18	15
Don't know	4	2	6	3	12

According to these data, we see that the vast majority of federal civil servants planned at that time to continue in government, with only minuscule proportions planning departures. It is interesting that, among the categories, executives showed the highest proportion of those planning to remain.

Replication of this survey today would no doubt yield different results. As this is being written, federal executives are said to be deeply distressed by relatively low salaries and other disappointments with the Senior Executive Service established during the Carter administration. In a survey conducted by the Office of Personnel Management in 1981, 72 percent of Senior Executive Service members questioned expressed dissatisfaction with their salaries, and 52 percent were considering departure from government because of this factor. Another one-third said they would probably look for a new job.[43]

Yet these top executives do not necessarily speak for all federal bureaucrats. While the OPM survey showed most Senior Executive Service members displeased with their pay, it also found that 67 percent of employees at Grades 13 through 15 were satisfied with it. On the specific issue of plans to seek alternative employment, in a large 1979 study conducted by OPM ($N = 20,000$), some 226 questions were posed, one of which asked if respondents agreed or disagreed with the statement: *"During this next year, I will probably look for a new job outside of this organization."* Twenty-three percent agreed, 59 percent disagreed, and 18 percent were undecided. Of the hundreds of other questions included in that study, the six shown in table 5.9 seem most pertinent to our discussion.[44]

TABLE 5.9. QUESTIONS FROM OPM SURVEY ON JOB SATISFACTION,
FEDERAL EMPLOYEES

	Agree	Undecided	Disagree
In general, I like working here.	86%	6%	8%
I enjoy doing my work for the personal satisfaction it gives me.	84	8	8
My job gives me the opportunity to use my own judgment and initiative.	84	6	10
My supervisor encourages subordinates to participate in important decisions.	47	16	37
In this organization conflict that exists between groups gets in the way of getting the job done.	41	11	48
There are feelings among members of my work group which tend to pull the group apart.	36	13	51

We see that preponderant majorities of the sampled federal bureaucrats said they liked their work and obtained personal satisfaction from it. Contrary to notions of a repressive atmosphere, a vast majority also saw the job as permitting discretion and initiative. Also, the proportion of the respondents perceiving their supervisors as encouraging participation in decisions exceeded that not doing so. With respect to hostility within the organization, more disagreed than agreed with statements describing a damaging extent of intergroup and intragroup conflict.

To summarize, this empirical evidence may not portray the bureaucratic workplace as aglow with unadulterated joy. At the same time, it does not comport with the image of the bureaucrat as an alienated, powerless, fearful, and suffocated poseur. Extent of bureaucratization does not correlate with personality tests of alienation or measures of powerlessness in organizations. Indeed, it may under certain circumstances reduce the sense of alienation. Business employees do not consistently feel more satisfied or less restricted than personnel in government agencies. In general, government bureaucrats are positive about their jobs, believe they can take initiatives and exert influence, and feel personally rewarded by the work they do. High-level federal civil servants may be dissatisfied over pay, but that sentiment cannot be extrapolated into generalized dissatisfaction within the federal work force. In fact, most sampled civil servants endorse their career choice strongly, either retrospectively or prospectively.

We still face the question whether these bureaucrats—supposedly suffering from truncated personalities, left-side brain dominance, paralysis of fear, and psychic imprisonment—are capable of judging their own condition. Unfortunately, there is no sure answer. Critical theorists insist they are deluded, and if that cannot be disproved, we must accept the surveys with some accompanying faith.

To be sure, selective evidence to the contrary can be offered. Douglas La-Bier, a psychologist engaged in private practice in Washington, D.C., points to obvious personality damage among some of his bureaucrat-patients. Even more interesting are cases of bureaucrats who are outwardly symptomless but nevertheless psychopathic; these LaBier explains as a consequence of being all too well adjusted to an excessively power-oriented setting.[45] Offering another kind of selective evidence, Kenneth Lasson presents fascinating vignettes based on the career experiences of six federal officials, all of whom suffer from severe frustrations over not achieving career or policy objectives.[46]

The patient files of a psychologist and the personal frustrations of a half dozen men and women make exciting reading, but to me they are less worrisome than, for example, surveys showing widespread alienation over executive salaries. The other side of this personal view is that considerable encouragement can be derived from the positive statements made by large proportions of representative samples of the bureaucratically harnessed. Hoodwinked or not, these individuals look upon their workplace as usually tolerable, often satisfying, and occasionally challenging. Either we should accept these statements at face value or admit that imprisonment within the organizational ethic is painless indeed.

Clearly, for some the Weberian harness truly chafes. Bureaucratic employment calls for closely interdependent activity among people. It means external goal setting, supervision, and evaluation. The bureaucrat normally does not fully control a field of action in which he or she can perform autonomously and claim sole credit for the results. For many people, including this author, this is indeed painful (I once tried working in bureaucracy and personally could not stand it). Perhaps bureaucratic employment would also be intolerable for many of the professors, journalists, and politicians who criticize bureaucracy, all of whom enjoy wide operating freedoms in their respective occupations. But those of us who comment on life in the bureaucracy from the outside depend on it nonetheless. Thus we can be thankful for the millions who find the bureaucratic setting acceptable—to whom reductions in force are a more frightening prospect than destruction of their personalities.

THE BUREAUCRATS' REPUTATION

Bureaucrats are ordinary people, we have no evidence that their "mentality" is malicious or even distinctive, and they are not necessarily crushed by bureaucracy as an employer. But how are they regarded by the general public? As we all know, the organs of mass culture usually depict them, somewhat contradictorily, as lazy and incompetent on the one hand and malicious and aggrandizing on the other. In other words, we are supposed to consider them both passively inadequate and actively malevolent. But *do* we?

TABLE 5.10. PREFERENCE FOR GOVERNMENT
VERSUS BUSINESS EMPLOYMENT

	Fortune Survey 1940	Gallup Poll 1947	Detroit Study 1954
U.S. government	40%	41%	56%
Private firm	50	40	30
No preference or opinion	10	19	14

The prestige, or lack of it, of public employment was first taken up as a research topic by Leonard White in the late 1920s. In chapter 2 we noted his finding that 58 percent of interviewed Chicagoans thought more of employment in business firms than at city hall. Another poll, conducted by *Fortune* in 1940, seemed to sustain that finding. A study conducted in Detroit in 1954 by Janowitz and Wright came to a somewhat different conclusion. They found a substantial preference for government versus private employment, thus raising the question whether the relative prestige of the two sectors was shifting over time in favor of the public sector. The figures cited in table 5.10 on page 104 are from Janowitz and Wright.[47]

Janowitz and Wright made another interesting point. Public disdain for bureaucrats is by no means uniform across the population. As one compares attitudes by income, social class, education, race, and sex, the prestige of government employees is lower on the part of respondents who are higher in income, status, and education, and also for whites versus blacks and men as over against women. Table 5.11 reveals these trends.

TABLE 5.11. RATINGS OF PRESTIGE OF GOVERNMENT EMPLOYEES

Respondent Characteristics	Prestige of Government Employees Rated	
	High	Low
Income:		
Under $2,000	30%	21%
$2,000-$3,999	31	24
$4,000-$5,999	33	27
$6,000-$7,999	20	35
Over $8,000	16	44
Class:		
Lower lower	37	21
Upper lower	31	26
Lower middle	25	36
Upper middle	14	43
Education:		
0-6 years	27	15
7-8 years	35	24
9-11 years	31	26
12 years	31	33
More than 12	14	47

TABLE 5.11 *(Continued)*

Race:		
Black	44	18
White	26	31
Sex:		
Female	31	24
Male	26	34

The work of Kilpatrick and associates done in the early 1960s, mentioned earlier, is another landmark study on this subject. In addition to surveying federal bureaucrats, they polled on a nationwide basis samples of employed persons outside the federal government. Respondents were asked to describe their "general idea" of a U.S. civil service employee on the one hand and a person employed by a large private business on the other. On analyzing the overall tone of the replies, the researchers found, first, that far more people view civil servants in a favorable light rather than an unfavorable one. The proportions between these two were 51 and 10 percent, respectively (with the remainder undecided). Furthermore, Kilpatrick and co-authors noted that public images of the business employee had a similar favorable-unfavorable relationship (i.e., 56 versus 4 percent). Finally, they discovered the same differentiation in status and gender (race was not reported on as a variable) found by Janowitz and Wright, as shown in table 5.12.[48]

These surveys, dated and nondefinitive as they are, indicate that more empirical work is needed in this area. But in a tentative and preliminary way, they suggest two conclusions. First, when queried in certain ways, the American public does not appear as disdainful of bureaucrats as the projected media image would indicate. Loaded, dichotomous-answer polls along the lines of the Gallup survey questions noted in chapter 1 are probably misleading. Indirect approaches to assessing the prestige of bureaucrats via questions on employment preference have the effect of shifting the respondents' focus from a broad societal "problem" to a more tangible issue. Open-ended descriptions of government employees, which are then content analyzed, tap sentiment that is somewhat removed from "bureaucracy" as an abstraction.

The second conclusion is that members of the public with more income, status, and education, and also those who are white and male, seem less respectful of public officials. A nationwide survey of public images of postal window clerks, sponsored by the Postal Service in 1977, similarly found the impressions of higher-income respondents and men to be less favorable.[49] In

TABLE 5.12. GENERAL EMPLOYED PUBLIC'S
EVALUATION OF CIVIL SERVANTS

Respondent Characteristics	Proportion Describing Civil Servants	
	Favorably	Unfavorably
Education:		
High school not completed	60%	3%
High school completed	52	9
Some college	42	16
College graduate	30	27
Sex:		
Female	59	8
Male	48	11
Teachers:		
High school	49	13
College	30	24
Students:		
High school	63	7
College seniors	33	24
Graduate students	26	32
Business executives	20	39

other words, antibureaucratic sentiment may possess something of an upper-status or dominant-group orientation. Perhaps this explains, at least in part, the divergence between the abstract image of bureaucracy expressed in our culture and the widespread acceptance of it on a personal experience level encountered in chapter 2. The surveys described there measure public opinion "democratically," in that lower-status respondents are included in samples in approximate proportion to their presence in the population. Cultural expressions on bureaucracy and bureaucrats, by contrast, are perforce initiated by opinion leaders—namely, the country's writers, journalists, politicians, businessmen, and professors. These persons are, disproportionately, high-income, well-educated, white males.

Several possible reasons could be advanced for an elitist or dominant-group bias against bureaucrats. One is sociological: Bureaucrats are looked down on by the upper strata because they are perceived as lower-class clerks or mediocre performers who could not succeed in the professions or business. Another possible explanation is economic: Upper-class groups have more to lose and less to gain from government relative to the lower strata, and government's taxing and spending effects are somewhat redistributive on a net basis. Also, a political explanation could be at work. Probusiness conservatives who are ideologically opposed to government in the first place tend to come from upper socioeconomic levels. Then too, a possible psychological explanation might be that assertive and confident upper-status males blanch at the idea of being dependent on or instructed by anyone, let alone "mere bureaucrats." Driven by less inflated egos, lower-status persons and women may view bureaucracy more as a symbol of assistance than coercion.

Leonard White asserted that as a result of his studies in Chicago, he "became convinced that the morale of thousands of city employees and officials was deeply affected by their conception of what the public thinks about them."[50] It is difficult not to share this opinion about bureaucrats in general today, although systematic evidence on this point is unavailable. Certainly many individual government employees with whom one talks are in a state of sad dismay over the barrage of media and politician attacks mounted against them, especially if they come from nominal bosses like the President of the United States. An oceanographer at the Defense Department commented late in the Carter Presidency, "There has alway been this high-handed, 'screw 'em' attitude by this administration toward the federal worker. We feel ignored and dumped on."[51] Sentiment seems just as angry on the part of federal employees over President Reagan's gibes at them as self-serving protectors of existing social programs. Showing less rancor but just as much hurt, an official at Interior reflected,

> Most of us bureaucrats are not building empires, and few of us will end up personally wealthy. We get good pay and benefits, but probably nothing special when compared to our opposite numbers in business and the professions.
>
> Many of us see the anti-civil servant clamor as mindless blame-casting, but I don't think that we are bitter. A feeling of frustration, perhaps, and of being let down, but not bitter. . . .
>
> The civil service is not some foreign power. Nor is it an invading army. It is doing, in the best way it can, the jobs that have been assigned it. We make mistakes like most people, and we have louts and lazies among us. But we think it's nonsense for those who are giving the marching orders—the voters, the Congress, and the President—to ridicule us for following them.[52]

Perhaps the extremism of the attacks will eventually cause a backlash of sympathy toward government workers. Already some newspaper editorialists and columnists are beginning to take a softer line. "Well, maybe it's time to challenge the stereotype, to say something nice about the faceless millions who labor for government all over the country," admits one columnist.[53] "If half the things muttered about public employees were spoken about any religious or racial group," points out another, "the speaker would be dismissed as a hopeless bigot." He adds, "Public employees must be the last remaining group in our society without its own anti-defamation department."[54]

More could be at stake here than simply unjust attacks on a sizable component of the national population. The important issue is whether the flow of antibureaucracy diatribe actually damages the quality of performance in government. It may, for example, induce young people to seek more appreciated careers outside the public sector. I have known social workers who, tired of being vague about their occupation when attending parties, finally quit for a more respected field. Less anecdotal evidence is found in statistics from certain federal agencies that show rising turnover rates, more early retirements, and smaller pools of qualified recruits. Who knows, the time may even come when the stereotype of "the bureaucrat" becomes in part self-fulfilling, as disgusted government employees lose heart and simply serve out their time with a minimum of effort and emotional investment.

Yet the opposite possibility is also plausible—the attacks may make little real difference in the long run. Sociologists have discovered that even bartenders and garbage collectors, despite their status in society, do not lack self-esteem. More to the point is the fact that many "bureaucrats" perceive themselves as not that at all, but chemists, foresters, engineers, librarians, or whatever—who just happen to work for government. Moreover, it is reassuring to realize that antibureaucrat talk has been a mainstay of the popular culture for generations, yet the bureaucratic apparatus has kept on working reasonably well all this time. Also, current personnel problems being faced in government may have more to do with low salaries and job uncertainty than media hype.

In short, the consequence of damaged performance through lowered morale may not have occurred. But then again, it may have, or could do so in the future. Is bureaucrat-baiting worth the risk?

CHAPTER 6

BIGNESS AND BADNESS RECONSIDERED

A long-standing debate in antitrust policy is whether "bigness is badness." The issue is whether bigness in corporations is itself a sin, or whether to be "bad" companies must actually commit sin. That distinction is never drawn in public debates on government bureaucracy. The assumption is always made by its cultural, political, and academic critics that bureaucracy is both big *and* bad. Unlike the business world, where one cannot avoid noting the existence of Mom and Pop stores as well as giant corporations, bureaucracy is equated with a bloated and suppressive giantism only. Furthermore, bureaucracies are considered inherently sinful, as part of being both too big and plagued by inherent moral defects such as lust for turf and power. In this chapter we investigate these charges of bigness and badness, especially as they relate to the broader context of the political system.

We begin the chapter by noting how large most American public bureaucracies really are. Attention is then given to their supposed tendencies to expand and also to deteriorate over time. Next, political activism by bureaucracies, that is, attempts to advocate agency interests and missions, is appraised. The chapter concludes with reflections on the implications of bureaucratic power for socioeconomic inequity and policy drift.

The Size of Bureaucracy

If anything is associated with bigness, it is government bureaucracy. Huge size is often given, by conservatives and liberals alike, as one of the underlying, principal problems of American public administration. But to what extent is bigness truly pervasive in the U.S. public sector? Let us try to measure the size of bureaucracy on the basis of numbers of employees, recognizing that inflation and proxy administration all but destroy the usefulness of budgets or expenditures as a measure.

Aggregate employment statistics for government seem to offer undeniable proof of giantism. With a total employment of 18 million, American bureaucracy is by this overall measure probably the fourth largest in the world, just behind Russia, China, and India. Moreover this aggregate size was, at least up to the Reagan administration, growing in both absolute and relative terms. Thirty years ago, public sector employment in this country was half of what it is today. The number of public employees per 1,000 population has risen from 58 in 1950 to 63 in 1960 to 78 in 1970. In 1981, according to one analysis, it reached 82. This compares to 109 in Britain, 83 in France, 76 in West Germany, and 45 in Japan.[1]

But how much do these statistics tell us about the size of *individual* bureaucracies? Surprisingly little is said on this subject in the literature of public administration. Empirical studies of organizations that use size as a variable are of little help since they deal with specialized samples. Generalized commentaries on the bigness of bureaucracy usually allude simply to the overall size of giants like the Department of Defense or the Postal Service. The total employment within these entities has good shock value but falls very short of giving us a typical picture. Obviously not all public organizations are nearly so big, especially at state and local levels of government where most bureaucracies and bureaucrats exist and operate.

Another problem with analyses based on total organization size is that this measure does not relate to citizens' immediate experience with bureaucracy. The work environment of an accountant at the Oceana Naval Air Station in Virginia Beach, Virginia, is not "the Pentagon" but a bureaucracy of 850 civilians who work in a compound on Oceana Boulevard in that city. Similarly, the bulk mailer complaining of delayed postal pickups in Oklahoma City does not deal with the totality of the U.S. Postal Service but with a local postal staff some 2,000 strong. That is much different, and the difference should be incorporated in our calculations and conceptions of bureaucratic size.

Obtaining data on employment size at the level of identifiable, operational bureaucracies is not easy. Of the approximately 80,000 governments in America, only one—the federal government—provides suitable information in one place. Centralized state and local employment figures consist only of census data collected by territorial jurisdiction and to some extent function, not by organizational unit. This means that computations cannot be definite or complete.

On the federal level, the most usable data for our purposes are reports compiled by the Office of Personnel Management on federal civilian employment, broken down by agency, county, and metropolitan area.[2] These figures at least tell us where people work, in county or city terms. This information does not necessarily describe the size of organizational units, however, since agencies may have more than one unit operating in a given geographic area. Also scattered field personnel in one county or metropolis may see themselves as "belonging" to a unit elsewhere. Thus, this kind of size data is not ideal for our purposes, but even so it is capable of giving us added insights into the size of bureaucracies as identified by those who use them.

This OPM information was used to develop figures on civilian employment as of December 1977 for 20 agencies: the three military departments plus "other Defense agencies"; the eleven civilian departments existing at that time; and the Veterans Administration, General Services Administration, National Aeronautics and Space Administration, Civil Service Commission, and Environmental Protection Agency. These agencies collectively employ about 70 percent of the federal civilian work force. Integrated with these figures were separate data for the individual post offices of the country, obtained directly from the Postal Service. This was done because several post offices exist in most counties, and the OPM data would have aggregated them. Unfortunately, the postal data apply to a more recent time, January 1981; but by incorporating them we enlarge the coverage of our figures to around 95 percent of federal civilians.

The material in table 6.1 gives, in the far left column, a series of size ranges by numbers of civilian employees. In the second column are found the numbers of bureaucratic units per employment size range in the twenty federal agencies mentioned. These figures were derived by noting the number of coun-

TABLE 6.1. NUMBERS OF FEDERAL BUREAUCRACIES
BY EMPLOYMENT SIZE RANGE

Size Range	Number Units in 20 Agencies	Number Post Offices	Total Number Units	Percent Units in This Range
1-4	5,652	20,340	25,992	57.2
5-9 (P.O. 5-10)	1,762	5,255	7,017	15.4
10-24 (P.O. 11-25)	3,145	2,644	5,789	12.7
25-49 (P.O. 26-50)	1,573	1,061	2,634	5.8
50-99 (P.O. 51-99)	924	578	1,502	3.3
100-199	617	360	977	2.2
200-299	254	118	372	.8
300-499	253	78	331	.7
500-999	250	88	338	.7
1,000-1,999	173	45	218	.5
2,000-4,999	156	33	189	.4
5,000-9,999	37	10	47	.1
10,000 and up	22	3	25	.06
TOTALS	14,818	30,613	45,431	99.9

ties (or cities if outside counties) throughout the United States in which each agency had employees of a certain size class. To illustrate, employment totals of 2,000 to 4,999 for any of the twenty agencies mentioned are found in 156 counties (or cities) of the country. One example among these 156 is Madison County, Alabama, where NASA employs 3,850 — at the George C. Marshall Space Flight Center in Huntsville. The third column of the table gives the number of post offices falling into each size range (with some slight incompatibility in range limits). The two right-hand columns sum these figures and show each range's proportion of the total number of organizations.

In analyzing these data we see that of the more than 45,000 units so identified, almost 26,000, or more than half (57 percent), employ not more than four persons! Eighty-five percent have fewer than 25 employees. Only about 1 percent, or 479 entities, are on the scale of 1,000 employees or more.

This incredible finding is partly an artifact of the separate counting of remote and tiny operations attached to units in nearby counties. Examples would be minuscule field stations, small audit teams, and rural service representatives. Yet unit size is also overstated by these data. Some large or urban counties contain more than one military base or agency facility. Also, bureaus headquartered in the District of Columbia are not differentiated from their departmental parents. Still other exaggerating distortions are the exclusion of small agencies other than the twenty-one covered, a failure to count branch post offices separately, and treatment of the residual category "other Defense agencies" as one.

Thus the data are certainly not perfect, but their imperfections may balance each other out somewhat to give us a reasonably accurate view of the relative numbers of federal bureaucracies in various size ranges. At the least, they help us realize how misleading is the notion of bureaucracies being necessarily mammoth. Some are huge, true — we see that 25 units had 10,000 or more employees, for example. But the vast majority of them are small, even tiny. The mean size of the 45,431 units analyzed is a mere 57.5 employees.

Another interesting aspect of these data is what they tell us about the size of organizations in which most bureaucrats work. The figures presented in table 6.2, developed from the same OPM and postal data, indicate aggregate employment at selected size levels. We see, for example, that 391,179 federal civilian employees worked in organizational units whose size was 10,000 personnel or more. These constituted 15 percent of all employees accounted for. Approximately half (actually 49.5 percent) worked in bureaucracies operating with 2,000 or more personnel; stated another way, the "median" federal bureaucrat labors alongside some 1,940 other people. This perspective suggests a somewhat larger scale to bureaucracy, but nonetheless that scale does not

TABLE 6.2. FEDERAL EMPLOYMENT AT SELECTED
LEVELS OF BUREAUCRATIC SIZE

Size Category by No. Employees	Aggregate Employment in Category	Percent of Total Employment
10,000 and up	391,179	15.0
5,000 and up	722,530	27.7
2,000 and up	1,292,228	49.5
1 and up (all units)	2,611,020	100.0

come close to the giantism implied by figues usually tossed around on the subject.

Still, a minority of the bureaucracies reflected in the data are shown to be very big, and one is naturally curious as to what these might be. While we could expect that most are departmental headquarters in Washington, only 20 of the 72 bureaucracies employing 5,000 or more fall into this category. Thirteen others consist of large urban post offices. Seven more are big field installations of certain civilian departments: VA facilities in Chicago and Los Angeles, Treasury operations in New York, the Mint at Philadelphia, HEW operations in Chicago, Social Security City in Baltimore, and Interior's bureau offices in Denver. The remaining 32 bureaucracies, collectively employing 65 percent of all the employees of these larger units, are military establishments. Outside Dayton, Ohio, for example, 15,000 civilians are employed at Wright-Patterson Air Force Base. Some 24,000 work at San Diego's naval installations. Although we often think of the military establishment as a uniformed bureaucracy concentrated in Washington or abroad, its civilians in mufti constitute many of the largest concentrations of the federal work force found across the country.

As mentioned, the only centrally available employment data for local government bureaucracy is census information. Unfortunately for our purposes, it is collected by governmental unit and not organization. This means we have numbers of public employees per municipality or county but not bureaucracy. Even so, an analysis of these figures yields some insights that parallel what was found at the federal level. The data given in table 6.3, which are from the 1977 Census of Governments,[3] consist of numbers of local jurisdictions falling into each of several size ranges, with size measured by numbers of full-time equivalent employees.

As in the case of federal organizations, we see that a great many of these governments are very small in work force terms. In fact, 30,913 units, or 39 percent of the total, have no full-time equivalent employees whatsoever! This

TABLE 6.3. NUMBERS OF LOCAL GOVERNMENT UNITS
BY EMPLOYMENT SIZE RANGE

			Number of Governmental Units			
Size Range	Counties	Munici-palities	Town-ships	Special Districts	School Districts	All Kinds
0	2	4,424	8,673	17,534	280	30,913
1-24	129	9,427	7,069	6,904	3,175	26,704
25-49	333	1,658	375	623	2,363	5,352
50-99	660	1,288	251	411	2,787	5,397
100-199	708	896	158	269	2,696	4,727
200-399	491	544	151	117	2,071	3,374
400-599	216	184	70	60	693	1,223
600-799	119	112	37	24	351	643
800-999	84	58	15	15	214	386
1,000 and up	298	287	28	53	493	1,159
TOTALS	3,040	18,878	16,827	26,010	15,123	79,878

datum projects an image of smallness that even surpasses that found at the federal level. Apparently such units exist on paper only or are staffed by unpaid, contractual, or loaned personnel. These "zero size" jurisdictions, together with those employing less than 25 staff, constitute no less than 72 percent of the total. Smallness is particularly characteristic of township government and special districts, 94 percent of which (in each category) had less than 25 employees. To an amazing extent, then, local government in the United States has little or even no bureaucracy measured this way.

The relatively few, bigger local governments do have plenty of bureaucrats, however. Given in table 6.4 are data on units employing 1,000 and more

TABLE 6.4. LOCAL GOVERNMENT UNITS EMPLOYING 1,000 OR MORE

Unit Type	Percent Units Employing 1,000 and Up FTE	Percent Total Employment in Units Employing 1,000 and Up FTE
Counties	9.8	51
Municipalities	1.5	68
Townships	.2	17
Special Districts	.2	38
School Districts	3.3	39
All Units	1.5	52

personnel. The middle column shows that these bigger governments comprise relatively small percentages of the total numbers of units in each category. Aggregatively, only 1.5 percent of local governments of all categories employ 1,000 or more. The right-hand column indicates the percentage of total, full-time equivalent employment in these bigger governments for each jurisdiction type; all such units together employ 52 percent of local government personnel. Thus, the "median" local bureaucrat works in a government employing slightly more than 1,000. A government that size will naturally have numerous departments, hence this figure does not have the same meaning as our measures of federal employment by organizational unit.

To summarize these findings on the size of bureaucracy, bigness by no means predominates when measured by work force size. Most administrative or governmental units for which data are available are very small, even tiny. Eighty-five percent of federal installations and 72 percent of local governments have less than 25 employees. About half of federal bureaucrats work in units of less than 2,000 employees. A similar proportion of local government employees work in jurisdictions employing 1,000 or fewer personnel. Some bureaucracies are certainly mammoth, but organizational fragmentation and diversity of size are the true hallmarks of American bureaucracy.

GROWTH, AGING, AND BADNESS

A major reason for the popular notion that governmental bureaucracies are invariably huge is the belief that they have an endemic, inexorable tendency to grow. Thus, the implicit reasoning goes, with the passage of time they *must* become enormous.

Probably every introductory course in public administration taught in the English language (and no doubt other tongues as well) spends a half hour or so on Parkinson's Law. Parkinson has discovered, as we know, that "work expands so as to fill the time available for its completion." Beyond that axiom a rather elaborate process is described by Parkinson of how civil servants, imagining themselves to be overworked, appoint two subordinates rather than one to avoid the creation of rivals. The subordinates eventually do the same, and the organization proceeds to pyramid in size. By means of explicit but mysterious formulas, Parkinson predicts that staff expansion "will invariably prove to be between 5.17 percent and 6.56 percent, irrespective of any variation in the amount of work (if any) to be done."[4] Is this good fun designed to brighten an otherwise dull subject, or is there something to it? Do bureaucrats conspire to create jobs out of petty self-protection? Does bureaucracy, for whatever reason, steadily and inevitably expand, even if not always by Parkinson's rates?

Certainly many people believe it does. Taxpayers witness the escalation of government budgets each year. Conservatives suspect crass vote buying is carried on by liberal politicians who promise new programs to every down-and-outer. Liberals visualize unending subsidies to business and an unnecessarily swollen Pentagon bureaucracy. Everyone has reasons to be convinced of an ever-growing bureaucracy, with or without Parkinson's Law.

In addition, students of organization have spun out theories supporting chronic bureaucratic expansion. Their arguments focus on internal organizational needs and processes, in a kind of dead-serious Parkinsonianism. One of the most prominent theorists in this area is Anthony Downs, who writes: "In fact, all organizations have inherent tendencies to expand. What sets bureaus apart is that they do not have as many restraints upon expansion, nor do their restraints function as automatically."[5]

Downs offers many reasons for his contention. Growth in agencies permits attraction of better personnel, he argues, and also increases the power, income, and prestige of leaders. In addition, expansion reduces internal conflicts within the organization and enlarges the probability of long-term survival. Government bureaus are seen by Downs as particularly susceptible to unimpeded growth since a lack of competitive market pressures excuses officials from the need to weigh the marginal returns of further spending against their marginal costs.

Like most other theorists of organizational growth, Downs sees many bad things happening as the bureaucracy expands. These include "wasted motion" or nonproductive effort given over to supervising others instead of doing the job. Also, authority is delegated or "leaked" from the top, and as a result powers of control and coordination significantly erode. What follows is an attempt to counteract declining control by imposing ever larger staff-monitoring agencies. These only introduce rigidity, however, by creating more rules, requiring more reports, and stimulating operating units to spend more time evading control. The end point is that administrative operations become, according to Downs, rigid, ossified, and incapable of fast or novel actions. "Thus the bureau becomes a gigantic machine that slowly and inflexibly grinds along in the direction in which it was initially aimed. It still produces outputs, perhaps in truly impressive quantity and quality. But the speed and flexibility of its operations steadily diminish."

Any line of reasoning that posits bureaucratic growth as inevitable and its consequences as undesirable leads us to a concept of decay. Here organization theorists invariably buttress their arguments by employing biological analogies of aging and the life cycle, with Downs as no exception. His "life cycle of bureaus" begins with entrepreneurial activity by zealots, whose agitation leads to the formation of new bureaus, usually by breaking off from old ones. These, then, seek to achieve sufficient autonomy early so that they can pass an "initial survival threshold." Rapid growth at the beginning of the cycle attracts "climber" bureaucrats who promote even faster expansion for career reasons, creating an "accelerator effect." Eventually, however, young bureaus run into obstacles, such as opposition from other bureaus, declining public interest in their functions, and reduced performance because of large size. Later, a "decelerator effect" is felt as climbers abandon the no longer expanding organizations, and "conserver" types are attracted.

Such over-the-hill bureaucracies do not die or shrivel up. They live on almost interminably, says Downs, ever expanding and continuously suffering the ravages of the aging process. The organization's memory becomes more and more crowded with experiences in dealing with varied situations, and it thus develops increasingly elaborate rules. These displace original goals. Structural complexity also increases, and sunk costs in existing procedures rise. Inertia and resistance to change increase, and conserver leadership becomes more dominant. Concomitantly, these officials become personally older with an increasing career stake in not rocking the boat. The proportion of administrators to production workers rises as the latter, but not the former, are cut back periodically; also this is encouraged by the growing need to coordinate large size. The effect of all these tendencies is Downs' "Law of Increasing Conservatism": "All organizations tend to become more conservative as they get older, unless they experience periods of very rapid growth or internal turnover." Bureaucracies do not live forever, Downs says, but they are "unlikely to die once they have become firmly established." The reasons for this are continuing support of benefiting clienteles, the absence of economic criteria for survival, a lack of motivation by neighboring bureaus to kill them off, and the survival advantage of sheer size.[6]

Another well-known model of aging in public administration is Marver Bernstein's life cycle of regulatory commissions. It parallels Downs' theories in several ways but was particularly designed for independent commissions created to regulate business and industry. Bernstein believes four distinct lifetime phases are experienced by such commissions, namely, Gestation, Youth, Maturity, and Old Age. The first phase is dominated by the battle for statutory enactment, while the second phase is initially characterized by a crusading attempt to implement the new law. But soon reformist interest recedes, and regulated interests begin to penetrate the agency. As commissions move into Maturity, open conflict is replaced by settled procedures of adjudication. Also, a policeman role is transformed to one of concerned manager of the affected industry, commission and business elites exchange jobs, and agencies and regulated interests form political coalitions. During the Old Age phase, budgets and operating efficiency decline, and bases of support narrow. "Capture" of the commissions by regulated groups becomes complete, and their combined interests are now deeply entrenched. Bernstein holds out the possibility of subsequent revival of these gerontological wrecks, but this would require a genuine scandal or emergency. No regulatory function of a commission has ever been eliminated, he says (writing in 1955 before the era of deregulation), and the phase of Old Age probably will not terminate until such upheaval occurs.[7]

These theories, then, present a most pessimistic picture. Bureaucracy is seen as possessing not merely Parkinson-like problems of petty self-protection but an entire series of unfortunate characteristics that get worse and worse with time, with no inevitable death to put an end to it all.

Before accepting the bad news as valid, let us look at some empirical data, starting with the subject of bureaucratic expansion. Writing at the end of the first year of the Reagan administration, it seems almost too obvious to point out that government agencies *can* be reduced in size. Budgetary cutbacks and reductions in force are occurring throughout American public administration at all levels these days, except for the military establishment and related agencies. In fact, total government employment in this country dropped by more than 300,000 in 1981, with federal civilian (nonpostal) employment going down by 60,000. I wonder if the theorists of bureaucratic expansionism wish that during the economizing era of the 1980s they could retract their confident models of an earlier time.

But were those theorists right *prior* to the Reagan administration? Did numbers of agency personnel *always* get bigger as time passed? Note the figures in table 6.5.[8]

TABLE 6.5. CIVILIAN EMPLOYMENT,
SELECTED FEDERAL AGENCIES

	1960	1965	1970	1975	1980
Dept. of Defense (000 omitted)	1,047	1,034	1,194	1,042	988
Dept. of State (000 omitted)	38	40	40	30	24
NASA (000 omitted)	10	34	33	26	25
Interstate Commerce Commission	2,381	2,427	1,755	2,115	2,067
Civil Aeronautics Board	755	846	682	728	822

In the Department of Defense, the nation's largest overall administrative organization, civilian employment not only failed to grow steadily over the twenty years shown, it did not grow at all. Long-term declines are visible in the State Department and ICC, while up-and-down oscillations occurred in the work forces of NASA and the CAB. If various imperatives and laws exist to keep bureaucracy constantly growing, where were they over the past twenty years for these particular bureaucracies?

Personnel growth can seem even less inexorable if examined in the light of population growth, the variable that determines how many citizens bureaucracy must serve with the resources granted it. Indeed when per capita figures for particular functional areas are examined over time, bureaucratic expansion takes on another perspective. Although numbers of city police in the country jumped from 299,000 in 1970 to 365,000 in 1980, on a per thousand population basis that increase was from 1.5 to 1.6. Similarly, numbers of city firemen increased in this period from 169,000 to 190,000, but the per thousand population rise was only from .83 to .84. Proportionate figures reflecting numbers of clients to be cared for are also of interest from this standpoint (see table 6.6).[9]

TABLE 6.6. EMPLOYEES PER 1,000 CLIENTS, SELECTED FIELDS

	1960	1970	1979
VA employees per 1,000 living veterans	7.2	6.1	7.5
Welfare workers per 1,000 AFDC recipients	37.1	25.9	35.3

As noted, the theories of Downs and others not only predict expansion in bureaucracy but also anticipate that bigness brings problems. In an aging metaphor, performance is supposed to deteriorate over time.

We can test for adverse effects of growth and aging in two ways in actual organizations: cross-sectional comparisons between organizations of differing size and age, and longitudinal comparisons of identical organizations over time. Let us look first at three empirical studies employing cross-sectional comparison, followed by four others using longitudinal analysis.

In a study of county bureaucracy, Christenson and Sachs surveyed the public by mail in a hundred counties of North Carolina. Respondents were asked to rate the quality of various county services such as libraries, schools, law enforcement, parks, and medical services. Approximately 8,900 returned questionnaires were used to construct a "quality of services" index, and levels on this index were correlated against the number of public employees in the county as well as the number of administrative units in the county in relation to population. The resulting coefficients were .48 and − .47. In other words,

those who perceived superior services tended to live in counties with more employees and more consolidated government. Christenson and Sachs concluded that their work "supports the proposition that a greater number of public
employees results in a higher perception of quality in public services. In the
provision of services, the quantity of employees and the quality of services go
hand in hand."[10]

In another cross-sectional comparison dealing with North Carolina, the
Research Triangle Institute's Center for Population and Urban-Rural Studies
gathered systematic program measurement data for the governments of 87
communities within the state. The data measured levels of effort, effectiveness, and performance by town and city governments in police protection, fire
protection, street maintenance, and garbage collection. The communities
were stratified in six population-size ranges with the differences between them
sufficient to reflect wide variation in size of municipal bureaucracy. Table 6.7
shows a selection of the resulting comparisons.[11]

TABLE 6.7. PROGRAM MEASUREMENT DATA,
NORTH CAROLINA COMMUNITIES, BY POPULATION SIZE

	Less than 2,500	2,500- 3,999	4,000- 7,999	8,000- 19,999	20,000- 49,999	Over 50,000
Average fire response time (minutes)	3.6	4.4	3.2	1.8	3.7	2.7
Fire property loss per capita ($)	73	10	20	15	14	16
Average police response time (minutes)	3.6	3.8	3.4	3.2	4.0	3.8
Crime clearances per $1,000 expenditures	.27	.27	.27	.52	.38	.51
Street miles maintained per street employee	3.1	2.4	4.1	4.6	4.7	4.1
Households served per garbage collection employee	213	249	208	289	312	329

We see that by no means were larger communities with their larger bureaucracies performing more poorly. To the contrary, the productivity of police in terms of clearing crimes and of refuse collectors in terms of serving
households was substantially greater in the bigger municipalities. Smaller

towns were relatively unimpressive with respect to fire loss sustained per capita and street miles maintained per employee. Fire and police response times
seemed unrelated to community size.

The third cross-sectional study focuses on organizational age rather than
size. In one of the many "Aston" studies of intercorrelations of organizational
variables conducted by social scientists at the University of Birmingham, D.S.
Pugh and associates examined 52 organizations located in the English Mid-
lands. Most were private firms, but eight government departments were included in the sample. These organizations varied in age from 29 to 170 years.
When the variable of age was correlated against other factors, the results were
usually not meaningful, interestingly enough. Age had no significant association with organizational size ($r = .16$), for example, or with a combined variable called "structuring of activities" that included extent of specialization,
standardization, and formalization ($r = .09$). This is hardly compatible with
Downs' theories of expansionism or increased structural complexity and rule
elaboration in the aging organization. Also, no relationship was found between age and "line control of workflow," a combined variable measuring ratios of subordinates, formalization of performance recording, and percentage
of superordinates ($r = -.02$); this fails to confirm Downs' notion of a bur-
geoning control structure. The investigators did discover one reasonably high
correlation with age, its relationship to "concentration of authority"—it was,
however, inverse ($r = -.38$). The older organizations, instead of engaging in
greater attempts at coordination and control, were characterized by more decentralization and autonomy and less standardization of personnel procedures.[12]

Turning now to research incorporating longitudinal study, Marshall
Meyer examined structural characteristics and other features of 254 finance
agencies in U.S. state and local governments. Most of these were studied at
two points in time, 1966 and 1972, and comparisons were made over these six
years. Also, Meyer compared agencies by era of origin, and for this purpose he
divided them into three categories: pre-1900, 1900-39, and post-1940. Given in
table 6.8, by both year of data collection and era of origin, are data on size as
measured by numbers of employees and the presence of two measures of elaboration of personnel administration.[13]

In support of theories linking age with size and extent of formalization,
the agencies both grew bigger and became more elaborated in their personnel
procedures between 1966 and 1972. Meyer points out, however, that the Intergovernmental Personnel Act of 1970 was passed in the intervening period and
could have had a major effect on personnel procedures. In addition, new techniques of program budgeting were coming into vogue around the country at

TABLE 6.8. CHARACTERISTICS OF FINANCE AGENCIES,
BY YEAR OF MEASUREMENT AND ERA OF ORIGIN

	Era of Origin		
	Pre-1900	1900-39	Post-1940
Mean Size:			
1966	137	89	95
1972	169	107	123
Uniform personnel code:			
1966	55%	71%	73%
1972	65	72	84
Written promotion criteria:			
1966	49%	68%	67%
1972	59	72	73

the time, which might have affected size of staff. Not in support of the aging theories is the fact that the younger post-1940 agencies were not the smallest in the sample and the older pre-1900 units were the least formalistic in procedures.

With respect to issues raised by Bernstein's theory of a life cycle for regulatory commissions, I conducted a study some years ago in which attempts were made to measure the intensity of federal regulation of business. Trends in this regard were assessed by several means, one of which was numbers of regulatory commission employees per 10,000 persons then employed in the industries regulated by that commission. A second measure was also proportionate to the regulatory task, namely, costs of regulation (essentially the summed expenditures of 86 federal agencies) per $10,000 nonfarm business product as shown in the national income accounts. Third, calculations were made of numbers of inspections per inspection site, numbers of investigations per complaint or other stimulus, and numbers of regulatory violations found per inspection or review. Employment measures were computed for the CAB, ICC, Federal Communications Commission, and Federal Power Commission; inspection and investigation frequencies were calculated for the CAB, FCC, Federal Trade Commission, Securities and Exchange Commission, Antitrust Division, and Bureau of Mines.[14]

With few exceptions, I found that most measures of regulatory intensity increased in the middle or late 1950s, flattened out or declined in the early '60s, and then declined further through to the early '70s. A striking feature of the data was the extent to which trend lines of the different measures and agencies were roughly isomorphic in shape and synchronized in timing. The decline in intensity noted was certainly compatible with Bernstein's expectations of industry capture, but the increases shown—all appearing well after any "Youth" phase—were not. Moreover, the agencies studied were all different in age at the time of the analysis, ranging from 35 to 86 years. Thus all should have been in different phases of development; yet they were moving largely in concert, apparently as a result of national political forces at work.

Another empirical test of the Bernstein thesis was conducted by Meier and Plumlee. They developed a series of quantitative measures related to political support for agencies from Congress and the President, cross-recruitment between the regulators and regulated, and various manifestations of organizational rigidity. Time-series data were gathered from the year of origin for eight agencies: CAB, FCC, FTC, National Labor Relations Board, Federal Aviation Administration, National Transportation Safety Board, Occupational Safety and Health Administration, and Packers and Stockyard Administration. On political support, the researchers discovered that appropriations, personnel, and budgetary growth rates tended to be high early in the history of the agencies, but primarily because they were starting from scratch. Later, the rates did not consistently decline, as Bernstein would predict, but instead fluctuated. On cross-recruitment, Meier and Plumlee found that appointments from industry usually decreased, rather than increased, with age. In like manner, retirement of agency leaders to regulated industry usually became less frequent with time. "None of the data unambiguously support the contention that regulators and the industry form a more symbiotic relationship as time passes," the researchers concluded. "In most cases the data directly refute the hypothesis."[15]

As for the contention that aging produces rigidity, Meier and Plumlee found that the proportion of agency leaders with legal training tended to rise as time passes (the legal profession may wish to question this choice of measure). Also, the age of top executives rose over time for several agencies, but slowly. No important relationships were found between organizational age and the variables of leader turnover, percentage of top appointees with prior substantive expertise, end-of-year case backlogs, and number of cases handled per employee. The authors conclude that "the future does not look bright for an aging theory of regulatory agency decay."

Life-cycle theorists do not follow their organic analogy with complete faithfulness, of course, since they do not see death as inevitable. In fact, they regard bureaucratic dying as nearly impossible. Again, the contention is almost embarrassing in the Reagan era when numerous federal agencies and even whole departments are threatened with destruction. But was it true prior to the 1980s?

Herbert Kaufman has studied this matter. He examined survival and termination in units of the ten civilian departments of the federal government in existence in 1973 plus entities of that age in the Executive Office of the President. Tracing administrative survival forward from 1923, Kaufman found that by 1973, 148 of the 175 organizations present in 1923 — or 85 percent — were still alive. Twenty-seven had been terminated, mainly by internal departmental action rather than statute, executive order, or reorganization plan. Thus, bureaucracies were not necessarily immortal even before Reagan. The statistical probabilities of survival over long periods were not bad, however; Kaufman calculates their death rate per 10,000 at 27.6, approximately half the rate (56.8) for business firms over that period.[16]

Investigating the causes of bureaucratic death, Kaufman found the major reasons to be competition, changes in leadership and policy, obsolescence, and completion of mission. Whether age is a cause of death or a means of survival remains an open question, says Kaufman. A faint tendency exists for younger organizations to expire more often than older ones; nonetheless, a comparison of the ages of dying and surviving organizations shows little discernible difference. In fact, no contrasting features of the two groups yields the means by which one can predict death. Although aging organizations supposedly become more rigid and hence more perishable, the fact that older units did not experience a higher death rate "casts doubt on the allegation of inevitable sclerosis. Organizational old age does not seem invariably to bring on greater rigidity."

In conclusion, systematic studies of bureaucracy once again cast serious doubt on prominent theories purporting to explain it. Available evidence does not support concepts of constantly expanding government bureaus or inevitable bureaucratic decay. Moreover, merely noting that bureaucracies "survive" over long periods does not save the theories. The implication of that choice of verb is that bureaucratic lifetimes exceed their needed length. The organizations presumably can then hold on by being both big and bad. But another way to look at temporal endurance by bureaucracies is to recognize that the tasks they are given — enhancing the public's health, providing for its welfare, protecting its safety, and working in behalf of its prosperity — are never finished and hence never concluded. Indeed, if bureaucracies did not usually survive, we would be in trouble. As Secretary of Commerce Malcolm Baldrige said in fighting off efforts by OMB Director David Stockman to eliminate three of his bureaus, these organizations "are not like an erector set that one can fool around with on the living room floor and quickly build up again."[17]

THE POLITICAL POWER OF BUREAUCRACY

Yet are not bureaucracies *political* actors in their own right and hence anxious not only to defend their existence — a kind of minimal political objective — but also to exercise political power in an active and aggressive way? Even if "badness" does not exist with respect to deteriorating performance, is it not manifest in the corrupting influences of power?

Bureaucracy does, of course, possess political power. That point is not in dispute. The fact that agencies implement legislation does not translate into passiveness with regard to formulating policy. Although bureaucrats are not elected, they are not apolitical. Similarly, the commitment of civil service professionals to serve elected officials does not mean they are without their own political aims. Even though the founding text of the field of public administration, an essay written in 1887 by Woodrow Wilson, states that administration "is removed from the hurry and strife of politics,"[18] anyone who has entered the portals of a bureaucracy knows that this is not true. (Wilson knew this also, and said so soon thereafter.)

"The lifeblood of administration is power." Thus begins another famous essay in public administration, by Norton Long.[19] Administrative agencies wield power because they constitute mobilizations of resources that can be used to allocate political values, that is, determine public policy. They develop distinctive institutional points of view on what policies are deemed "in the public interest." They push unabashedly within political arenas to advance these viewpoints. Moreover, agencies are supported by external political groups as well as opposed by them, and thus they engage fully in the political conflict that inevitably envelopes those possessing power.

With bureaucracies constituting political as well as administrative institutions, then, the question is not whether they possess political clout, but how much clout. As would be expected, critics of bureaucracy believe the amount is far too great. To them, bureaucracy at the least commands dangerous concentrations of political power and in all likelihood is capable of sabotaging democracy itself.

The classic statement on the subject is that of Max Weber. Weber was a brilliant conceptualizer of bureaucracy but not personally enamored of it. He believed the phenomenon to be imperative to modern life, but at the same time was disturbed by authoritarian tendencies in the German Empire of his day and the role of the Prussian bureaucracy developed by Bismarck. One of Weber's famous lines on the point was quoted in the first chapter: "Bureaucracy has been and is a power instrument of the first order — for the one who controls the bureaucratic apparatus." Another famous statement: "Under normal conditions, the power position of a fully developed bureaucracy is always overtowering. The political master finds himself in the position of the dilettante who stands opposite the expert, facing the trained official who stands within the management of administration."[20]

Are these fears, expressed in relation to authoritarian Prussia at the turn of the century, applicable to the United States of the 1980s? One could easily build a case that, indeed, American bureaucracy possesses too much power. Its aggregate size would seem to clinch that case. Compared to the administrative branch of government, the other political branches are puny by comparison. Probably 90 percent of government spending, at the least, finances administrative departments, not legislatures, the judiciary, or the chief executive. How could anything so preponderant be in politics and not constitute a super-power?

Yet this line of argument can be deceptive. The Postal Service with its 660,000 employees does not always have an easy time with its regulator, the Postal Rate Commission, which employs about 70 people. The same is true in the relationship between the National Transportation Safety Board and the Department of Transportation and the large personnel departments and corresponding small civil service boards found in state and local governments around the country. The relatively puny size of legislative committees (even with staffs) has nothing whatever to do with the power they exercise over bureaucracies through statute, appropriations, and legislative oversight. The same logic applies to the courts, which also have great power over administration, even to the extent of declaring statutory authority or past actions unconstitutional.

Moreover, as we have seen, certain bureaucracies are very large, but a great many are surprisingly small organizations. Also, they are highly diversified. Each has its separate identity, mission, interest, and political arena. Differences and rivalries, more than common ground, exist among them. The issue of "bureaucratic power" concerns such individual bureaucracies, not a single abstract "bureaucracy" in the sense of an integrated civil service. To argue otherwise is to assume that separate bureaucratic institutions somehow secretly conspire with one another in politics, as in the manner of cells of collaborators in an underground movement.

Approaching the subject on this basis, then, one individual agency's extent of political power has no necessary relationship to another's. Some organizations are literally dangerous because of their extended power, as was the FBI under J. Edgar Hoover; others are pathetically weak, as is another federal law enforcement agency, the Bureau of Alcohol, Tobacco and Firearms. Power levels may dramatically shift over time as well. We have in recent years, for example, witnessed a tremendous expansion in the political power of the Office of Management and Budget. The opposite is true with the Virginia State Highway Commission, a powerhouse of the Byrd machine that is today a remnant of its former self. The CIA enjoyed great power in the 1950s and '60s, lost it in the '70s, but is regaining it in the '80s. The Federal Trade Commission, conversely, has gone through an almost perfect opposite set of power shifts over these same decades. Some of the most fascinating literature in public administration tells about public sector entrepreneurs like Hoover, Admiral Rickover, and Robert Moses, but the long-standing empires built by these titans are enthralling precisely because they stand out as unusual.[21]

Political power not only varies, it is also elusive. Critics of bureaucracy like to point out that this kind of organization possesses indispensable resources of great value to others, such as expertise and information. This, it is then said, makes bureaucracies without peer in terms of power. They are in a position to bargain ruthlessly with those who must have this expertise and information. Another line of deductive argument points to the discretion possessed by bureaucrats. Since legislators and judges cannot plan and decide everything, they must give ample latitude to bureaucrats. This range of discretion widens as increasingly technical matters are administered, giving bureaucrats more and more power as society becomes increasingly complex.

But power is not simply a commodity to be exchanged or a choice to be exercised. The phenomenon is not that self-contained; power rests in complex bilateral or multilateral relationships. A bureaucracy cannot "trade" a report or secret unless other parties want it and the conditions of exchange happen to be right. Similarly, discretion cannot be freely exercised just because it is formally possible to do so—the anticipated reactions of others must be weighed. A further complication is the intangible, unmeasureable nature of power. Its outward form may be deals and options, but its true extent relates to mutual perceptions of intent and capacity to help or hurt. These calculations are subjective and uncertain. The nonclarity of the situation itself may create power, especially in perceptions of the "power" of adversaries. This is particularly so if they seem remote. Bureaucracy often seems plentifully remote to its adversaries, but the reverse is true as well. To an administrator charged with making a significant impact in a policy arena filled with entrenched interests, the prospects may appear bleak indeed.[22]

Having noted these various characteristics of bureaucratic power, how much need we worry about it? Can it be controlled?

Treatments of this subject usually begin with the observation that bureaucracy is subject to multiple controls. These controls include direction by the chief executive, statutory enactment and amendment, the budget process, personnel controls, the appropriations process, external auditing, inspectors general and ombudsmen, judicial appeal and intervention, and legislative oversight, investigation, veto, and confirmation of appointees.

If this list seems long, it is. But then the analysts do not appreciate the obvious implications of their lengthy survey. Instead of pointing to the multiple restrictions faced by bureaucracy, they emphasize how *each* kind of control is plagued with inadequacies. It is noted, for example, that the chief executive faces a formidable job directing scores of administrative departments because of a wide "span of control." They also observe that the budget and appropriations processes often involve merely incremental adjustments, that oversight and audit bodies rely on limited staff, and that most judicial review of administration does not disturb the substance of decisions.

This is all true. But the perspective of such a critique is only that of the controllers and not of the controlled. From the standpoint of firing-line administators, constraints are not individually imperfect but collectively cumulative. Agency heads face all the controls at once, at least in the sense of anticipated reactions. Meanwhile, they are expected to build a creditable record of achievement. Recently Herbert Kaufman studied, by firsthand observation, the behavior and attitudes of six federal bureau chiefs. With respect to the "autonomy" they enjoyed as heads of supposedly independent "fiefdoms," Kaufman concluded that "Congress clearly had the upper hand in dealing with them," and that "at one time or another, and to one extent or another, they bowed to virtually all the groups with authority over them; the web of constraints was extremely confining."[23]

Actually, a measure of agency autonomy may be looked on as not subversive to the Republic but as a sine qua non for effective public administration. By means of it, legitimate purposes served by the organization—whether aviation safety, environmental protection, or urban planning—can be kept from derogation while under the pressures of competing purposes. This is not "runaway bureaucracy," and it is surely to be preferred to perfect efficacy on the part of all mechanisms of bureaucratic control; in that situation the grip of constraint, applied from all sides at once, would be paralyzing.

What is perhaps ideal—and probably often obtains to one degree or another—is a system of multiple controls subject to flexible resistance and evasion. This pattern permits the transmission of various influences from differing sources yet enables the administrative unit to maneuver as needed and operate as a viable political entity. Bureaucracy is not like the dike that will collapse if we do not plug up every leakage of external control. The better metaphor is the vessel at sea, which is subject to the varied influences of wind, current, and radioed commands from the shore, but still sets its own immediate course.

I recognize that this model is strongly counter to traditional thinking in public administration where one of the foremost concerns has always been control by the chief executive. Indeed, the field's orthodoxy calls for an "integrationist" or "strong chief executive" approach to administrative organization. Underlying this orientation is the belief that the mayor, city manager, governor or President must be given ample tools to "manage" the executive branch for which legal responsibility is held. This is why public administration has long championed specialized staff bodies surrounding the chief executive; the imposition of intricate budgetary, personnel, and information-system controls; and the need for single-head departments and agencies. The intention, in effect, is "public management"—directing a series of many bureaucracies collectively as if they were one organization (i.e., "the executive branch"). The design is then tied to democratic theory by contending that only by having a single elected official responsible for administration—Weber's "political master," if you will—can the voters have the means for registering disapproval of actions of bureaucracy.

The perspective behind this view is, once again, of the controller and not the controlled. Well-buried assumptions in the field of public administration favor advancement of the power of top management and downplay the need for constituent agencies to possess operating and policy autonomy. It is only when tragedies like Watergate occur that even the field's fathers realize that it is sometimes good that a President encounters bureaucratic resistance to his schemes. As for the argument of democratic control, it can be pointed out that other controllers than the chief executive are elected, such as legislators and —in state and local government—sometimes auditors, judges, and even department heads. Moreover, popular influences can be effected upon administration through other means, such as staffing for point of view and collegial administration. With respect to the latter, I have argued elsewhere that the departmental policy boards and commissions used in several states should not be considered the reorganizer's enemy but an acceptable administrative option, on the grounds that they perform a unique representational function and assist departmental autonomy by absorbing political heat.[24]

Another orthodox perspective on controlling bureaucratic power that distorts our thinking is the assumption that bureaucrats never wish to conform with external influences. Officials want autonomy, of course, but as actors within interdependent networks of power, they want security as well. They do not only seek to win fights but also hope to build trust. This is not out of altruism but from a desire to create stability and dependability among relationships over time. Hence, if we watch bureaucrats after a new administration is elected to office, we find them attempting to discover and follow that administration's wishes, not merely working out ways to ignore them. If we observe officials translating statutory language into programs, we discover them treating each word as a kind of holy writ, even though they may have previously tried mightily to get that writ amended. More subtly, we find that administrators, like other actors within a given political community—whether it be a city hall, a state capitol, or the corridors of Washington—continuously absorb the mood cues currently circulating. Often these are verbally symbolized, by such words as "cost effectiveness," "program evaluation," "deregulation," or "cutback." This continuous socialization is neither mysterious nor ominous. Instead it is the natural result of interpersonal contact within the politico-administrative community, plus being subject to a common backdrop of media commentary that incessantly repeats the symbolic words.

Some of public administration's great early teachers also insisted that bureaucrats are influenced not only by external guidance but by internal norms. Carl Friedrich, in a famous published exchange with Herman Finer, pointed to the importance of a sense of responsibility toward one's professional norms.[25] Professionalism is not merely rigid resistance to the outside world; it is also the internalization of critical values developed over time in a specialized field—accounting, public health, civil engineering, city management, or whatever. Another teacher of Friedrich's generation, John Gaus, opened himself to the ridicule of cynics by proclaiming the presence of an "inner check" that influences the behavior of the administrator.[26] Today's great interest in the ethical dimensions of administration means that Gaus was not merely a naive professor but a thinker in the field who was ahead of his time.

A perspective on bureaucratic power somewhat outside the mainstream of the field is that of "bureaucratic politics." This approach does not fear bureaucratic power but seems almost to glorify it. Governments are viewed something like miniature systems of international relations in which sovereign administrative powers bargain, negotiate, enter coalitions, and even declare war. Exaggerated as it is, this approach contributes to our discussion the important point that bureaucratic power involves interagency conflict—and hence some mutual cancellation of effort by rivals. That such counterchecking could be an important curb on bureaucratic power is not conceded by anti-bureaucratic theorists, who regard all bureaucracies as the same abstract enemy. Also, it is a point ignored by public administration traditionalists, who envision a neatly managed executive branch where cooperation is enforced from the top.

But when we think of it, the diversity of bureaucracies and the scarcity of resources available to them almost inevitably combine to create interagency conflict. This is not outright war, as the bureaucratic politics school visualizes, nor is it efficient competition, as economists might imagine. Rather, it is sustained institutional rivalry. To illustrate, enforcement agencies and service bureaus take contrasting emphases in applying regulations. Environmental protection and economic development entities disagree on policies toward attracting industry. At the federal level, the Defense Department and State Department regularly take issue over national security policy, as do the Treasury Department, Council of Economic Advisers, and Federal Reserve over economic and budget policy. Then too, the annual budget process institutionalizes conflict over scarce expenditure dollars and personnel positions. In some governmental jurisdictions parallel struggles are carried on over accounting procedures, allotment of building space, use of the car pool, and chairmanships of interdepartmental committees.

Moreover, intraorganizational as well as interorganizational checkmating occurs. Many of the struggles just mentioned are carried on in parallel fashion within single organizations, among divisions and sections. In some cases the presence of unions also creates labor-management conflict that mightily affects supposedly integrated power relationships. Furthermore, officials occupying various positions find themselves almost inevitably involved in role conflict: Engineers naturally argue with planners, personnel officers automatically differ with program chiefs, junior executive staff anger department heads, computer technicians irritate data collection staff, directors of new programs are perceived as threatening by heads of old ones, and so on. Robert Michels may have enacted an "iron law" requiring a solidified oligarchy within bureaucracy, and James Burnham may have proclaimed a "managerial revolution" that installed a unified class of managers, but nonetheless enormous personal rivalry, turf conflict, and resource struggle go on inside bureaucracy.[27]

As a final comment on the issue of bureaucratic power, it is important to remember that its use and abuse are greatly affected by the cultural and political environments in which it operates. Karl Wittfogel's discourse on "oriental despotism" brilliantly argues that the organizational imperatives of the hydraulic (water-using) society inevitably lead to bureaucratized authoritarianism.[28] Yet it is the cultural and political setting of bureaucracies, not their innate nature or tasks, that leads to authoritarian or democratic administration. Public bureaucracies have existed in every form of polity known to human kind, from democratic Swiss cantons and New England towns to the totalitarian regimes of Hitler and Stalin. Antibureaucracy writers sometimes illustrate the horrors of bureaucracy by citing examples of administrative repression in Nazi Germany and Soviet Russia. But in so doing they practice guilt by association. Under a repressive regime, bureaucracies are of course the instruments of repression. Under a constitutional regime, bureaucracies operate under procedural as well as substantive constraints, as do other organs of government.

Thus we should not be surprised to discover that in individual countries the issue of bureaucratic power requires differing analyses and conclusions. In Britain the question is affected by a top level of administrators with upper-class origins or pretensions. In France, the Grands Corps and Ecole Nationale d'Administration are enormously powerful political forces. In former colonies of Africa and Asia, a tendency often exists for established bureaucratic institutions with a colonial origin to dominate newer political elements.[29] The point is, the context greatly counts, hence countries greatly differ.

In the United States, several features of our particular bureaucratic environment condition agency power. Federalism creates multiple layers of administrative jurisdiction and hence invites more fluidity than a centralized state would allow. The separation of powers concept assures the potential of competitive scrutiny of administration by powerful legislatures and independent judiciaries operating from autonomous political bases. The American press, largely free from governmental restraint, makes the ferreting out of bureaucratic scandal a principal objective. Very important in this regard is the Freedom of Information Act, which requires bureaucracies to spend huge sums to respond to requests for often highly sensitive materials. Other features of the American political scene that confront bureaucratic power are the proliferation of public interest lobbies, the ease of tort litigation against public officials, statutory encouragement of whistle-blowing, built-in mechanisms of client advocacy, and institutionalized citizen involvement in decision making. Within this context, U.S. bureaucratic power is probably more inhibited than in any other country on earth.

Inequity and Drift

With respect to the "badness" of omnipotence, then, depictions of bureaucracy as loose cannon rolling about democracy's deck are at odds with the realities of fluid, shared, and checked political power in American public administration. Occasionally a piece of artillery breaks loose from its moorings, but generally the restraints hold fast. In fact, we must be sure the ropes are not tied too securely, or we restrict the maneuvering room of these institutions.

In addition to runaway political power, bureaucracy is accused of two additional sins with respect to the political system: perpetuation of socioeconomic inequity and furtherance of policy drift.

The first accusation is essentially that bureaucracy inherently favors the powerful and wealthy elements of society. Bureaucracies are seen as formed by the establishment to serve its own interests. They are run by educated, articulate, middle-class people who do not empathize with the problems of the socioeconomically deprived. Their programs serve business and professional interests and not those of urban minorities and rural poor. Efforts at basic reconstruction of society are seen as an anathema to bureaucracy with its principal function being the perpetuation of a system of fundamental inequity among social classes.

The new public administration movement of the 1960s, discussed in connection with social change in chapter 4, placed this theme at the forefront of its concerns. Its proponents called on public administration to assume an aggressive and open posture in redistributing society's benefits and achieving social equity. This necessitated, for at least some associated with the movement, bypassing the machinery of elected representative government to achieve redistributionist ends. Majoritarian democracy was seen as corrupted by elitist influences, thus requiring circumvention of normal political controls and direct responsiveness by administrators to the needs of minorities. A frequently cited model here is liberal Supreme Court justices who ignore majority opinion to protect unpopular minorities. In the words of George Frederickson, "the new Public Administration might well foster a political system in which elected officials speak basically for the majority and for the privileged minorities while courts and the administrators are spokesmen for disadvantaged minorities."[30]

The second accusation to be discussed contends that bureaucracy is responsible in a major way for aimlessness within the polity. Just as the inequity charge is a product of the 1960s, this allegation is attuned to the '70s and '80s. It moves beyond concerns for socioeconomic maldistribution and emphasizes the faults of a pluralist political system. Democracy is seen as not only corrupt but rudderless, dominated by countless narrow interest groups, each pursuing its individual purpose. The outcome is still socioeconomic inequity, however; the powerful, rich, and highly organized actors regularly win all important struggles among interests. Even so, policies are not the outcome of overall, planned direction imposed by a small elite, but net resultants of a fluid and competitive bargaining process. As a consequence the polity drifts and stagnates rather than achieves purposeful movement in reordering society.

Public bureaucracies are often considered by those taking this position as at the heart of the problem. They are foremost actors themselves in policy struggles. They are perceived as defining their goals narrowly and inwardly without reference to broad policy or coherent direction for the polity as a whole. Moreover, they align themselves closely with like-thinking interest groups to form tight coalitions that control policy in individual areas. Theodore Lowi, who regards this situation as unacceptable "interest group liberalism," calls for dethroning the power of bureaucracies to take discretionary action and thus make fragmented policy. His proposals for "juridical democracy" call for curbing the delegation of broad powers to agencies; presidential veto of regulation; and greater emphasis on formal rule making, statutory codification, and sunset laws.[31]

Another writer who may be associated with this perspective is Guy Peters. He contends that following the breakdown of political parties and other democratic institutions in many societies, the result has been "bureaucratic government," namely, fragmented action by self-interested administrative institutions that does not add up to integrated governing. Bureaucracies, he says, "are almost inherently incapable of considering broad allocative and governance questions for the society."

> Bureaucracy may be capable of supplying government, but unlike political parties which supply government by "directionless consensus," government supplied by bureaucracy may be government by "nonconsensual directions." The government supplied will not go in any single direction, but in many, dependent upon the agency and its relationship to its clientele. For the same reason it will be nonconsensual and incoherent government. There would be no integrating ideology or philosophy, only a set of specific ideologies about specific policy problems.[32]

Other critics of bureaucracy have taken a parallel position that stresses the lack of underlying and unifying public values in administrative systems. Eugene Lewis argues that in a "bureaucratic age" citizenship is redefined in ways inimical to the democratic polity. Citizens do not play the role of guiding constituents but instead are transformed into clients to be served or victims to be repressed. As a result, government remains fractionated by narrow bureaucratic interests and is not provided with "broad valuative ends for the future or the transformation rules to achieve them."[33]

In still another critique, Dvorin and Simmons indict bureaucracy for failing to elicit meaningful values for the society. Administrative organizations merely mirror the values of their respective clienteles and, in that sense, are "amoral." Public administration as a field, Dvorin and Simmons further say, has concentrated on technical functioning while ignoring the broader issue of ultimate purpose of bureaucratic action. It is their view that the vast power of modern bureaucracies is precisely why these institutions must assume moral leadership to better society by pursuing human dignity.[34]

In essence, then, these two allegations charge bureaucracy with subverting the polity as a system. Bureaucracy prevents, or at least importantly discourages, the political system from reaching both its redistributionist and purposeful potential. From a history of ideas standpoint, this posture for public administration is fascinating in the way it turns the founding doctrine of the field around. Woodrow Wilson believed (or at least said) that politics corrupts bureaucracy when machine bosses engage in patronage, nepotism, and favoritism and thereby prevent administration from reaching its "scientific" potential. By contrast, these contemporary writers suggest that bureaucracy corrupts politics through restricting its egalitarian output and sabotaging its sense of direction.

A first point to be made in response to these attacks is that a sense of moral outrage over an inequitable society and nonpurposive polity is perfectly understandable. The question is whether we would wish to risk making matters worse by fashioning an administrative state that marched stridently forward toward utopia regardless of the consequences. Although Lowi insists upon curbing the powers of administration, some of the other critics advocate that bureaucrats ignore elections in behalf of a higher good and assume the mantle of moral leadership. Such behavior could, I should think, quickly become obnoxious if not downright menacing. A noninstrumental role for administration sounds innocent enough, but 1984 is upon us; the means of technocratic oppression are readily available, almost in the exact way Orwell said they would be. All we need is the appropriate joining of vision and power and a perfectly equitable and exquisitely purposeful state can be created. I, for one, worry about the absolute certainty and self-righteous resolution that the leaders of such a state would need to possess—Cromwell, not just Orwell, comes to mind.

Turning from the potential implications of these viewpoints to their analysis of the present situation, it is fair to ask how much blame ought to be placed on the shoulders of bureaucracy for existing inequity and drift. Administrative agencies are certainly guilty of playing the game of politics according to the rules currently in effect. Their interest in associating with and exploiting the present centers of power assuredly keeps them from manning many barricades. Their preoccupation with immediate policy arenas and mission objectives prevents them as well from being very interested in the big picture. To the extent that American society perpetuates injustice and flounders adrift, bureaucracy has no doubt aided and abetted the commission of these crimes.

Bureaucracy did not itself commit them, however. That is a most important point to keep in mind. Bureaucracy did not create our capitalist economy with its attendant inequalities. Bureaucracy did not lay down the historico-cultural legacies of racism and sexism that plague us today. Bureaucracy did not organize the single-interest lobbies that work Washington or the state cap-

itals, nor did it contribute to deterioration of the major political parties. Bureaucracy did not establish the constitutional separation of powers that assures
continuous opposition, political deadlock, and by necessity some incoherence
within government. Finally, bureaucracy did not set in motion the long-standing habits of freewheeling pragmatism that have discouraged ideological
thinking in American politics for most of our history.

Moreover, bureaucracy cannot be said to be incompatible with efforts to
attain socioeconomic equity or the experiencing of political purposefulness.
Bureaucracy is just as prominent in self-consciously egalitarian socialist soci-
ties as in capitalist, to say the least. Bureaucracy is a most important element
in the life of a country like Israel, a nation with purpose if ever there was one.[35]
Even in the United States we have had historical periods of relative emergence
of redistributionist policy and political purpose, such as the New Deal. Bureaucracy neither impeded Roosevelt nor disappeared under him. At other
times, such as during World War II and the Kennedy years, bureaucracy also
coexisted with a relatively strong sense of political direction. In the current
Reagan administration the American polity once again seems in relatively coherent motion in a certain general direction. The President may be reducing
the size and scope of bureaucracy, but he is hardly doing without it.

A final point is that, along with being implicated in inequity and drift, bureaucracy actively helps to alleviate each. Despite his concern for its adverse
effects on parliamentary rule, Weber himself noted that bureaucracy's concept
of treating citizens on an equal basis is contrary to notions of privilege and
thus helps to level social and economic differences. He also pointed to the role
of bureaucratic organization in making possible mass political parties, which
have at least the potential of providing political cohesion and direction.[36]

Certainly one can argue that current efforts to lessen socioeconomic inequities in the United States are insufficient. But the efforts that do exist are primarily carried on by public bureaucracy. And they are not puny in scale. More
income is probably redistributed by American revenue collection and human
service bureaucracies every year—in sheer absolute amount—than was transferred by all the great revolutions of history put together, at least at the time of
initial bloodletting. The writing of 36 million checks monthly at Social Security City is itself a staggering achievement that only a modern bureaucracy could
achieve. A more radical system of redistribution than Social Security would require just as efficient a mechanism, perhaps more so.

With respect to purposefulness, bureaucracy's contribution is equally
easy to overlook. It is found in the activity of planning. Public bureaucracy
may not plan for the whole political system, but it certainly does so for programs and areas of policy interest. Also, much sectoral and regional planning

occurs, providing some integration of foci, if only at a subsystem level. Planners cannot and should not steer society, but they are valuable for projecting trends, weighing scenarios, and institutionalizing the long view. The polity would surely be more directionless than it is now if all planning, instead of just most, were done by private corporations whose interests are narrowly defined.

A final contribution is in the form of political representation. We noted in chapter 5 that the composition of the bureaucracy mirrors quite faithfully that of the population as a whole. Far more important in political terms than this demographic representation is functional representation created by the program diversity of agencies. Because of the mammoth scope of tasks given bureaucracy in the modern society, virtually every interest has an administrative counterpart—whether it be agriculture, labor, the scientific community, war veterans, oil companies, schoolteachers, or beekeepers. Moreover, the interests represented are not merely those of the rich and well-born. Bureaucracies exist for enforcement of civil rights, promotion of minority employment, alleviation of urban poverty, protection of migrant workers, education of preschool blacks, safeguarding of the environment, advancement of solar energy, enhancement of worker safety, promotion of labor unions, and receipt of consumer complaints. Very few causes are completely without an administistative spokesman.

The advantage of bureaucracies as political representatives is that they are both informed and accountable. The first characteristic is needed for making a convincing case, the second for demonstrating legitimacy. Electoral representatives such as legislators are highly accountable but sometimes fall seriously short on specialized knowledge. Private interest groups, on whom the legislators often depend for information (and dollars), are well informed but often lack accountability to a source of legitimate authority. Public bureaucracies, by contrast, possess technical expertise *and* formal legal authority at the same time. This is a unique combination in terms of both efficaciousness and providing ties to a larger order. Without it, the society would be even less equitable and the polity more adrift.

CHAPTER 7

A BRIEF, A MYTH, A CHALLENGE

In this final chapter we undertake three tasks. First, the case for bureaucracy is briefly summarized. Second, an explanation is offered for why the failures and dangers of public bureaucracy are wildly exaggerated and its successes and contributions are greatly underestimated. Third, consideration is given to the possible next steps within the field of public administration in light of bureaucracy's strong case.

THE CASE FOR BUREAUCRACY: A BRIEF

Our starting point for making the case for bureaucracy is the proposition that its true nature is not outlined in Sunday supplement diatribes, nor even in the reasoned argument found in most scholarly writings on the subject. Rather, understanding the quality of American bureaucracy begins with exploring the meaning of actual government agencies for the millions of citizens that experience them every day. The question for these citizens is simply whether the administrative entities encountered do or do not deliver. These "students" of public administration do not approach the subject as a literary or academic plaything but as a set of concrete institutions upon which they depend for obtaining crucial information, providing vital services, alleviating personal problems, and maintaining a safe community. In such "study" the stakes are immediate and the impressions direct and fresh.

Direct reports from citizens on their experiences with bureaucracy — as distinct from generalized conventional wisdom on the subject — indicate that they perceive far more good than bad in their daily interactions with it. Client polls, public opinion surveys, exit interviews, and mailed questionnaires all repeat the basic finding that the majority of encounters are perceived as satisfactory. Bureaucracy is reported as usually providing the services sought and expected. Most of the time it lives up to acceptable standards of efficiency, courtesy, and fairness. Sometimes government agencies perform poorly, of course; innumerable acts of injustice, sloth, and plain rudeness are committed daily in government offices around the country. No one is claiming perfection for bureaucracy. At the same time, the basic conclusion of satisfactory citizen treatment as the *norm* rather than the *exception* flies radically in the face of most literature on the subject. Citizens have an understanding of bureaucracy that those of us who "know" about it professionally seldom seem to attain.

We found then, that the "water glass" of bureaucracy is perceived by its users as more full than empty. Some critics tend to discount such perceptions as inexact opinions of lay respondents who have been "set up" by the peculiarities of research designs. If so, the citizens were fooled consistently, because different designs yielded the same conclusion. Others say this acceptance reflects the organization's ability to impose an unrecognized ethic of control. The charge is unanswerable since no evidence of mental imprisonment constitutes its "evidence"; but in any case only a few academics are worrying about liberation. Moreover, if direct performance measures can be accepted at face value, several of these measures reveal surprisingly high proportions of success. Unmistakably, the indicators we have say that bureaucracy works most of the time.

Our insights into American bureaucracy are sharpened further when it is studied comparatively rather than as a whole or in isolation. We use the single noun "bureaucracy" but in so doing refer to a vast multitude of enormously varying institutions. The extreme heterogeneity of government agencies is underscored when formally identical or similar pairs of organizations are found, beneath the surface, to differ radically. The bankruptcy of stereotyped thinking about bureaucracy is made even clearer when we discover contrast in aspects of bureaucracy that by reputation are particularly locked into gray uniformity. We noted, for example, that welfare application forms and welfare waiting rooms vary enormously.

Then, too, we find that certain disparaging differentials thought to exist in relation to public bureaucracy disappear under close scrutiny. One of these is the long-standing allegation, made by urban liberals, that municipal bureaucracies deliberately discriminate against the poor and racial minorities. The evidence is overwhelming against this proposition. An even older denunciation of bureaucracy, advanced by probusiness conservatives, is that public bureaucracy performs poorly compared to the private sector. Comparison between public and private administration is difficult; but when it is possible to compare, business performance is by no means always shown to be superior to governmental. In fact, government is sometimes favored in measures of efficiency, productivity, and innovation.

Finally, a comparison of American bureaucracy to that of other countries underscores the fact that we in this country have much to be grateful for. Americans usually entertain more favorable perceptions of bureaucratic performance than do citizens of other countries. In the functional area in which every government in the world invests substantial resources—postal service—program statistics rank the United States as a world leader. Doubtless the most caustic critics of American bureaucracy sigh with relief when, after traveling abroad, they return to the relatively efficient public services found in the United States.

A major cause for chronic underestimations of American bureaucratic performance is our tendency to hold unrealistic expectations concerning it. Belonging to a culture used to optimism and problem solving, Americans tend to assume that if announced objectives are not met, something is "wrong." The initial feasibility of the goals tends to remain unconsidered. Belonging also to a business civilization, Americans are used to tangible indicators of achievement, that is, a "bottom line." But in bureaucracy goals tend to be idealistic, diffuse, and vague. They often conflict or even contradict. As a result, observers are easily led to conclude that "failure" has occurred because one or more objectives have not been met. Hence, in a way, public bureaucracy does not "fit" American culture too well, which is one reason why its cultural images are so negative. Although individual citizens have mostly satisfactory concrete experiences with bureaucracy, they too encounter divergence from time to time between personal goals and bureaucratic behavior. Regardless of whether this divergence is justified or not, it is transformed into an objectified symbol of contempt: "red tape."

The reasonably good record of American bureaucratic performance could be even better if more of it were direct in nature. But because of various reasons, U.S. public administration has become marked by extensive use of indirect means of implementation, especially via grants, contracts, and credit mechanisms. This "administration by proxy" operates under several severe handicaps including increased overall complexity and reduced control of resources. Agencies delegating the "proxy" often become little more than application processors and check writers that are held accountable for work they themselves do not perform. For their part, bureaucracies delegated the "proxy" must spend untold resources scurrying for grants, contracts, and loans; on receiving the awards, they must deal with the attached strings and respond to policy desires not necessarily initiated within their own political constituencies. Thus the administrative givers and receivers both end up working under added operational burdens and from an eroded political base.

Bureaucracy is further handicapped by the tendency of Americans to expect more from it than just a good job. Bureaucracy is supposed to manipulate successfully conditions in society so as to remove "problems," that is, things identified by someone as painful or unfortunate. But defining a problem does not make it removable. Moreover, because of intervening variables, bureaucracy may do everything possible to correct an external condition without removing it. A manufacturing firm can control the product it produces and is thus in a position to influence the terms on which its work is evaluated. A public bureaucracy, evaluated on the resultant effects of its output, must largely hope for the best.

Bureaucracy is often portrayed as incapable of fostering social change. This is in part also an inflated expectation in that bureaucracies must be recognized as dependent on power and authority external to themselves (even though also possessing both in ample amounts); they cannot be expected to overturn power structures that establish them in the first place. Beyond this limitation, public agencies constantly stimulate and implement changes, although the changes wrought may not always be the particular ones the critics themselves want. Even so, the kinds of substantive change encountered by different public bureaucracies are so manifold in character that somewhere in the society administrative "change agents" operate to please just about everybody, regardless of their position on the political spectrum.

Our misleading stereotypes of bureaucracy extend to the men and women who staff them, the bureaucrats. Yet a sixth of the working population are bureaucrats, broadly speaking. One needs a creative imagination indeed to classify all of these millions as dullards, lazy bums, incompetents, and malicious oppressors. Actually, apart from race and gender considerations, this sector of the population is very similar to the population at large in terms of demographics. Yet, despite the bureaucrats' "ordinariness," the academic model builders have for some forty years entertained the notion of an ominous "bureaucratic mentality." Under empirical examination such an attitudinal syndrome evaporates into thin air. Bureaucrats are no more authoritarian than any citizen, and their attitudes toward clients are a far cry from patronizing or oppressive.

Also, the academicians have labored mightily to portray the bureaucrat as a pathetic victim, subject to repressive controls and deep psychic damage while working under the well-worn nemesis of hierarchy. Certainly Weber's "tight harness" is too restrictive for some, including most of the professors who attack it. But for millions of others, working in bureaucracy is perceived as holding a fairly good job. Empirical studies show that bureaucrats experience no more (and perhaps less) alienation than other individuals, and by various measures, job satisfaction levels are reasonably high. Again, if the "psychic prison" prohibits recognition of deep alienation, only those few outsiders who can miraculously see through the delusion realize its true extent.

Several misconceptions also prevail about bureaucracy's tendencies with respect to organizational size, growth, and aging. Loose talk of giantism—often centering on the huge size of federal budgets and the largest federal agencies—misrepresents the range of bigness versus smallness found in administrative institutions within the public sector. The daily experiences of people with bureaucracy have little to do with gross expenditure totals or the aggregated vastness of the Department of Defense or Postal Service. What counts is the actual offices and institutions where citizens work and obtain services. Most of these entities are surprisingly small, even tiny, in terms of numbers of employees. According to our admittedly imperfect data, the vast majority of federal installations and local governments employ less than twenty-five people.

Moreover, bureaucracies by no means continually or inevitably grow in size. Some get bigger, some remain stable, others actually decline in numbers of employees. Much of the growth that occurs is due to population or workload expansion rather than Parkinson's Law or similar imperatives, whether jocular or not. Regardless of changes in size, no evidence is available to support contentions that bigness creates "badnesses" of inefficiency and rigidity. In fact, some empirical studies come to the opposite conclusion. Still another misconception is that bureaucracies never die and become ossified and captured with age. All of these venerable notions collapse when confronted by evidence.

Bureaucracy is often regarded as possessing uncontrollable political power and hence engaging in subversion of democracy. Certainly public agencies possess political power, as they must to perform at all. But this power is not unrestrained. Multiple controls exist, and bureaucrats have incentives to follow as well as lead. Bureaucracies check each other, and in the United States external sources of restriction operate in unusual number and with a particularly strong net effect. American bureaucracy may well be the most inhibited on earth.

Bureaucracy is accused of contributing to socioeconomic inequities in society and a sense of policy drift within the polity. The underlying notion here is that administration corrupts politics, a reversal of the causal direction propounded at an earlier time in the field of public administration. Such a view gives far too much credit to bureaucracy's influence. Public administrators may not mount revolutionary barricades or initiate moral crusades, but at the same time they are hardly to blame for the existence of either capitalism or pluralism. In fact, public bureaucracies help considerably to ameliorate the adverse consequences of each.

THE GRAND BUREAUCRATIC MYTH

If American bureaucracy turns out to be not so bad but actually satisfactory, why then do we commonly regard it as terrible? Why does such a chasm separate the reality of bureaucratic performance and our abstract images of it?

The explanation lies in a particularly dramatic instance of public myth creation. Americans have worked themselves into a state of believing—at a generalized level of conceptualization—that their government does not perform. The drastic nature of this myth is, when one thinks about it, quite amazing. The gap between bureaucracy's conceptual image and its actual performance constitutes not merely a few degrees of disagreement but a nearly inverse contradiction. We find what is probably the best-equipped public sector in the world, operating in one of the technologically most advanced societies on earth, regarded as incompetent. Just as startling, one of the most constitutionally delimited and democratically guided political systems in history is seen as engaging in repressive administration. The myth is not only grand in content, however; it is grand in effect. Its preposterous implications go almost unchallenged in a culture habituated by incessant questioning of every strongly held view. The inherent contradiction of a concurrently stupid and conspiring bureaucracy passes largely unnoticed. Furthermore, the patently ridiculous reduction of thousands of vastly different public organizations performing a huge array of tasks to a single stereotype of failure is seldom called to task.

A myth so grand can be that way only because it is somehow useful. The myth of terrible bureaucracy performs at least two functions in American society. One of these is validation, or granting reassurance to individuals whose views or constructions of reality do not square with the empirical world. An example of this kind of myth is the notion of white superiority, which reassures the racial bigot. A second illustration is the myth of the weaker sex, which reassures the male chauvinist.

One validating contribution by the bad-bureaucracy myth is reassurance of the individual who fails to achieve personal goals in interaction with public agencies. We have already discussed the prime symbolic component of this use of the myth, "red tape." Rejection of an application for assistance, a job, or a grant can be blamed on "the bureaucracy," regardless of its merits. So too can be the promotion that did not come through, the policy advice earnestly given but not accepted, and the continuous rewriting of one's prized memos. For this reason, it is not surprising that many antibureaucracy attacks come from expatriate public servants. Also understandable in this light is the charge levied by ambitious junior-level officials that bureaucracy is closed to new ideas.

The myth validates a number of occupational roles as well. If bureaucracy is depicted as a nest of vipers, the most aggressive investigative skills an enterprising journalist can get away with are acceptable. Encouraging an official to commit disloyalty to his or her employer and colleagues by leaking to a columnist or blowing the whistle is transformed into asking that individual to play the role of public interest hero. If bureaucracy is seen as captured by privileged groups or greedy corporations, interest group activists can convince themselves that militancy of the highest order is a sacred duty. Similarly, the myth of a wasteful bureaucracy gives meaning to life for armies of auditors, budget examiners, and management consultants. The myth that bureaucracy overreaches its authority also helps aides of chief executives, the staff of oversight committees, and investigators of "watchdog" agencies, who feel they are involved in nothing less important than defending the safety of the Republic.

A second function of the grand bureaucratic myth is justification. In this instance the myth not merely convinces its user of the validity of a strained version of reality but it convinces others. Examples of this kind of myth from ideological politics are "free enterprise" and "international communism" on the right wing and "monopoly capitalism" and "people's liberation" on the left.

In political terms the grand bureaucratic myth is a particularly versatile means of justification. Incumbent officeholders can point to an incompetent bureaucracy as the reason past policies did not achieve their touted ends. Candidates challenging incumbents can use bloated bureaucracy as an issue to address, without saying anything substantive or risking rebuttal or opposition. Conservatives can employ the myth as a rationale to reduce spending and taxes, cut back government regulation, decimate welfare programs, and push Proposition 13-type constitutional amendments. Liberals find it convenient as well; they can denounce bureaucracy as oppressing the poor, suppressing its employees, helping big business, and endangering civil liberties. With a little creativity even the extreme ends of the political spectrum are able to exploit the myth. The far right portrays public bureaucracy as the harbinger of communism, while the far left associates it with efficient management of Nazi concentration camps.

In both validation and justification, bureaucracy serves as a most effective enemy. Enemies are useful tools, as mentioned, and their uses include personal defense and political persuasion. They justify righteousness, intensify feelings, focus enmity, divert attention, and silence critics. And bureaucracy is the perfect enemy. It is abstract enough to fit anyone's value system, from the taxpayer's anger over the complexity of the revenue code to the environmentalist's disgust over compromised air-quality standards. Moreover, bureaucracy as an enemy is very dependable because it is never defeated and hence never disappears—thus never terminating its availability as an enemy. In addition, bureaucracy's imputed association with huge size, impersonalness, and mysterious technology, plus its connection with the sovereign power of the state, make it particularly ominous and hence potent as a target of hatred. Note the references to bureaucrats in the following statement against gun control:

The time to use your guns is when the government comes to get them.
When they come for the guns it is time to act. More than anything
else, this is what Washington fears. And along these lines, friends, if
you think the bureaucratic goons are arrogant now, imagine how they
would behave if they knew you were helpless.[1]

Bureaucracy probably performs validation and justification functions in
most nations and cultures of the world. No doubt some interesting variations
occur in this regard. In the Soviet Union, for example, the myth is of value because it deflects antiregime sentiment in a way nonthreatening to those in power. In many Third World countries it "explains" why development plans are
not realized. As for the United States, Americans' habitual suspicion of government and corresponding commitment to capitalism make public bureaucracy
particularly exploitable: A bureaucratic America stands as the antithesis of a
self-reliant, free, and entrepreneurial America. Unfortunate departures from
this romantic vision can be blamed on bureaucracy. Just as we noted that the
reality of bureaucracy does not "fit" American culture too well, its myth seems
tailor-made to it. Hence we should expect it to remain firmly in place on an in-
definite basis. At the risk of disappointing some readers, then, I shall not even
bother to issue some kind of noble call to "destroy" the grand bureaucratic
myth.

THE CHALLENGE FOR PUBLIC ADMINISTRATION

My call for action consists instead of rather modest recommendations to my
colleagues in the field of public administration.

Not everyone in the field has been taken in by the grand bureaucratic
myth. Michael Wriston has raised his voice "in defense of bureaucracy."[2] Herbert Kaufman has described the fear of bureaucracy as a "raging pandemic."[3]
Victor Thompson has observed that "most people do not suffer unduly at the
hands of the large, modern bureaucratic organization."[4] Zahid Shariff has
commented that "public administration is clearly the whipping boy."[5] Werner
Dannhauser has urged us to realize that "nothing will be gained and a great
deal can be lost by magnifying the bureaucracy problem out of all proportion."[6]
Lewis Mainzer has concluded that the quality of the American public service
"is no mean achievement":

Compared with governmental bureaucracies elsewhere or in other
times, it achieves an impressive record combining competence, dignity,
and responsibility. The variety in quality and style of American public

administration is incredible, the worst is admittedly bad, but a fair amount is quite decent and the best is impressively good. In a world so bungled, whatever worth has been achieved merits a restrained word of praise.[7]

These commentators are in the distinct minority. The field's conventional wisdom flows almost exclusively from the images and literatures surveyed in the first chapter of this book. As Alvin Gouldner noted some time ago, students of bureaucracy seem to revel in despair and pessimism, almost as if they enjoyed delivering to us the worst possible news about modern society: "Instead of assuming responsibilities as realistic clinicians, striving to further democratic potentialities wherever they can, many social scientists have become morticians, all too eager to bury men's hopes."[8]

Indeed, academic students of bureaucracy tend to regard the grand bureaucratic myth not with what might be expected from such outlandish falsity, that is, lighthearted bemusement or open ridicule.[9] Instead, most have embraced the myth. Many have even worked enthusiastically to dignify it with ponderous language, convoluted theory, and unending elaboration.

The underlying reason for this conduct may be, simply, intellectuals' innate need to wring hands and furrow brows. Ithiel de Sola Pool remarks how they usually assume "it is somehow more sophisticated and moral to criticize institutions than to justify them."[10] Analysts of academia have long noted this negativist tendency and have developed various theories to explain it. One is that intellectuals see themselves as guardians of society's values and thus become especially irate when these values are not completely realized. Another speculation is that the intellectuals' own ambiguous status in American society leads them to identify with the underprivileged.[11] A less generous interpretation might be that intellectuals like being in the position of indispensable saviors of an otherwise doomed order. Whatever its wellsprings, the tendency for unbalanced criticism is manifested in academic treatments of bureaucracy.

Charles Perrow offers the thought that the antibureaucracy academic tradition stems from the "exposé tradition" of sociology where a hidden, dark, and subterranean side of social reality was always presumed to exist.[12] The point is a good one, for many models of public bureaucracy originate from sociology. The initial model of Weber, dysfunctionalist constructs of Merton and Selznick, and innumerable subsequent extensions and critiques of those theories come to mind. Additional bureaucratic theory was derived from economics and urban studies where predispositions to believe in inefficient or ineffective public action also exist. When we think of it, in fact, precious little theory of bureaucratic behavior was initiated within public administration itself; even most models of public management are borrowed from business, while much decision and organization theory has been taken from sociology, economics, or psychology.

In other words, we might well conclude that most theories of public bureaucracy are imported doctrines from disciplines unsympathetic in the first place to what public administration is about. Unfortunately, the field has been unable to escape this legacy. Although presumably committed to an activist public sector that necessarily and creatively supplements the marketplace, the field of public administration then turns around and damns the institutions found there.

This paradox is particularly startling when we remember the field is supposed to be an applied one—or at least this has always been my assumption— whose ideal is integration of theory and practice. We all agree on this ideal, but deductive academic badgering of administrative institutions hardly helps its realization; no wonder administrative practitioners regard the public administration professorate with a jaundiced eye. It is as if teachers in medical schools insisted that practicing doctors are nothing but incompetent quacks, or the discipline of psychology told the world that psychotherapy is, after all, a fraud. Our colleagues in the schools of business could not imagine attacking the corporations the way we attack the bureaucracies; to them, these institutions are assumed to be basically worthwhile in the society, and thus worth knowing about, teaching about, and even assisting as vital elements of our world.

What should be done? I propose two things. First, the field of public administration must develop the intellectual self-confidence to extend more uninhibitedly its own body of knowledge about public bureaucracy. We need to move beyond forty years of dubious sociology and the antigovernment biases of market-oriented economists, exposé sociologists, and critical theorists. Bureaucracies should be studied honestly for what they are, rather than for what they are not. This means dealing adequately, in both theory construction and data collection, with the great scope of differentiation and variation that obtains in governmental administration. In examining bureaucratic activity we need to do more than confirm prior suspicions through selected information. We should endeavor to attempt, at least, openmindedness in approaching the subject and be willing to note successes as well as failures. Balanced scholarship may not be as exciting and "in" as pronouncing the system doomed, illegitimate, or facing generalized crisis. It requires, among other things, close study of ongoing routines, for only by noting the proportionate outcomes of large numbers of detailed transactions—the stuff of most bureaucratic work— can proportions of achievement be truly understood. It is the humdrum, daily routine of bureaucracy that determines its efficacy for citizens, after all, even though for academics this may be inherently uninteresting.

My second proposal is that, in our teaching, training, and consulting, we deemphasize grandiose nostrums and concentrate on particularized suggestions for improvement and refinement. As simple as this proposal is, it requires a substantial shifting of orientation. We are so accustomed to the belief that public bureaucracy has failed as a whole that we find it difficult not to approach public sector improvement in terms of wholesale revision. Because of the assumption of comprehensive breakdown, we are easily lured to across-the-board panaceas. These include cure-all, alphabetized techniques of management that come and go as frequently as the seasons—like PPB, ZBB, OD, and MBO. Another tendency is to decide the only way out of the mess is to sidestep bureaucracy entirely, i.e., via deinstitutionalization, volunteerism, privatization, voucher systems, or the negative income tax. The ultimate in grandiose answers is the notion popular a few years ago that in this "postindustrial state" we are already "beyond bureaucracy." The now antiquated sound of these words underscores the faddish, even flippant way we approach the subject.[13]

Practitioners are, I believe, tired of fads. They want more from the academic community. A constructive first step those interested in improving bureaucracy can take is to recognize, from the start, that bureaucracy has not comprehensively broken down. A second step is to affirm that all agencies, programs, and settings are highly individualized. Such an exhibition of realism would at least earn the academics a certain level of practitioner respect upon which to proceed. The third step would then be a concerted effort to tailor precise and individualized recommendations to specific situations. In other words, if the patient is very sick, operate. If the affliction is minor, a few pills will do. A routine checkup may even reveal the patient is in fairly good health. This all seems so obvious, yet all too often we have assumed that (1) all bureaucracies are deathly ill; (2) all have the same terrible malady; and (3) all must undergo the same drastic and newly discovered cure. No wonder many patients think they already know more than the doctor!

Let me add a postscript addressed not to my public administration colleagues but to everyone who experiences public bureaucracy, namely, all of us. As a traditional bête noire in our society, bureaucracy is often thought of as some kind of alien force. It is imagined as a "they" that opposes us and hence is apart from us. Actually, bureaucracy is very close. It is public institutions operating within our communities. It is public employees living in our neighborhoods. It is programs mandated by government officials for whom we personally voted. It is collective action in our behalf. In a meaningful sense, then, bureaucracy is *ours*. That is why the case for bureaucracy is important.

Notes

Chapter 1. Bureaucracy Despised and Disparaged (pp. 1-15)

1. H.H. Gerth and C. Wright Mills, eds., *From Max Weber* (New York: Oxford University Press, 1946), pp. 196-99.
2. Saul Pett, "The Bureaucracy," AP article published 14 June 1981.
3. Russell Baker, as quoted in John D. Weaver, *The Great Experiment* (Boston: Little, Brown, 1965), p. 15.
4. Jack Anderson, "How to Outsmart the Bureaucrats," *Parade,* 27 July 1980, p. 18.
5. Michael Nelson, "Bureaucracy: The Biggest Crisis of All," originally published in the *Washington Monthly* and reprinted in *The Culture of Bureaucracy,* ed. Charles Peters and Michael Nelson (New York: Holt, Rinehart and Winston, 1979), p. 43.
6. Mike Royko column published 16 September 1980.
7. Both questions were asked in 1977. The results of the first are from George H. Gallup, *The Gallup Poll: Public Opinion, 1972-1977* (Wilmington, Del.: Scholarly Resources, 1978), 2:1112. Information on the second question is from the *Washington Post,* 1 October 1978, p. A16.
8. William A. Niskanen, *Bureaucracy: Servant or Master?* (London: Institute of Economic Affairs, 1973); Gordon Tullock, *Private Wants, Public Means* (New York: Basic, 1970); James Buchanan et al., *The Economics of Politics* (London: Institute of Economic Affairs, 1978); George Gilder, *Wealth and Poverty* (New York: Basic, 1981).
9. Robert K. Merton, "Bureaucratic Structure and Personality," *Social Forces* 17 (1940): 560-68; Victor A. Thompson, *Modern Organization* (New York: Knopf, 1961); Michel Crozier, *The Bureaucratic Phenomenon* (Chicago: University of Chicago Press, 1964); Gordon Tullock, *The Politics of Bureaucracy* (Washington: Public Affairs Press, 1965); Anthony Downs, *Inside Bureaucracy* (Boston: Little, Brown, 1967); Guy Benveniste, *Bureaucracy* (San Francisco: Boyd & Fraser, 1971); Christopher Hodgkinson, *Towards a Philosophy of Administration* (Oxford: Basil Blackwell, 1978).

10. Carol H. Weiss and Allen H. Barton, eds., *Making Bureaucracies Work* (Beverly Hills, Calif.: Sage, 1980); George C. Edwards III and Ira Sharkansky, *The Policy Predicament* (San Francisco: Freeman, 1978); Eugene Bardach, *The Implementation Game* (Cambridge, Mass.: MIT Press, 1977); William S. Peirce, *Bureaucratic Failure and Public Expenditure* (New York: Academic Press, 1981).

11. Gerth and Mills, *From Max Weber,* pp. 228-29, 232-33.

12. Karl A. Wittfogel, *Oriental Despotism* (New Haven: Yale University Press, 1957); Ludwig Von Mises, *Bureaucracy* (New Haven: Yale University Press, 1944); Eric Strauss, *The Ruling Servants* (New York: Praeger, 1961); Henry Jacoby, *The Bureaucratization of the World* (Berkeley: University of California Press, 1973), p. 1.

13. Robert Michels, *Political Parties* (Glencoe, Ill.: Free Press, 1949); Philip Selznick, *TVA and the Grass Roots* (New York: Harper & Row, 1966); Bengt Abrahamsson, *Bureaucracy of Participation* (Beverly Hills, Calif.: Sage, 1977); Francis E. Rourke, ed., *Bureaucratic Power in National Politics* (Boston: Little, Brown, 1978).

14. Eugene Kamenka and Martin Krygier, *Bureaucracy: The Career of a Concept* (London: Edward Arnold, 1979); Ralph Miliband, *The State in Capitalist Society* (New York: Basic, 1969), chap. 5; Alan Wolfe, *The Limits of Legitimacy* (New York: Free Press, 1977), chap. 8; Martin Albrow, *Bureaucracy* (London: Pall Mall Press, 1970), chap. 4.

15. Downs, *Inside Bureaucracy;* Niskanen, *Bureaucracy: Servant or Master?*

16. Warren Bennis, *Beyond Bureaucracy* (New York: McGraw-Hill, 1973); Lynton K. Caldwell, "Biology and Bureaucracy: The Coming Confrontation," *Public Administration Review* 40 (January/February 1980): 1-12.

17. Frederick C. Thayer, *An End to Hierarchy and Competition: Administration in the Post-Affluent World,* 2nd ed. (New York: Franklin Watts, 1981); David Schuman, *The Ideology of Form* (Lexington, Mass.: Heath, 1978); Joseph Bensman and Bernard Rosenberg, "The Meaning of Work in Bureaucratic Society," in *Identity and Anxiety,* ed. Maurice R. Stein, Arthur J. Vidich, and David M. White (Glencoe, Ill.: Free Press, 1960); Michael P. Smith, "Self-Fulfillment in a Bureaucratic Society," *Public Administration Review* 29 (January/February 1969): 25-32; Ralph P. Hummel, *The Bureaucratic Experience* (New York: St. Martin's Press, 1977).

18. Strauss, *The Ruling Servants;* Hummel, *The Bureaucratic Experience;* Jeffrey M. Prottas, *People-Processing: The Street-Level Bureaucrat in Public Service Bureaucracies* (Lexington, Mass.: Heath, 1979).

19. Merton, "Bureaucratic Structure and Personality"; Frances Fox Piven and Richard A. Cloward, *Regulating the Poor* (New York: Random House, 1971); Glenn Jacobs, "The Reification of the Notion of Subculture in Public Welfare," *Social Casework* 49 (November 1968): 527-34; Orion F. White, Jr., "The Dialectical Organization: An Alternative to Bureaucracy," *Public Administration Review* 29 (January-February 1969): 32-42; Hummel, *The Bureaucratic Experience;* Yeheskel Hasenfeld and Daniel Steinmetz, "Client-Official Encounters in Social Service Agencies," in *The Public Encounter: Where State and Citizen Meet,* ed. Charles T. Goodsell (Bloomington: Indiana University Press, 1981), chap. 5.

20. Gideon Sjoberg, Richard A. Brymer, and Buford Farris, "Bureaucracy and the Lower Class," *Sociology and Social Research* 50 (April 1966): 325-37; Michael Lipsky, *Street-Level Bureaucracy* (New York: Russell Sage Foundation, 1980); Michael K. Brown, *Working the Street: Police Discretion and the Dilemmas of Reform* (New York: Russell Sage Foundation, 1981); Mitchell F. Rice, "Inequality, Discrimination and Service Delivery," *International Journal of Public Administration* 1, no. 4 (1979): 409-33; Jeffrey M. Prottas, "The Cost of Free Services," *Public Administration Review* 41 (September-October 1981): 526-34.

21. Robert B. Denhardt, "Toward a Critical Theory of Public Organization," *Public Administration Review* 41 (November-December 1981): 628-35; idem, *In the Shadow of Organizations* (Lawrence: Regents Press of Kansas, 1981); Gareth Morgan, "Paradigms, Metaphors, and Puzzle Solving in Organization Theory," *Administrative Science Quarterly* 25 (December 1980): 605-22; Gibson Burrell and Gareth Morgan, *Sociological Paradigms and Organizational Analysis* (London: Heinemann, 1979).

22. James Q. Wilson, "The Bureaucracy Problem," *Public Interest* 6 (Winter 1967): 6.

23. Christopher C. Hood, *The Limits of Administration* (London: Wiley, 1976), p. 205.

24. Alvin W. Gouldner, "Metaphysical Pathos and the Theory of Bureaucracy," *American Political Science Review* 49 (June 1955): 501.

25. Nicos P. Mouzelis, *Organization and Bureaucracy* (Chicago: Aldine, 1967), p. 67.

26. Stephen Miller, "Bureaucracy Baiting," *American Scholar* 47 (Spring 1978): 205.

27. Ibid., p. 212.

28. Gouldner, "Metaphysical Pathos," p. 507.

29. Thompson, *Bureaucracy and the Modern World,* chap. 5.
30. Charles Perrow, *Complex Organizations* (Glenview, Ill.: Scott, Foresman, 1972), pp. 32-35, 52-58.

CHAPTER 2. The Water Glass Viewed Differently (pp. 16-37)

1. Richard Steiner, "Client: Master or Servant," *Midwest Review of Public Administration* 8 (October 1974): 260, 262-63.
2. Robert Morris and Ilana Hirsch Lescohier, "Service Integration: Real Versus Illusory Solutions to Welfare Dilemmas," in *The Management of Human Services,* ed. Rosemary C. Sarri and Yeheskel Hasenfeld (New York: Columbia University Press, 1978), p. 28.
3. Leonard D. White, *The Prestige Value of Public Employment in Chicago* (Chicago: University of Chicago Press, 1929), pp. 145-47.
4. *Illinois Municipal Review* 55, no. 9 (September 1976): 5.
5. Office of Management Services, City of Dallas, "1978 Dallas City Profile: Results and Findings" (Dallas, 1978), pp. 7, 13, 14.
6. Milwaukeee County Department of Social Services, "Some Statistical Highlights: Consumer Survey, 1977" (Milwaukee, 1977).
7. Bureau of Social Welfare, Maine Department of Health and Welfare, "Service Impact Analysis" (Augusta, 1972), pp. 52, 124.
8. Thomas Tissue, "Response to Recipiency under Public Assistance and SSI," *Social Security Bulletin* 42 (November 1978): 9-10.
9. Institute for Social Research, University of Michigan, "Quality of Service Measurement: Program and Instrumentation, Final Report" (Ann Arbor, 1975), pp. 7, 22, 27.
10. University of Wisconsin Extension, "Statewide Citizens Survey" (Madison, 1976).
11. David W. Ahern and Norman J. Fogel, "Citizen Satisfaction with City Services and Support for Urban Political Systems" (paper presented to Southern Political Science Association, Gatlinburg, Tenn., 1979), table 1.
12. Michael R. Fitzgerald and Robert E. Durant, "Citizen Evaluations and Urban Management: Service Delivery in an Era of Protest," *Public Administration Review* 40 (November-December 1980): 588.
13. Elinor Ostrom and Gordon Whitaker, "Does Local Community Control of Police Make a Difference?" *American Journal of Political Science* 17 (February 1973): 68-69.
14. Joel F. Handler and Ellen Jane Hollingsworth, "The Administration of

Welfare Budgets: The Views of AFDC Recipients," *Journal of Human Resources* 5 (Spring 1970): 215.

15. Roy G. Francis and Robert C. Stone, *Service and Procedure in Bureaucracy* (Minneapolis: University of Minnesota Press, 1956), p. 177.

16. U.S. Congress, Subcommittee on Intergovernmental Relations of the Senate Committee on Government Operations, *Confidence and Concern: Citizens View American Government, A Survey of Public Attitudes*, 93rd Cong. 1st sess. (1973), Committee Print, pt. 1, pp. 173-75; pt. 2, pp. 301, 303, 305, 311, 313, 315, 319, 321.

17. Daniel Katz, Barbara A. Gutek, Robert L. Kahn, and Eugenia Barton, *Bureaucratic Encounters* (Ann Arbor: Institute for Social Research, University of Michigan, 1975), pp. 64, 68, 69, 221. See also their "Americans Love Their Bureaucrats," *Psychology Today* 9 (June 1975): 66-71.

18. Katz et al., *Bureaucratic Encounters,* pp. 65, 118, 121-26, 186-87.

19. Barbara J. Nelson, "Clients and Bureaucracies: Applicant Evaluations of Public Human Service and Benefit Programs" (paper presented to American Political Science Association, Washington, D.C., 1979), pp. 6-8, fig. 6.

20. Nelson, "Clients and Bureaucracies," fig. 5.

21. Stuart M. Schmidt, "Client-Oriented Evaluation of Public Agency Effectiveness," *Administration & Society* 8 (February 1977): 412, 421-22.

22. Charles T. Goodsell, "Client Evaluation of the Bureaucratic Encounter" (paper presented to American Political Science Association, New York, 1978), pp. 14-16. For various published comments from this project, see Goodsell, "Conflicting Perceptions of Welfare Bureaucracy," *Social Casework* 61 (June 1980): 354-60; idem, "Client Evaluation of Three Welfare Programs," *Administration & Society* 12 (August 1980): 123-36; idem, "The Contented Older Client of Bureaucracy," *Journal of Aging and Human Development* 14, no. 1 (1981-82): 1-9.

23. U.S. Postal Service, Customer Service Department, "National Study: Changing Household Customer Attitudes," May 1971.

24. Brian Stipak, "Using Clients to Evaluate Programs," *Computers, Environment and Urban Systems* 5 (1980): 137-54; idem, "Citizen Satisfaction with Urban Services: Potential Misuse as a Performance Indicator," *Public Administration Review* 39 (January-February 1979): 46-52; Barbara A. Gutek, "Strategies for Studying Client Satisfaction," *Journal of Social Issues* 34, no. 4 (1978): 44-56; Barbara J. Nelson, "Client Evaluations of Social Programs," in *The Public Encounter: Where State and Citizen Meet,* ed. Charles T. Goodsell (Bloomington: Indi-

ana University Press, 1981), chap. 2; for a contrary view, see Jeffrey L. Brudney and Robert E. England, "Urban Policy Making and Subjective Service Evaluation: Are They Compatible?" *Public Administration Review* 42 (March-April 1982): 127-35.

25. Social Systems Research Corporation, "An Evaluation of Contracted Social Services" (report prepared for Bureau of Social Welfare, Maine Department of Health and Welfare, Augusta, 1974), pp. 36, 42, 47.

26. Blanche D. Blank et al., "A Comparative Study of an Urban Bureaucracy," *Urban Affairs Quarterly* 4 (March 1969): 344.

27. Margo Koss et al., *Social Services: What Happens to the Clients?* (Washington, D.C.: Urban Institute, 1979), p. 9.

28. Data on AFDC in this and the succeeding two paragraphs are from Roby H. Campbell and Marc Bendick, Jr., *A Public Assistance Data Book* (Washington, D.C.: Urban Institute, 1977), pp. 278, 281, 284, 290, 293, 313, 319, 322, 325.

29. U.S. Department of Agriculture, Food and Nutrition Service, "Participation in the Food Stamp Program as Shown by Quality Control Reviews, July-December 1976" (Washington, 1977).

30. U.S. Department of Labor, *Unemployment Insurance Statistics,* July-September 1979, table 14.

31. U.S. Postal Service, *Annual Report,* 1980, p. 8.

32. U.S. Postal Service, Rates and Classification Department, "Origin-Destination Information System Quarterly Statistics," *Postal Quarterly* 1 (1981): 4-5.

33. U.S. Postal Service, Management Information Systems and Customer Service Departments, "Window Clerk Transaction Studies," 1980.

34. Technical Assistance Research Program, "Feasibility Study to Improve Handling of Consumer Complaints: Evaluation Report" (report prepared for Office of Consumer Affairs, Department of Health, Education, and Welfare, Washington, D.C., 1975), pp. 6-7.

CHAPTER 3. Some Suspicions, Some Surprises (pp. 38-60)

1. Guy Benveniste, *Bureaucracy* (San Francisco: Boyd & Fraser, 1977), p. xvi.

2. James D. Thompson, "Authority and Power in 'Identical' Organizations," *American Journal of Sociology* 62 (November 1956): 290-301.

3. James L. Price, "Use of New Knowledge in Organizations," *Human Organization* 23 (Fall 1964): 224-34.

4. William E. Turcotte, "Control Systems, Performance, and Satisfaction in Two State Agencies," *Administrative Science Quarterly* 19 (March 1974): 60-73.

5. Tana Pesso, "Local Welfare Offices: Managing the Intake Process," *Public Policy* 26 (Spring 1978): 305-30.

6. See, for example, Michael Lipsky, *Street-Level Bureaucracy* (New York: Russell Sage Foundation, 1980), pp. 89, 95; Jeffrey M. Prottas, *People-Processing: The Street-Level Bureaucrat in Public Service Bureaucracies* (Lexington, Mass.: Heath, 1979)), p. 24; idem, "The Cost of Free Services," *Public Administration Review* 41 (September-October 1981): 526-34; Frances Fox Piven and Richard A. Cloward, *Regulating the Poor* (New York: Pantheon, 1971), pp. 149, 165; Barry Schwartz, *Queuing and Waiting* (Chicago: University of Chicago Press, 1975).

7. Charles T. Goodsell, "The Phenomenology of Welfare Waiting Rooms" (paper presented to Southwestern Political Science Association, Dallas, 1981).

8. Nancy A. Mavrogenes, Earl F. Hanson, and Carol K. Winkley, "But Can the Client Understand It?" *Social Work* 22 (March 1977): 110-12; Marc Bendick, Jr., and Mario G. Cantu, "The Literacy of Welfare Clients," *Social Service Review* 52 (March 1978): 56-68.

9. Charles T. Goodsell, Raymond E. Austin, Karen L. Hedblom, and Clarence C. Rose, "Bureaucracy Expresses Itself: How State Documents Address the Public," *Social Science Quarterly* 62 (September 1981): 576-91.

10. See, for example, Gideon Sjoberg, Richard A. Brymer, and Buford Farris, "Bureaucracy and the Lower Class," *Sociology and Social Research* 50 (April 1966): 325-37; Saad Z. Nagi, "Gate-Keeping Decisions in Service Organizations: When Validity Fails," *Human Organization* 33 (Spring 1974): 47-58; Richard A. Cloward and Frances Fox Piven, "The Professional Bureaucracies: Benefit Systems as Influence Systems," in *Blacks and Bureaucracy,* ed. Virginia B. Ermer and John H. Strange (New York: Crowell, 1972), pp. 206-22; Julius A. Roth, "Some Contingencies of the Moral Evaluation and Control of Clientele: The Case of the Hospital Emergency Service," *American Journal of Sociology* 77 (March 1972): 839-56.

11. Paul R. Dimond, Constance Chamberlain, and Wayne Hillyard, *Dilemma of Local Government* (Lexington, Mass.: Heath, 1978); Robert K. Yin and Douglas Yates, *Street-Level Governments* (Lexington, Mass.: Heath, 1975).

12. Michael Lipsky, "Toward a Theory of Street-Level Bureaucracy," in *Theoretical Perspectives on Urban Politics,* ed. Willis D. Hawley et al. (Englewood Cliffs, N.J.: Prentice-Hall, 1976), p. 209. See also Lipsky's book cited in note 6 and his "Street-Level Bureaucracy and the Analysis of Urban Reform," in Ermer and Strange, *Blacks and Bureaucracy,* pp. 171-84. A similar position is taken by Michael K. Brown in "The Allocation of Justice and Police-Citizen Encounters," in *The Public Encounters: Where State and Citizen Meet,* ed. Charles T. Goodsell (Bloomington: Indiana University Press, 1981), chap. 6.

13. Herbert Jacob, "Contact with Government Agencies: A Preliminary Analysis of the Distribution of Government Services," *Midwest Review of Political Science* 16 (February 1972): 123-46; Nicholas P. Lovrich and G. Thomas Taylor, "Neighborhood Evaluation of Local Government Services," *Urban Affairs Quarterly* 12 (December 1976): 197-222; Doh C. Shin, "The Quality of Municipal Service: Concept, Measure and Results," *Social Indicators Research* 4 (May 1977): 207-29.

14. Daniel Katz, Barbara A. Gutek, Robert L. Kahn, and Eugenia Barton, *Bureaucratic Encounters* (Ann Arbor: Institute for Social Research, University of Michigan, 1975), p. 89.

15. Howard Schuman and Barry Gruenberg, "Dissatisfaction with City Services: Is Race an Important Factor?" in *People and Politics in Urban Society,* ed. Harlan Hahn (Beverly Hills, Calif.: Sage, 1972), p. 370.

16. John C. Comer, "'Street-Level' Bureaucracy and Political Support," *Urban Affairs Quarterly* 14 (December 1978): 215.

17. Joel D. Aberbach and Jack L. Walker, "The Attitudes of Blacks and Whites Toward City Services," in *Financing the Metropolis,* ed. John P. Crecine (Beverly Hills, Calif.: Sage, 1970), chap. 18.

18. *Hawkins* v. *Town of Shaw,* 303 F. Supp. 1162 N.D. Miss. (1969), 303 F. 2nd 1286 5th Cir. (1971).

19. Frank Levy, Arnold J. Meltsner, and Aaron Wildavsky, *Urban Outcomes: Schools, Streets, and Libraries* (Berkeley: University of California Press, 1974), chap. 2.

20. Kenneth R. Mladenka, "Responsive Performance by Public Officials," in Goodsell, *The Public Encounter,* chap. 8.

21. Philip B. Coulter, "Measuring Inequity of Service Delivery: A Case Study of Tuscaloosa, Alabama" (paper presented to Southwestern Political Science Association, Dallas, 1981), pp. 16-19.

22. Robert L. Lineberry, *Equality and Urban Policy: The Distribution of Municipal Public Services* (Beverly Hills, Calif.: Sage, 1977).

23. Coulter, "Measuring Inequity of Service Delivery," pp. 11-14.

24. Lineberry, *Equality and Urban Policy,* pp. 113-17.
25. Kenneth R. Mladenka and Kim Quaile Hill, "The Distribution of Bene-
    fits in an Urban Environment: Parks and Libraries in Houston," *Urban
    Affairs Quarterly* 13 (September 1977): 78-81; Mladenka, "The Urban
    Bureaucracy and the Chicago Political Machine: Who Gets What and
    the Limits to Political Control," *American Political Science Review* 74
    (December 1980): 992-93.
26. Bryan D. Jones, *Service Delivery in the City: Citizen Demand and
    Bureaucratic Rules* (New York: Longman, 1980), pp. 116-17, 132-35.
27. Levy et al., *Urban Outcomes,* chap. 1.
28. John C. Weicher, "The Allocation of Police Protection by Income
    Class," *Urban Studies* 8, no. 4 (1971): 218.
29. Kenneth R. Mladenka and Kim Quaile Hill, "The Distribution of
    Urban Police Services," *Journal of Politics* 40 (February 1978): 124.
30. Robert E. Worden, "Street-Level Bureaucrats and the Distribution of
    Urban Services: Patrol Officers and Police Services" (paper presented to
    Southwestern Political Science Association, Dallas, 1981), pp. 9-10.
31. Michael G. Maxfield, Dan A. Lewis, and Ron Szoc, "Producing Offi-
    cial Crimes: Verified Crime Reports as Measures of Police Output,"
    Social Science Quarterly 61 (September 1980): 231-33.
32. Richard E. Sykes and John P. Clark, "A Theory of Deference Exchange
    in Police-Civilian Encounters," *American Journal of Sociology* 81 (No-
    vember 1975): 598.
33. Naomi Kroeger, "Bureaucracy, Social Exchange, and Benefits Received
    in a Public Assistance Agency," *Social Problems* 23 (December 1975):
    189.
34. Schwartz, *Queuing and Waiting,* p. 122.
35. William A. Niskanen, *Bureaucracy: Servant or Master?* (London: Insti-
    tute of Economic Affairs, 1973); Ludwig Von Mises, *Bureaucracy*
    (New Haven: Yale University Press, 1944); Allen H. Barton, "A
    Diagnosis of Bureaucratic Maladies," *American Behavioral Scientist* 22
    (May-June 1979): 483-92.
36. For a summary of literature, consult Hal G. Rainey, Robert W. Back-
    off, and Charles H. Levine, "Comparing Public and Private Organiza-
    tions," *Public Administration Review* 36 (March-April 1976): 233-44.
    For an insightful practical commentary on this by a businessman and
    administrator, see W. Michael Blumenthal, "Candid Reflections of a
    Businessman in Washington," *Fortune* 99 (29 January 1979): 36-49.
37. Mark Green, "A Question of Leadership," syndicated by LA Times-
    Washington Post Service, 24 May 1981.

38. E.S. Savas, "Municipal Monopolies Versus Competition in Delivering Urban Services," in *Improving the Quality of Urban Management,* ed. W. Hawley and D. Rogers (Beverly Hills, Calif.: Sage, 1974), p. 478.

39. William J. Pier, Robert B. Vernon, and John H. Wicks, "An Empirical Comparison of Government and Private Production Efficiency," *National Tax Journal* 27 (December 1974): 653-56.

40. Cotton M. Lindsay, "A Theory of Government Enterprise," *Journal of Political Economy* 84 (October 1976): 1070, 1073.

41. Lawrence G. Hrebiniak and Joseph A. Alutto, "A Comparative Organizational Study of Performance and Size Correlates in Inpatient Psychiatric Departments," *Administrative Science Quarterly* 18 (September 1973): 373.

42. Noralou P. Roos, John R. Schermerhorn, and Leslie L. Roos, Jr., "Hospital Performance: Analyzing Power and Goals," *Journal of Health and Social Behavior* 15 (June 1974): 87.

43. B. Peter Pashigian, "Consequences and Causes of Public Ownership of Urban Transit Facilities," *Journal of Political Economy* 84 (December 1976): 1239-59.

44. David G. Davies, "The Efficiency of Public Versus Private Firms: The Case of Australia's Two Airlines," *Journal of Law and Economics* 14 (April 1971): 149-65.

45. *Roanoke Times & World News,* 21 December 1980.

46. John E. Fisher, "Efficiency in Business and Government," *Quarterly Review of Economics and Business* 2 (August 1972): 37.

47. Sam Peltzman, "Pricing in Public and Private Enterprises: Electric Utilities in the United States," *Journal of Law and Economics* 14 (April 1971): 124, 143.

48. Sar A. Levitan and Robert Taggart, *The Promise of Greatness* (Cambridge, Mass.: Harvard University Press, 1976), p. 41.

49. Eugene Haas, Richard H. Hall, and Norman J. Johnson, "The Size of the Supportive Component in Organizations: A Multi-Organizational Analysis," *Social Forces* 42 (October 1963): 13.

50. Lorraine E. Prinsky, "Public vs. Private: Organizational Control as a Determinant of Administrative Size," *Sociology and Social Research* 62 (April 1978): 405.

51. Nancy Hayward and George Kuper, "The National Economy and Productivity in Government," *Public Administration Review* 38 (January-February 1978): 2.

52. U.S. Office of Personnel Management, *Measuring Federal Productivity,* February 1980, pp. 21, 23, 25.

53. U.S. Postal Service, *Annual Report,* 1980, p. 5.

54. J. David Roessner, "Incentives to Innovate in Public and Private Organizations," *Administration & Society* 9 (November 1977): 359.

55. Peter M. Blau, *The Dynamics of Bureaucracy* (Chicago: University of Chicago Press, 1963), pp. 246-47.

56. Louis K. Bragaw, *Managing a Federal Agency: The Hidden Stimulus* (Baltimore: Johns Hopkins University Press, 1980).

57. Fisher, "Efficiency in Business and Government," pp. 45-46.

58. I have challenged this definition in "The New Comparative Administration: A Proposal," *International Journal of Public Administration* 3, no. 2 (1981): 143-55.

59. Fred W. Riggs, *Administration in Developing Countries* (Boston: Houghton Mifflin, 1964), chap. 8.

60. Antoinette Catrice-Lorey, "Social Security and Its Relations with Beneficiaries: The Problem of Bureaucracy in Social Administration," *Bulletin of the International Social Security Association* 19 (1966): 286-97.

61. Michel Crozier, *The Bureaucratic Phenomenon* (Chicago: University of Chicago Press, 1964).

62. Wallace S. Sayre, "Bureaucracies: Some Contrasts in Systems," *Indian Journal of Public Administration* 10 (April-June 1964): 219-29.

63. Gabriel A. Almond and Sidney Verba, *The Civic Culture* (Boston: Little, Brown, 1963), pp. 70, 72.

64. Samuel J. Eldersveld, V. Jagannadham, and A.P. Barnabas, *The Citizen and Administrator in a Developing Democracy* (Glenview, Ill.: Scott, Foresman, 1968), p. 293; Eldersveld, "Bureaucratic Contact with the Public in India," *Indian Journal of Public Administration* 11 (April-June 1965): 231.

65. Sidney Verba and Norman H. Nie, *Participation in America: Political Democracy and Social Equality* (New York: Harper & Row, 1972), p. 374.

66. Otwin Marenin, "Law Enforcement and Political Change in Post-Civil War Nigeria" (paper presented to American Society for Public Administration, San Francisco, 1980), p. 33.

67. Data supplied by U.S. Postal Service, Office of International Postal Affairs.

68. Lee Sigelman, "Measuring Government Productivity: A Comparative Approach," manuscript, n.d.

69. "If You Think Postal Service Is Bad in U.S., Look Abroad," *U.S. News & World Report* 76 (18 March 1974): 94-96.

70. Charles T. Goodsell, "The Program Variable in Comparative Administration: Postal Service," *International Review of Administrative Sciences* 42, no. 1 (1976): 33-38.

71. Charles T. Goodsell, "Cross-Cultural Comparison of Behavior of Postal Clerks Toward Clients," *Administrative Science Quarterly* 21 (March 1976): 140-50; idem, "An Empirical Test of 'Legalism' in Administration," *Journal of Developing Areas* 10 (July 1976): 485-94.

CHAPTER 4. Great (but Impossible) Expectations (pp. 61-81)

1. Peter F. Drucker, "The Deadly Sins in Public Administration," *Public Administration Review* 40 (March-April 1980): 103-4.

2. James Q. Wilson, "The Bureaucracy Problem," *Public Interest,* no. 6 (Winter 1967): 4-5.

3. See "Ripley's Believe It or Not" published in the Sunday comics on 15 April 1979.

4. Alvin W. Gouldner, "Red Tape as a Social Problem," in *Reader in Bureaucracy,* ed. Robert K. Merton et al. (New York: Free Press, 1952), p. 418.

5. Paul H. Appleby, *Big Democracy* (New York: Alfred Knopf, 1945), p. 64.

6. Amory Lovins, "Is 'Red Tape' a Code Word for Law?" *Washington Post,* 3 August 1979.

7. Herbert Kaufman, *Red Tape* (Washington, D.C.: Brookings Institution, 1977), pp. 7-13ff.

8. See Gouldner's comment on privacy and red tape in "Red Tape as a Social Problem," pp. 412-13.

9. Jeffrey M. Prottas, *People-Processing: The Street-Level Bureaucrat in Public Service Bureaucracies* (Lexington, Mass.: Heath, 1979), p. 3.

10. Michael Hill, *The State, Administration and the Individual* (Totowa, N.J.: Rowman & Littlefield, 1976), p. 79.

11. Charles Perrow, *Complex Organizations: A Critical Essay* (Glenview, Ill.: Scott, Foresman, 1972), pp. 24-25, 30.

12. "'Son of Sam' Requests VA Ruling for Service-Connected Benefits," *Washington Post,* 21 April 1980.

13. Peter M. Blau and Marshall W. Meyer, *Bureaucracy in Modern Society,* 2nd ed. (New York: Random House, 1971), p. 148.

14. Michael Inbar, *Routine Decision-Making: The Future of Bureaucracy* (Beverly Hills, Calif.: Sage, 1979), p. 204.

15. Benjamin D. Singer, "Incommunicado Social Machines," *Social Policy* 8, no. 3 (November-December 1977): 89.

16. Christopher C. Hood, *The Limits of Administration* (London: Wiley, 1976), pp. 202-3.

17. Deil S. Wright, "Intergovernmental Relations," in *Contemporary Public Administration,* ed. Thomas Vocino and Jack Rabin (New York: Harcourt Brace Jovanovich, 1981), chap. 8, p. 194.

18. Frederick Mosher, "The Changing Responsibilities and Tactics of the Federal Government," *Public Administration Review* 40 (November-December 1980): 542.

19. Ibid., p. 546.

20. Jeffrey L. Pressman and Aaron Wildavsky, *Implementation* (Berkeley: University of California Press, 1973), pp. 132-33.

21. Catherine Lovell and Charles Tobin, "The Mandate Issue," *Public Administration Review* 41 (May-June 1981): 318-31.

22. Walter Williams, *Government by Agency: Lessons from the Social Program Grants-in-Aid Experience* (New York: Academic Press, 1980).

23. Roger Cobb and Charles D. Elder, *Participation in American Politics* (Boston: Allyn and Bacon, 1972), pp. 82-89.

24. Wilson, "The Bureaucracy Problem," p. 6.

25. Aaron Wildavsky, *Speaking Truth to Power: The Art and Craft of Policy Analysis* (Boston: Little, Brown, 1979), p. 48.

26. Ibid., p. 4.

27. Mark H. Moore, "Statesmen in a World of Particular Substantive Choices," in *Bureaucrats, Policy Analysts, Statesmen: Who Leads?* ed. Robert A. Goldwin (Washington, D.C.: American Enterprise Institute, 1980), p. 33.

28. Sar A. Levitan and Robert Taggart, *The Promise of Greatness* (Cambridge, Mass.: Harvard University Press, 1976), pp. 275-78.

29. Peter Savage, "Contemporary Public Administration: The Changing Environment and Agenda," in *Public Administration in a Time of Turbulence,* ed. Dwight Waldo (Scranton, Pa.: Chandler, 1971), p. 44.

30. Richard T. LaPiere, *Social Change* (New York: McGraw-Hill, 1965), pp. 408-13.

31. H. George Frederickson, "Toward a New Public Administration," in *Toward a New Public Administration,* ed. Frank Marini (Scranton, Pa.: Chandler, 1971), chap. 11, p. 312.

32. Frederickson's expanded views on these matters are found in his *New Public Administration* (University, Ala.: University of Alabama Press, 1980).

33. Victor A. Thompson, *Without Sympathy or Enthusiasm* (University, Ala.: University of Alabama Press, 1975), p. 66.

34. Richard L. Simpson, "Beyond Rational Bureaucracy: Changing Values and Social Integration in Post-Industrial Society," *Social Forces* 51 (September 1972): 5.

35. Dwight Waldo, "Some Thoughts on Alternatives, Dilemmas, and Paradoxes in a Time of Turbulence," in Waldo, *Public Administration in a Time of Turbulence*, pp. 274-76.

36. LaPiere, *Social Change*, pp. 452-57.

37. Charles T. Goodsell, *Administration of a Revolution* (Cambridge, Mass.: Harvard University Press, 1965).

CHAPTER 5. Bureaucrats as Ordinary People (pp. 82-109)

1. Ralph P. Hummel, *The Bureaucratic Experience* (New York: St. Martin's Press, 1977), pp. 2-3.

2. John D. Weaver, *The Great Experiment* (Boston: Little, Brown, 1965), p. 273.

3. Norton E. Long, "Bureaucracy and Constitutionalism," *American Political Science Review* 46 (September 1952): 814.

4. Steven Thomas Seitz, *Bureaucracy, Policy, and the Public* (St. Louis: Mosby, 1978), p. 113.

5. Milton C. Cummings, M. Kent Jennings, and Franklin F. Kilpatrick, "Federal and Nonfederal Employees: A Comparative Social-Occupational Analysis," *Public Administration Review* 27 (December 1967): 399.

6. State and local percentages calculated from N. Joseph Cayer and Lee Sigelman, "Minorities and Women in State and Local Government: 1973-75," *Public Administration Review* 40 (September-October 1980): 445.

7. Kenneth John Meier, "Representative Bureaucracy: An Empirical Analysis," *American Political Science Review* 69 (June 1975): 532.

8. Matthew Hutchins and Lee Sigelman, "Black Employment in State and Local Governments: A Comparative Analysis," *Social Science Quarterly* 62 (March 981): 82.

9. Meier, "Representative Bureaucracy," pp. 537-39.

10. Frank J. Thompson, "Civil Servants and the Deprived: Socio-Political and Occupational Explanations of Attitudes Toward Minority Hiring," *American Journal of Political Science* 22 (May 1978): 335. The

correlation of minority status and receptivity to hiring minorities was statistically significant but lower than that of three belief variables.

11. Kenneth John Meier and Lloyd G. Nigro, "Representative Bureaucracy and Policy Preferences: A Study in the Attitudes of Federal Executives," *Public Administration Review* 36 (July-August 1976): 466-67.

12. Ralph Miliband, *The State in Capitalist Society* (New York: Basic, 1969), pp. 119-29 and passim.

13. The data on political views are from Seitz, *Bureaucracy, Policy, and the Public,* p. 113; the data on policy views are from Meier, "Representative Bureaucracy," p. 541.

14. Herbert McClosky, "Consensus and Ideology and American Politics," *American Political Science Review* 58 (June 1964): 365-69; Bob L. Wynia, "Federal Bureaucrats' Attitudes Toward a Democratic Ideology," *Public Administration Review* 34 (March-April 1974): 158-59.

15. Charles S. Hyneman, *Bureaucracy in a Democracy* (New York: Harper, 1950), p. 20.

16. Robert Merton, "Bureaucratic Structure and Personality," *Social Forces* 17 (1940): 560-68.

17. Joseph Bensman and Bernard Rosenberg, "The Meaning of Work in Bureaucratic Society," in *Identity and Anxiety: Survival of the Person in Mass Society,* ed. Maurice R. Stein, Arthur J. Vidich, and David M. White (Glencoe, Ill.: Free Press, 1960), pp. 181-97.

18. Hummel, *The Bureaucratic Experience,* pp. 22, 25.

19. Charles Peters, "Can Anything Be Done About the Federal Bureaucracy?" *Washington Post Magazine,* 1 October 1978, p. 14.

20. Melvin L. Kohn, "Bureaucratic Man: A Portrait and an Interpretation," *American Sociological Review* 36 (June 1971): 461-74. Also source for the following two paragraphs.

21. Another study, supporting Kohn's findings, showed that senior managers working in larger, more bureaucratized British companies tended to be more flexible and risk-prone individuals. Tony Ellis and John Child, "Placing Stereotypes of the Manager into Perspective," *Journal of Management Studies* 10 (October 1973): 235-55.

22. James F. Guyot, "Government Bureaucrats Are Different," *Public Administration Review* 22 (December 1962): 195-202.

23. Julius S. Brown, "Risk Propensity in Decision Making: A Comparison of Business and Public School Administrators," *Administrative Science Quarterly* 15 (December 1970): 473-81.

24. Samuel M. Meyers and Jennie McIntyre, "Welfare Policy and Its Consequences for the Recipient Population: A Study of the AFDC Program,"

Department of Health, Education, and Welfare, Social and Rehabilitation Service, December 1969, pp. 94, 215.

25. The data given from this survey have not been published previously, although some reference is made to them in Charles T. Goodsell, "Conflicting Perceptions of Welfare Bureaucracy," *Social Casework* 61 (June 1980): 354-60.

26. Fred Reed, "Military Minds," *Washington Post*, 2 October 1979.

27. H.H. Gerth and C. Wright Mills, eds., *From Max Weber* (New York: Oxford University Press, 1946), p. 228.

28. Bensman and Rosenberg, "The Meaning of Work in Bureaucratic Society," p. 184 and passim.

29. Hummel, *The Bureaucratic Experience,* pp. 49-51, 83-88, 92-109.

30. Frederick C. Thayer, *An End to Hierarchy and Competition: Administration in the Post-Affluent World,* 2nd ed. (New York: Franklin Watts, 1981), pp. A1-A16, 46-52.

31. Guy Benveniste, *Bureaucracy* (San Francisco: Boyd & Fraser, 1977), especially chap. 5.

32. Robert B. Denhardt, *In the Shadow of Organizations* (Lawrence: Regents Press of Kansas, 1981), p. 9. See also his "Toward a Critical Theory of Public Organization," *Public Administration Review* 41 (November-December 1981): 628-35. For other references to this orientation, consult Gibson Burrell and Gareth Morgan, *Sociological Paradigms and Organizational Analysis* (London: Heinemann, 1979); and Morgan, "Paradigms, Metaphors, and Puzzle Solving in Organization Theory," *Administrative Science Quarterly* 25 (December 1980): 605-22.

33. David Ewing, *Freedom Inside the Organization* (New York: McGraw-Hill, 1977), pp. 3, 59.

34. George Konrád, *The Case Worker* (New York: Harcourt Brace Jovanovich, 1974), pp. 168-69.

35. Charles Bonjean and Michael Grimes, "Bureaucracy and Alienation: A Dimensional Approach," *Social Forces* 48 (March 1970): 365-73.

36. Gerald H. Moeller and W.W. Charters, "Relation of Bureaucratization to Sense of Power Among Teachers," *Administrative Science Quarterly* 10 (March 1966): 444-65.

37. Dennis W. Organ and Charles N. Greene, "The Effects of Formalization on Professional Involvement: A Compensatory Process Approach," *Administrative Science Quarterly* 26 (June 1981): 237-51.

38. J.B. Rhinehart, R.P. Barrell, A.S. DeWolfe, J.E. Griffin, and F.E. Spaner, "Comparative Study of Need Satisfactions in Governmental

and Business Hierarchies," *Journal of Applied Psychology* 53 (June 1969): 230-35.

39. Bruce Buchanan, "Red-Tape and the Service Ethic: Some Unexpected Differences Between Public and Private Managers," *Administration & Society* 6 (February 1975): 423-44; idem, "Government Managers, Business Executives, and Organizational Commitment," *Public Administration Review* 34 (July-August 1974): 342.

40. Hal G. Rainey, "Reward Expectancies, Role Perceptions, and Job Satisfaction Among Government and Business Managers: Indications of Commonalities and Differences," *Academy of Management Proceedings*, 1979, pp. 357-61.

41. Clarence Stone and Robert Stoker, "Deprofessionalism and Dissatisfaction in Urban Service Agencies" (paper presented to Midwest Political Science Association, Chicago, 1979), pp. 47-48. Percentage figures furnished by Professor Stone.

42. Franklin P. Kilpatrick, Milton C. Cummings, and M. Kent Jennings, *The Image of the Federal Service* (Washington, D.C.: Brookings Institution, 1964), p. 188.

43. "The Federal Report," *Washington Post,* 21 August 1981. For information on another such survey, see the same newspaper for 15 October 1981.

44. Office of Personnel Management, *Federal Employee Attitudes, 1979: Survey Questions and Response.* Exact percentages furnished by OPM.

45. Douglas LaBier, "Passions at Work" (paper presented to American Political Science Association, Washington, D.C., 1980). See also his "Uncle Sam's Working Wounded," *Washington Post Magazine,* 17 February 1980, pp. 6-14.

46. Kenneth Lasson, *Private Lives of Public Servants* (Bloomington: Indiana University Press, 1978).

47. Morris Janowitz and Deil Wright, "The Prestige of Public Employment: 1929 and 1954," *Public Administration Review* 16 (Winter 1956): 17, 19.

48. Kilpatrick et al., *The Image of the Federal Service,* p. 210.

49. U.S. Postal Service, Customer Services Department, "Perceptions of Postal Window Clerks," 1978.

50. Leonard D. White, *The Prestige Value of Public Employment in Chicago* (Chicago: University of Chicago Press, 1929), p. 1.

51. "U.S. Workers Primed to Send Carter a Message," *Washington Post,* 20 April 1980.

52. Don Goldman, "Need a Fall Guy? Blame a Bureaucrat," *Washington Post,* 2 December 1979.

53. Bob Willis, "Bureaucrat Is Often Unjustly Maligned," *Roanoke Times & World News,* 16 September 1980.
54. Mark Shields, "Very Special Agents," *Washington Post,* 4 April 1981.

CHAPTER 6. Bigness and Badness Reconsidered (pp. 110-38)

1. "Minigovernment: Japan Keeps Its Bureaucracy to Limited Size," *Washington Post,* 27 June 1981.
2. Office of Personnel Management, *Federal Civilian Work Force Statistics: Annual Report of Employment by Geographic Area* (31 December 1977). Information tabulated from this source was compiled by Susan E. Sparks.
3. Bureau of the Census, *1977 Census of Governments,* vol. 3, no. 2, *Compendium of Public Employment,* table 24, pp. 428-29.
4. C. Northcote Parkinson, *Parkinson's Law and Other Studies in Administration* (Boston: Houghton Mifflin, 1957), p. 12. For a scathing denunciation of Parkinson and also the originators of the "Peter Principle," see George D. Beam, "The Parkinson-Peter Pasquinade," *Bureaucrat* 9 (Summer 1980): 69-80.
5. Anthony Downs, *Inside Bureaucracy* (Boston: Little, Brown, 1967), pp. 16-17.
6. Ibid., pp. 5-14, 17-23, 140-43, 158-60.
7. Marver H. Bernstein, *Regulating Business by Independent Commission* (Princeton: Princeton University Press, 1955), pp. 74-95. The word "capture" was not used by Bernstein but introduced later by others.
8. *Statistical Abstract of the United States,* 1974, p. 236; 1980, p. 281.
9. *Statistical Abstract of the United States,* 1980, pp. 282, 319, 354, 381; 1981, pp. 269, 307, 309, 343, 368.
10. James A. Christenson and Carolyn E. Sachs, "The Impact of Government Size and Number of Administrative Units on the Quality of Public Services," *Administrative Science Quarterly* 25 (March 1980): 96, 99-100.
11. Research Triangle Institute, Center for Population and Urban-Rural Studies, and North Carolina Department of Natural Resources & Community Development, Division of Community Assistance, "Comparative Performance Measures for Municipal Services," December 1978.
12. D.S. Pugh, D.J. Hickson, C.R. Hinings, and C. Turner, "The Context of Organization Structures," *Administrative Science Quarterly* 14 (March 1969): 91-114.

13. Marshall W. Meyer, *Change in Public Bureaucracies* (Cambridge: Cambridge University Press, 1979), pp. 171, 176.

14. Charles T. Goodsell, "Intensity of Federal Regulation of Business," *Business and Government Review* 11 (March-April 1970): 17-23; idem, "Recent Oscillations in the Regulatory State" (paper presented to Southwestern Political Science Association, Dallas, 1973).

15. Kenneth J. Meier and John P. Plumlee, "Regulatory Administration and Organizational Rigidity," *Western Political Quarterly* 31 (March 1978): 80-95, with quotations from pp. 91 and 95.

16. Herbert Kaufman, *Are Government Organizations Immortal?* (Washington, D.C.: Brookings Institution, 1976), pp. 23-24, 34-35, 46, 53. For following paragraph, see pp. 60-61, 68-69.

17. "Budget 'Agreement' on Trade Agencies," *Washington Post,* 14 December 1981.

18. Woodrow Wilson, "The Study of Administration," in *Public Administration and Policy,* ed. Peter Woll (New York: Harper & Row, 1966), p. 28.

19. Norton E. Long, "Power and Administration," *Public Administration Review* 9 (Autumn 1949): 257.

20. H.H. Gerth and C. Wright Mills, *From Max Weber* (New York: Oxford University Press, 1946), pp. 228, 232.

21. See in this regard Eugene Lewis, *Public Entrepreneurship: Toward a Theory of Bureaucratic Political Power* (Bloomington: Indiana University Press, 1980).

22. Note on this point Herbert Kaufman, "Fear of Bureaucracy: A Raging Pandemic," *Public Administration Review* 41 (January-February 1981): 4.

23. Herbert Kaufman, *The Administrative Behavior of Federal Bureau Chiefs* (Washington, D.C.: Brookings Institution, 1981), p. 161.

24. Charles T. Goodsell, "Collegiate State Administration: Design for Today?" *Western Political Quarterly* 34 (September 1981): 447-60.

25. Carl J. Friedrich, "Public Policy and the Nature of Administrative Responsibility," *Public Policy* 1 (1940): 3-24.

26. John M. Gaus, Leonard D. White, and Marshall E. Dimock, *The Frontiers of Public Administration* (New York: Russell and Russell, 1936), pp. 39-40.

27. Robert Michels, *Political Parties* (New York: Free Press, 1962); James Burnham, *The Managerial Revolution* (New York: John Day, 1941).

28. Karl A. Wittfogel, *Oriental Despotism* (New Haven: Yale University Press, 1957).

29. Fred W. Riggs, "Bureaucrats and Political Development: A Paradoxical View," in *Bureaucracy and Political Development,* ed. Joseph La-Palombara (Princeton: Princeton University Press, 1963), pp. 120-67.

30. H. George Frederickson, "Toward a New Public Administration," in *Toward a New Public Administration,* ed. Frank Marini (Scranton, Pa.: Chandler, 1971), p. 329.

31. Theodore J. Lowi, *The End of Liberalism,* 2nd ed. (New York: Norton, 1979), chap. 11.

32. B. Guy Peters, "The Problem of Bureaucratic Government," *Journal of Politics* 43 (February 1981): 82.

33. Eugene Lewis, *American Politics in a Bureaucratic Age: Citizens, Constituents, Clients and Victims* (Cambridge, Mass.: Winthrop, 1977), p. 174.

34. Eugene P. Dvorin and Robert H. Simmons, *From Amoral to Humane Bureaucracy* (San Francisco: Canfield Press, 1972), chap. 1.

35. Gerald E. Caiden, *Israel's Administrative Culture* (Berkeley: University of California Press, 1970).

36. Gerth and Mills, *From Max Weber,* pp. 211, 224.

CHAPTER 7. A Brief, a Myth, a Challenge (pp. 139-49)

1. Alan Stang, "American Liberty and Your Right to Your Gun," *American Opinion* 22 (September 1979): 103. For a general discussion of "enemies," see David Finlay, *Enemies in Politics* (Chicago: Rand McNally, 1967).

2. Michael J. Wriston, "In Defense of Bureaucracy," *Public Administration Review* 40 (March-April 1980): 179-83.

3. Herbert Kaufman, "Fear of Bureaucracy: A Raging Pandemic," *Public Administration Review* 41 (January-February 1981): 1-9.

4. Victor A. Thompson, *Without Sympathy or Enthusiasm* (University, Ala.: University of Alabama Press, 1975), p. 87.

5. Zahid Shariff, "Contemporary Challenges to Public Administration," *Social Science Quarterly* 62 (September 1981): 564.

6. Warner J. Dannhauser, "Reflections on Statesmanship and Bureaucracy," in *Bureaucrats, Policy Analysts, Statesmen: Who Leads?* ed. Robert A. Goldwin (Washington, D.C.: American Enterprise Institute, 1980), p. 132.

7. Lewis C. Mainzer, *Political Bureaucracy* (Glenview, Ill.: Scott, Foresman, 1973), p. 151.

8. Alvin W. Gouldner, "Metaphysical Pathos and the Theory of Bureaucracy," *American Political Science Review* 49 (June 1955): 507.

9. One example, however, is George D. Beam, "The Parkinson-Peter Pasquinade," *Bureaucrat* 9 (Summer 1980): 69-80.

10. Ithiel de Sola Pool, "The Language of Politics: General Trends in Content," in *Propaganda and Communication in World History,* ed. Harold D. Lasswell (Honolulu: University Press of Hawaii, 1980), p. 180.

11. Fred J. Evans, "Toward a Theory of Academic Liberalism," *Journal of Politics* 42 (November 1980): 993-1030.

12. Charles Perrow, *Complex Organizations: A Critical Essay* (Glenview, Ill.: Scott, Foresman, 1972), p. 180.

13. Note Zahid Shariff, "The Persistence of Bureaucracy," *Social Science Quarterly* 60 (June 1979): 3-19.

Selected Bibliography

Appleby, Paul H. *Big Democracy.* New York: Alfred Knopf, 1945.

Barton, Allen H. "A Diagnosis of Bureaucratic Maladies." *American Behavioral Scientist* 22 (May-June 1979): 483-92.

Beam, George D. "The Parkinson-Peter Pasquinade." *Bureaucrat* 9 (Summer 1980): 69-80.

Bensman, Joseph, and Bernard Rosenberg. "The Meaning of Work in Bureaucratic Society." In *Identity and Anxiety,* edited by Maurice R. Stein, Arthur J. Vidich, and David M. White. Glencoe, Ill.: Free Press, 1960.

Benveniste, Guy. *Bureaucracy.* San Francisco: Boyd & Fraser, 1977.

Blau, Peter M. *The Dynamics of Bureaucracy.* Chicago: University of Chicago Press, 1963.

Denhardt, Robert B. *In the Shadow of Organizations.* Lawrence: Regents Press of Kansas, 1981.

Downs, Anthony. *Inside Bureaucracy.* Boston: Little, Brown, 1967.

Dvorin, Eugene P., and Robert H. Simmons. *From Amoral to Humane Bureaucracy.* San Francisco: Canfield Press, 1972.

Fisher, John E. "Efficiency in Business and Government." *Quarterly Review of Economics and Business* 2 (August 1972): 35-47.

Frederickson, H. George. *New Public Administration.* University, Ala.: University of Alabama Press, 1980.

Gerth, H.H., and C. Wright Mills, eds. *From Max Weber.* New York: Oxford University Press, 1946.

Goodsell, Charles T. "Conflicting Perceptions of Welfare Bureaucracy." *Social Casework* 61 (June 1980): 354-60.

———. "Looking Once Again at Human Service Bureaucracy." *Journal of Politics* 43 (August 1981): 763-78.

———, ed. *The Public Encounter: Where State and Citizen Meet.* Bloomington: Indiana University Press, 1981.

Gouldner Alvin W. "Metaphysical Pathos and the Theory of Bureaucracy." *American Political Science Review* 49 (June 1955): 496-507.

———. "Red Tape as a Social Problem." In *Reader in Bureaucracy,* edited by Robert K. Merton et al. New York: Free Press, 1952. Pp. 410-18.

HILL, MICHAEL. *The State, Administration and the Individual.* Totowa, N.J.: Rowman & Littlefield, 1976.

HOOD, CHRISTOPHER C. *The Limits of Administration.* London: Wiley, 1976.

HUMMEL, RALPH P. *The Bureaucratic Experience.* New York: St. Martin's Press, 1977.

HYNEMAN, CHARLES S. *Bureaucracy in a Democracy.* New York: Harper, 1950.

INBAR, MICHAEL. *Routine Decision-Making: The Future of Bureaucracy.* Beverly Hillls, Calif.: Sage, 1979.

JACOBY, HENRY. *The Bureaucratization of the World.* Berkeley: University of California Press, 1973.

JONES, BRYAN D. *Service Delivery in the City: Citizen Demand and Bureaucratic Rules.* New York: Longman, 1980.

KAMENKA, EUGENE, and MARTIN KRYGIER. *Bureaucracy: The Career of a Concept.* London: Edward Arnold, 1979.

KATZ, DANIEL; BARBARA A. GUTEK; ROBERT L. KAHN; and EUGENIA BARTON. *Bureaucratic Encounters.* Ann Arbor: Institute for Social Research, University of Michigan, 1975.

KAUFMAN, HERBERT. *Are Government Organizations Immortal?* Washington, D.C.: Brookings Institution, 1976.

_____. "Fear of Bureaucracy: A Raging Pandemic." *Public Administration Review* 41 (January-February 1981): 1-9.

_____. *Red Tape.* Washington, D.C.: Brookings Institution, 1977.

KOHN, MELVIN L. "Bureaucratic Man: A Portrait and an Interpretation." *American Sociological Review* 36 (June 1971): 461-74.

LASSON, KENNETH. *Private Lives of Public Servants.* Bloomington: Indiana University Press, 1978.

LEVY, FRANK; ARNOLD J. MELTSNER; and AARON WILDAVSKY. *Urban Outcomes: Schools, Streets, and Libraries.* Berkeley: University of California Press, 1974.

LEWIS, EUGENE. *American Politics in a Bureaucratic Age: Citizens, Constituents, Clients and Victims.* Cambridge, Mass.: Winthrop, 1977.

_____. *Public Entrepreneurship: Toward a Theory of Bureaucratic Political Power.* Bloomington: Indiana University Press, 1980.

LINEBERRY, ROBERT L. *Equality and Urban Policy: The Distribution of Municipal Public Services.* Beverly Hills, Calif.: Sage, 1977.

LIPSKY, MICHAEL. *Street-Level Bureaucracy.* New York: Russell Sage Foundation, 1980.

LONG, NORTON E. "Bureaucracy and Constitutionalism." *American Political Science Review* 46 (September 1952): 808-18.

———. "Power and Administration." *Public Administration Review* 9 (Autumn 1949): 257-64.

MEIER, KENNETH JOHN. "Representative Bureaucracy: An Empirical Analysis." *American Political Science Review* 69 (June 1975): 526-42.

MERTON, ROBERT K. "Bureaucratic Structure and Personality." *Social Forces* 17 (1940): 560-68.

MEYER, MARSHALL W. *Change in Public Bureaucracies.* Cambridge: Cambridge University Press, 1979.

MILLER, STEPHEN. "Bureaucracy Baiting." *American Scholar* 47 (Spring 1978): 202-22.

MOUZELIS, NICOS P. *Organisation and Bureaucracy.* Chicago: Aldine, 1967.

NAGI, SAAD Z. "Gate-Keeping Decisions in Service Organizations: When Validity Fails." *Human Organization* 33 (Spring 1974): 47-58.

NISKANEN, WILLIAM A. *Bureaucracy: Servant or Master?* London: Institute of Economic Affairs, 1973.

PEIRCE, WILLIAM S. *Bureaucratic Failure and Public Expenditure.* New York: Academic Press, 1981.

PERROW, CHARLES. *Complex Organizations: A Critical Essay.* Glenview, Ill.: Scott, Foresman, 1972.

PETERS, B. GUY. "The Problem of Bureaucratic Government." *Journal of Politics* 43 (February 1981): 56-82.

PRESSMAN, JEFFREY L., and AARON B. WILDAVSKY. *Implementation.* Berkeley: University of California Press, 1973.

PROTTAS, JEFFREY M. *People-Processing: The Street-Level Bureaucrat in Public Service Bureaucracies.* Lexington, Mass.: Heath, 1979.

RAINEY, HAL G.; ROBERT W. BACKOFF; and CHARLES H. LEVINE. "Comparing Public and Private Organizations." *Public Administration Review* 36 (March-April 1976): 233-44.

SCHWARTZ, BARRY. *Queuing and Waiting.* Chicago: University of Chicago Press, 1975.

SHARIFF, ZAHID. "Contemporary Challenges to Public Administration." *Social Science Quarterly* 62 (September 1981): 555-68.

SIMPSON, RICHARD L. "Beyond Rational Bureaucracy: Changing Values and Social Integration in Post-Industrial Society." *Social Forces* 51 (September 1972): 1-6.

SJOBERG, GIDEON; R.A. BRYMER; and B. FARRIS. "Bureaucracy and the Lower Class." *Sociology and Social Research* 50 (April 1966): 325-37.

STRAUSS, ERIC. *The Ruling Servants*. New York: Praeger, 1961.

THAYER, FREDERICK C. *An End to Hierarchy and Competition: Administration in the Post-Affluent World*. 2nd ed. New York: Franklin Watts, 1981.

THOMPSON, VICTOR A. *Bureaucracy and the Modern World*. Morristown, N.J.: General Learning Press, 1976.

_____. *Modern Organization*. New York: Knopf, 1961.

_____. *Without Sympathy or Enthusiasm*. University, Ala.: University of Alabama Press, 1975.

TULLOCK, GORDON. *The Politics of Bureaucracy*. Washington: Public Affairs Press, 1965.

VON MISES, LUDWIG. *Bureaucracy*. New Haven: Yale University Press, 1944.

WALDO, DWIGHT, ed. *Public Administration in a Time of Turbulence*. Scranton, Pa.: Chandler, 1971.

WEAVER, JOHN D. *The Great Experiment*. Boston: Little, Brown, 1965.

WHITE, LEONARD D. *The Prestige Value of Public Employment in Chicago*. Chicago: University of Chicago Press, 1929.

WHITE, ORION F., JR. "The Dialectical Organization: An Alternative to Bureaucracy." *Public Administration Review* 29 (January-February 1969): 32-42.

WILDAVSKY, AARON B. *Speaking Truth to Power: The Art and Craft of Policy Analysis*. Boston: Little, Brown, 1979.

WILSON, JAMES Q. "The Bureaucracy Problem." *Public Interest* 6 (Winter 1967): 3-9.

WRISTON, MICHAEL J. "In Defense of Bureaucracy." *Public Administration Review* 40 (March-April 1980): 179-83.

Index

DATE DUE

GAYLORD			PRINTED IN U.S.A.